SPIRITUAL COMFORT

by

John Colquhoun, D.D.
Minister of the Gospel, Leith

"Comfort ye, comfort ye My people, saith your God. Speak ye comfortably to Jerusalem. " Isaiah 40:1–2

"Although thou sayest thou shalt not see Him, yet judgment is before Him; therefore trust thou in Him." Job 35:14

"My heart trusted in Him, and I am helped; therefore my heart greatly rejoiceth, and with my song will I praise Him." Psalm 28:7

Edited by Rev. Don Kistler

Soli Deo Gloria Publications
. . . for instruction in righteousness . . .

Soli Deo Gloria Publications
P.O. Box 451, Morgan, PA 15064
(412) 221-1901/FAX (412) 221-1902

*

This edition of *Spiritual Comfort,* in which grammar,
spelling, and formatting changes have been made,
is taken from the second edition published
in Edinburgh in 1814, and is © 1998 by
Don Kistler and Soli Deo Gloria.

*

ISBN 1-57358-075-9

Contents

Foreword

One of the invariable hallmarks of men whose ministry has been widely used to strengthen the people of God is that they themselves have heeded the apostolic exhortation, "Let the word of Christ dwell in you richly as you teach" (Colossians 3:16). Not only does their preaching illustrate what Paul meant by "the open manifestation of the truth" (2 Corinthians 4:2), but it becomes clear in their preaching that they themselves have fed on Scripture, meditated on it, sucked the goodness from it, and submitted their minds and wills to its truth in such a way that the power of the Word has seeped into their emotions and affections and transformed them.

John Colquhoun, whose name is less well-known today than it ought to be, must be numbered among such company. The fruit of his ministry was evident in his hearers' lives. A well-known story tells how, one Saturday night at an inn between Glasgow and Edinburgh, Alexander Moody Stuart encountered two young men who reappeared late on Sunday evening. On making inquiry, he discovered that these ordinary working-class youngsters used the inn as their weekend resting place on their regular one-hundred-mile journey between Glasgow (where they lived) and Edinburgh (where they went to sit under the rich evangelical ministry of John Colquhoun). This was in a time of a long six-day work week, and on foot—a fitting tribute to a minister who as a youngster had once walked fifty miles in order to purchase a Christian book!

Personal Background

Born in the parish of Luss in Dunbartonshire, Scotland, on January 1, 1748, the son of a local farmer, Colquhoun received his early education at the local school supported by the Society for Promoting Christian Knowledge (SPCK). Here he was singularly blessed by the mentorship of a Christian teacher. He attributed his conversion as a youngster to the effect of the Shorter Catechism's question, "What is effectual calling?" Thereafter his teacher introduced him to Thomas Boston's great work, *Human Nature in Its Fourfold State* (a work which more than, perhaps, any other molded the understanding of generations of Scots). This was the book young John was prepared to trudge those fifty long miles in order to purchase. It not only sharpened his own understanding of the grace of God in the gospel, it shaped the whole course and tenor of his ministry.

At the age of twenty, constrained by a sense of call to the ministry, Colquhoun matriculated in the University of Glasgow. His studies lasted for the next ten years, and it was not until 1780 that he was licensed as a preacher of the gospel. In 1781 he was ordained to his first and only pastoral charge in the New Church (St. John's), South Leith (near Edinburgh). Here he ministered with prolonged faithfulness and zeal for almost fifty years, dying in 1827.

Latter-Day Marrow Theology

It will become quickly evident to readers of this re-published work by John Colquhoun that his ministry had a certain quality about it and a distinctive flavor.

What was it about his understanding of the gospel which made his hearers and readers "taste" the gospel in a special way in his preaching and writing?

The answer undoubtedly lies in the influence on him of the so-called "Marrow Brethren," men—like Thomas Boston, the Erskine brothers (Ralph and Ebenezer), and others—who earlier in the century had been profoundly influenced by the controversial book attributed to Edward Fisher, *The Marrow of Modern Divinity* (London, 1645). Thomas Boston had "happened" upon it early in his ministry, and it had immediately clarified his understanding of the gospel. It soon became not only a resource book for evangelicals, but in many ways a rallying point for those who lamented the moderatism which had become so prevalent in the Kirk. The famous "Marrow Controversy" ensued and, in 1720, the book (for a reprint of which Thomas Boston wrote interpretive notes) was, for all practical purposes, proscribed reading for members of the Church of Scotland under suspicion of Antinomian and Arminian tendencies.

What brought Boston, and later John Colquhoun, such delight in the Marrow teaching was its emphasis on grace as free, full, divine, and genuine. As Boston recognized, its effect was to destroy the fundamental legalism of the human heart and its propensity to turn the God of unconditional grace ("while we were yet sinners Christ died for us") into a God of negotiated terms ("if you do A and B then I will begin to be gracious to you").

Colquhoun grasped the deep implications of this teaching, in terms of the way in which it illumined the endemically legalistic nature of the human heart and

simultaneously magnified the wonder of the love of
God in Christ for sinners. His discovery for himself of
the unfettered character of the grace of God in the
gospel put the grace of God into his heart, and then
into his ministry, and thus into his preaching. As a re-
sult, those who heard his sermons tasted a rich, liberat-
ing, satisfying gospel—something which, in the
Scottish axiom, is "better felt than telt." Such an experience is readily understood only by those who have actually had it.

That John Colquhoun drank deeply from this
reservoir is evident even from the titles of his works, all
of which were published first in Edinburgh: the present reprint, *A Treatise of Spiritual Comfort* (1813); *A
Treatise on the Law and the Gospel* (1816); *A Treatise on the
Covenant of Grace* (1818); *A Catechism for the Instruction
and Direction of Young Communicants* (1821); *A View of
Saving Faith* (1824); *A Collection of the Promises of the
Gospel* (1825); *A View of Evangelical Repentance* (1825). A
collection of his *Sermons, Chiefly on Doctrinal Subjects*
(1836) was published posthumously. He remained a
"Marrow man" to the end of his days, and with charac-
teristic wit he used to tell students for the ministry that
"I daurna advise ye tae read *The Marrow,* for the
Assembly condemned it. But though they condemned
The Marrow, they didna condemn Tammes Boston's
notes on it—and that's a book ye should read!"

A Treatise on Spiritual Comfort

The present work, now thankfully published, stands
in a great tradition of evangelical writings which rec-
ognize that the Christian life is not an easy path. Its
predecessors include such great works as Richard

Sibbes's *The Bruised Reed* (based on Isaiah 42:3), Thomas Goodwin's *A Child of Light Walking in Darkness* (based on Isaiah 50:10), William Bridge's *A Lifting Up for the Downcast* (based on Psalm 42:11), and other similar expositions of spiritual discouragement and depression, and their biblical remedies. In this respect, Colquhoun wrote as a latter-day Puritan, speaking to his contemporaries as a physician of the soul whose skills were well-honed by a profound knowledge of Scripture and the human heart.

Colquhoun had, however, a particular concern which arose out of his observation of the impact of the loss of spiritual assurance ("comfort"), first, on the sanctification of the Christian, and, then, inevitably, the corresponding decline in the influence of his or her life on others who might be seeking Christ for themselves. Having a firm grasp on the principle that the real quality of our witness is determined by a certain ethos and tenor, a melody (or lack of it) played by our spirits, he saw with great insight the inevitable connection between spirituality and witness.

As readers will soon discover, John Colquhoun explores and analyzes the nature, causes, and cure of such a condition. Insight abounds in which he marries together the wisdom he had quarried from the Puritans and the Marrow Brethren, Boston and his circle. But so rare is such a wisdom in our day that it sometimes seems like news brought from some explorer who has traveled in hitherto-uncharted territory. Thus Colquhoun makes distinctions with which we moderns tend to be impatient and dismiss as "scholastic"—for example, the distinction between the seed and the experience of assurance. Unafraid to search out, test, and (if necessary) destroy hypocrisy, he distinguishes temporary from permanent foundations, and true from false joy. His analysis is serious and penetrating: discontentment and impatience (surely the diseases of late-twentieth-century westerners) arise from the "inordinate love of some earthly comfort"; vain thoughts are the perennial enemy of true spirituality.

Insight abounds, too, into the subtle activity of the powers of darkness. Standing on the shoulders of John Bunyan's *Pilgrim's Progress*, Colquhoun is sensitive to the fact that Christians may be plagued by blasphemous thoughts, arising from the activity of Satan. Drawing on the wisdom of Owen and the Marrow brethren he sees how common, and also how dangerous, are the "hard thoughts of God" which lie hidden in our nature, since they were first injected there by Satan at the Fall.

The remedies prescribed are no less impressive in their spiritual wisdom and humanity. Avoid isolation; meditate frequently on God's grace—but let the meditation be "short and easy." Colquhoun was not a spiritual therapist who made the mistake of replacing old burdens with new legalisms.

Undergirding all lies a deep sense of the sovereign grace and wisdom of God. He can be trusted even when He cannot be understood. He is working out His purposes through whatever incomprehensible and untidy providences mark (and seem to mar) our lives. The sensitivity of this point of *Spiritual Comfort* underlines Colquhoun's grasp of the principle that the heavenly Father is never doing merely one thing at a time, but is working *all things* together for the good of *all those* who love Him and are callrd according to *His* purpose (Romans 8:28). Mingled with a balanced and healthy introspection lacking in so many contemporary "how to get your life together tidily" manuals is a recognition of the chief end: that in Christ we come to *know* God, and to *enjoy* Him forever. This is the path to recovery in that it remedies our endemic problem, which is, as Luther noted, that we are by nature focused inward *(incurvatus in se)*, centered on self rather than living out of our true center in God. For Colquhoun brings us to see our sinfulness in order to help us to see our need of the gospel, in order, in turn, to lead us to drink the living waters of grace which the Spirit brings to us from within Christ, its spring, and from the Father, its deep, eternal source. In this, the rediscovery and knowledge of the triune God of grace, lies all true spiritual comfort, strength, and vitality.

But I must not allow my enthusiasm for John Colquhoun, and the permanent value of his writings, to delay your encounter with him any further. You do not need to take my word for the value of these pages; read them for yourself and be enriched.

Sinclair B. Ferguson
Charles Krahe Professor of Systematic Theology
Westminster Theological Seminary, Philadelphia

Advertisement

It has often occurred to me that, as spiritual consolation in this valley of tears is highly necessary to support and encourage the hearts of exercised Christians, and so to make them advance with alacrity in the love and practice of true holiness, as well as to engage them to perform every particular duty with increasing cheerfulness and resolution, so they need to be instructed often in the unspeakable importance of such comfort, and in the means of attaining its increase.

Under the forcible impression of these sentiments, and from a desire to contribute my feeble endeavors to promote the consolation and edification of believers, I engaged in the following work. It has been my aim at the same time to avoid a plan which may be defective in its parts, or irregular in their distribution—to render the subject easy and intelligible, and so to adapt the work to the capacities even of the weakest and most illiterate Christians. I do not presume to have fully attained these objects. How far I have succeeded, and wherein I have failed in the attempt, it does not become me to say. The judicious and candid reader will determine.

If anything contained in the following pages shall, by the blessing of Him who is the Consolation of Israel, be rendered useful but to one disconsolate believer, my labor will be amply compensated.

John Colquhoun
February 18, 1813

Introduction

The persons for whose use this treatise is more immediately intended are they who have, by the Holy Spirit, been convinced of their guilt, malignity, and demerit, of the sin which dwells *in* them, as well as of the iniquities that are committed *by* them; who have also been convinced of the utter insufficiency of their own righteousness for their justification in the sight of God, and who have been enabled to embrace Jesus Christ as their righteousness and strength. All who fit this description are earnestly desirous of advancing in holiness; but many of them seem to be far from being duly sensible of the high importance of spiritual consolation to the love and practice of holiness. They are soon apprehensive of danger if they feel iniquities prevailing against them; but they yield without alarm to that dejection of spirit which is often occasioned, either by inward conflicts or outward trials, not considering that disquietude of soul paves the way for despondency, and despondency for utter despair; all which are, to a high degree, injurious to the spiritual welfare of the soul. Trouble of mind, especially when it proceeds to the length of despondency, strengthens the unbelief and enmity of the heart against God, and so disqualifies the Christian from performing acceptably the duties incumbent upon him. Although God does not suffer any of His children ever to fall into the horrible gulf of absolute despair, yet some of them have brought themselves to the very brink of it so as greatly to dishonor their holy profession, to injure their own souls, and to hurt the souls of many around them who are always too ready to impute their dejection of spirit to the holy religion which they profess. Thus, they often discourage the hearts of some who are seeking Jesus, and strengthen the prejudices of others who are enemies to Him.

The sovereign antidote to that sinful and grievous distemper of mind is the spiritual and holy consolation which is offered and promised in the gospel. Much of the sacred Volume was written for this end, that the saints might be comforted, and that they "through patience and comfort of the Scriptures might have hope" (Romans 15:4). God, in the exceeding riches of His grace, has given in His Word, and confirmed by His oath, many great and precious promises in order that all "who have fled for refuge, to lay hold upon the hope set before them" might not only have consolation, but strong consolation. He has spoken in His holiness on purpose that they might rejoice, that they might be so "filled with all joy and peace in believing" (Romans 15:13), as to serve Him with gladness (Psalm 100:2); and, hereby, to recommend faith and holiness to all around them.

Such pleasure does the Lord Jesus take in the prosperity of His servants, and so deeply is He concerned for their happiness, even in this valley of tears, that He has commanded them "to comfort one another" (1 Thessalonians 4:18), "to comfort yourselves together" (1 Thessalonians 5:11), and especially "to comfort the feeble-minded" (1 Thessalonians 5:14). And, doubtless, if private Christians are bound to comfort one another, much more is it the duty of ministers of the gospel to imitate the Apostles of Christ in being helpers of their joy (2 Corinthians 1:24). Accordingly, this solemn charge is given, and is again, and a third time, repeated to those, " 'Comfort ye, comfort ye My people,' saith your God. 'Speak ye comfortably to Jerusalem, and cry unto her, that her warfare is accomplished, that her iniquity is pardoned' " (Isaiah 40:1–2).

That I therefore may, in obedience to that high command, be instrumental in administering comfort to such afflicted and discouraged believers as may be disposed to read this treatise, I shall, in dependence on the Spirit of truth, endeavor:

First, to discourse of spiritual comfort in general.

Second, I shall consider the great importance and usefulness of it to believers.

In the third place, I shall show the way in which many of them lose the comfort which they formerly attained.

Fourth, I shall point out some of the sad consequences of their having forfeited their usual comfort.

In the fifth place, I shall briefly consider the nature and signs of melancholy.

Next, I shall unfurl some of the designs of God in permitting any of His saints to lose their wonted consolation.

Afterwards, I shall show how disconsolate Christians may recover their former comfort.

Next, I shall point out the means which they ought to employ in order to attain increasing comfort.

And, in the last place, I shall give some directions by observing which exercised believers may become established in spiritual consolation.

1

Of Spiritual Comfort in General

Comfort, in its general usage, is that refreshing pleasure or enlivening satisfaction of spirit by which a man is upheld and strengthened against all evils, whether felt or feared; or, it is that inward solace which supports and invigorates the heart under trouble of every kind. There are three sorts of comfort: natural, sinful, and spiritual. Natural comfort is the refreshment of our natural spirits by the good creatures of God, the gifts of His bounty. When God gives us rain from heaven, and fruitful seasons, He thereby fills our hearts with food and gladness (Acts 14:17). There is comfort in every creature of God. When we are hungry, food comforts us; when thirsty, drink refreshes us; when cold, clothes warm us; and when in affliction or in want of advice, friends encourage us. But, besides these common and necessary gifts of Providence, every sense has something peculiar to itself which affords it comfort. The eyes have beautiful colors to give them pleasure. The ears, besides ordinary sounds, have melodious sounds to delight them. The taste has not only the suitableness of common food, but the sweetness of honey to please it; and the smell, besides common odors, has fragrant flowers to regale it.

Sinful or unholy comfort is the pleasure which sinners take in gratifying their lusts, or the delight which

1

they have in abusing the gifts of divine bounty. Sometimes the true Christian is ready to wonder how wicked men can, at any time, feel themselves comfortable; but he has no cause to wonder, for the very commission of sin is a momentary comfort to their depraved nature. "It is as sport to a fool to do mischief" (Proverbs 10:23). To commit iniquity is agreeable to their sinful nature and, therefore, is a comfort to it. Indeed, were it not for the frequent opportunities which they have of gratifying some lust, either of the flesh or of the mind, life would be an insupportable burden to them. "Evil men," said Solomon, "sleep not, except they have done mischief; and their sleep is taken away, unless they cause some to fall" (Proverbs 4:16). Ah, how inexpressibly dreadful is the condition of that man to whose heart it is a pleasure, a comfort, to sin against a holy and a gracious God! Sinful comfort also is the pleasure that self-righteous persons take in relying either on their own righteousness wholly, or partly on the righteousness of Christ and partly on their own, for their justification and title to eternal life, and the delight which hypocrites feel in reflecting on their counterfeit graces and attainments.

Spiritual or holy comfort is that inward solace or satisfaction which supports, strengthens, and exhilarates holy souls, and which they have in and from the Lord Jesus, their Covenant-Head, by the exercise of faith, hope, love, and the other graces of the Holy Spirit (Romans 5:1–5). Or, it is that spiritual delight, that holy joy, which cheers and invigorates the hearts of believers under all their inward and outward troubles. It is this only that deserves the name of pure, solid, and durable consolation. If it is a comfort to the wicked man amidst all his afflictions to gratify his carnal and ungodly lusts, it cannot, surely, but be a real and even a great consolation to a holy man, under all the trials of life, to exercise his spiritual graces and perform his holy duties.

The word "comfort" is in Scripture used in a twofold sense. It is sometimes employed to express that which gives consolation itself, which is received from it, or enjoyed by means of it. First, it is employed in Scripture to express that which gives or is a means of giving consolation to the soul of an afflicted believer, whether it be a person (Colossians 4:11), or a thing in which, by the blessing of Christ, comfort is hidden and by which it is afforded (Psalm 119:76), or a word or reason suggesting to the mind the Christian matter of consolation (Psalm 119:50). Each of these is called "comfort" because it is a means or instrument of dispensing consolation to the saints.

Second, the term is, by the Spirit of inspiration, more frequently employed to express the consolation itself which believers receive whether by means of persons, of things, or of reasons, and which they feel or enjoy in their souls. It is in this last sense, chiefly, that I propose in this treatise to discourse of spiritual comfort.

In order to illustrate the general nature of this inestimable blessing, I shall present it to the view of the devout reader under the following particulars:

1. *Spiritual comfort usually supposes trouble of some kind, either felt or feared, or the prospect of some difficult duty to the performance of which the believer needs to be encouraged.* It is under affliction or uneasiness that the heart of the Christian needs to be comforted. The Lord Jesus

accordingly said, "Blessed are they that mourn, for they shall be comforted" (Matthew 5:4). He made the first promise of the Holy Spirit as a Comforter to His disciples when, in the prospect of His departure from them, sorrow had filled their hearts (John 16:6–7). "God," said the Apostle Paul, "comforteth us in all our tribulation, that we may be able to comfort them who are in any trouble" (2 Corinthians 1:4). He calls Him "the God who comforteth them that are cast down" (2 Corinthians 7:6). The soul, that it may be qualified for spiritual consolation, must be quickened and humbled. It is the spirit of the humble and the heart of the contrite ones that the high and lofty One will revive with holy comfort (Isaiah 57:15). Indeed, the oil of spiritual joy is such that no vessel but a contrite heart can hold it. The design of imparting divine consolation is to cheer and invigorate the drooping spirit. The office of the Comforter is to relieve the disconsolate soul (Lamentations 1:16). It is impossible for those who have never felt the uneasiness of a wounded conscience to value or desire the joy of God's salvation.

The soul, that it may need and be prepared for true consolation, must not only be quickened and humbled, but be under some affliction, either felt or apprehended. Comfort, according to an apostolic direction, is to be administered to "the feeble-minded" (1 Thessalonians 5:14), to such as are ready to stagger under the cross and be overtaken by the temptations of Satan and the world, or discouraged because of the corruptions of their own hearts. It is trouble that renders spiritual consolation necessary as well as desirable. If the believer were not feeble and incapable of being supported by a created arm, the office of a divine

Comforter would be unnecessary. If he had not a painful as well as a spiritual sense of his want of heavenly consolations, earthly comforts would be more acceptable to him than they are; and if his heart were not prepared for them by being humbled as well as afflicted, they would no more refresh it than a shower of rain would refresh a rock. Accordingly, Christ seldom communicates sensible comfort to the saints but when they are either in inward or outward trouble.

It is by their being troubled that they become disconsolate, and so become fit for being consoled. And it is their sharpest afflictions that often serve to prepare them for the sweetest consolations. He, therefore, brings them usually into the wilderness before He speaks comfortably to them (Hosea 2:14). It may be proper here to remark that, as divine comfort is the opposite of trouble (Luther says, "All things come from Christ to His Church in contraries. He is righteousness, but it is felt in sin. He is life, but it is in death. He is consolation, but it is in calamity." Augustine likewise observes that "the Christian's life runs on between these two: our crosses and God's comforts"), so it must be more powerful and effectual than either outward or inward trouble; for there is no prevailing but by that which is the stronger. It must be more forceful to raise up the dejected soul than the grievance is to cast it down; otherwise it cannot at the time be comfort to it.

2. There are three degrees of spiritual comfort. The lowest degree is peace of conscience, the next is joy, and the highest is triumph.

Peace of conscience is that inward serenity or tranquility of mind which arises from the faith and sense of being justified in the sight of God, or of being in a state of union with Christ and of conformity to Him. "Being justified by faith," said the Apostle Paul, "we have peace with God through our Lord Jesus Christ" (Romans 5:1). The peace with which the God of hope fills the hearts of the saints is peace in believing (Romans 15:13). It arises also from the sense or consciousness of peace with God. When the blood of Christ is by faith applied to the conscience, the conscience is purged by it from dead works (Hebrews 9:14), and the heart also is, at the same time, sprinkled by it from an evil conscience (Hebrews 10:22).

The subject of spiritual peace is a conscience that is purged. Purity and peace are connected together in the conscience, and they are both necessary to render it a good conscience (1 Timothy 1:5). When the conscience is sprinkled with the blood of Jesus, it is thereby set free from the dread of avenging wrath. The mind is not as formerly disturbed with alarming fears of God's indignation, nor disquieted by His judgments (Proverbs 1:33). This is accompanied, usually, with a cordial acquiescence in the will of the Lord, founded on a persuasion of His wisdom and sovereignty, of His holiness and goodness. And so far as a man attains this holy acquiescence in the divine will, he is secure from disappointment and free from uneasiness. Now this peaceful serenity of soul is the first degree of spiritual comfort. When the Lord Jesus would comfort His disconsolate disciples, He said, "These things I have spoken to you, that in Me ye might have peace" (John 16:33).

Joy is a higher degree of holy consolation. Spiritual joy is that gladness of heart which flows from the lively exercise of faith, feasting upon Christ in the offers and promises of the gospel. The Apostle Paul prayed thus for the believers at Rome: "Now, the God of hope fill you with all joy and peace in believing" (Romans 15:13), and the Apostle Peter said to the Christians of the dispersion, "Believing, ye rejoice" (1 Peter 1:8). It is a holy delight in living upon Christ and in walking in Him, and it is effected by the Holy Spirit shedding abroad in the heart, like a fragrant perfume, the love of God. When He graciously condescends to administer that reviving medicine, it elevates and enlarges the fainting soul. Arising as it does from the beginning of enjoyment, and from the hope of the full and endless enjoyment of God in Christ, it strengthens, and so comforts, the drooping heart. "The joy of the Lord is your strength" (Nehemiah 8:10). Peace is negative, joy is positive comfort. The former is as the calming of the storm; the latter as the breaking out of the sun. That is a mitigation of trouble; this, a sense of positive enjoyment. When a condemned criminal knows that he is pardoned, he has peace; but when he is advanced to preferment besides, he has joy.

Triumph is the highest degree of consolation. The saints triumph when they so greatly rejoice as almost to shout for joy on account of the victory given them over their spiritual enemies. They triumph when, more than conquerors through Him who loved them, they exult or rejoice in their almighty Redeemer with rapturous delight. This was often the attainment of the holy Apostle Paul, and of his fellow laborers in the gospel. 2 Corinthians 2:14: "Thanks be unto God which always causeth us to triumph in Christ."

A lofty description of their triumph he gives in

Romans 8:31–39. How high did heavenly consolation rise in the soul of that holy Apostle when he was writing that sublime passage! In like manner does the believer triumph when, in his pursuit of more communion with Christ and conformity to Him, he is enabled to vanquish great opposition. In some happy moments of his life, his joy, like a river swelled by impetuous rains, bursts all its banks and carries all the joys and all the sorrows of this world before it. It is then, especially, that it may be called "joy unspeakable and full of glory" (1 Peter 1:8). It is glorious in itself, and is attended with glorying in the Lord Jesus. When the heart of the Christian is elevated to this degree of consolation, he glories in the Lord. All that is in this world is brought under him; the greatest calamities cannot daunt him. He sets Christ, and God in Christ, against all enemies and all evils, whether external or internal. This triumphant glorying in the Lord is like that of the holy Psalmist, who said, "My soul shall make her boast in the Lord" (Psalm 34:2). It is remarkable that these three degrees of spiritual comfort are, by our Apostle, mentioned in a single passage in Romans 5:1–3: "We have peace with God through our Lord Jesus Christ . . . we rejoice in hope . . . and not only so, but we glory in tribulations also."

3. *Spiritual consolation is, according to the covenant of grace, given to believers by God the Father, by Christ the second Adam, and by the Holy Spirit.* God the Father gives it by sovereign and judiciary authority, Christ the Mediator by gracious dispensation, and the Holy Spirit by effectual operation. God the Father ordains it for His children (Isaiah 26:12). Christ, the last Adam, administers it; and the blessed Spirit, as the Spirit of

Christ, applies it to them.

Holy consolation is given them by God the Father. None but Jehovah Himself can pour consolation into a troubled soul. All true comfort is, originally and fundamentally, in Him. He it is whom the Apostle Paul calls "the God of all comfort, who comforteth the saints in all their tribulation" (2 Corinthians 1:3–4), and "the Father, who hath loved us, and hath given us everlasting consolation" (2 Thessalonians 2:16). He also calls Him "the God of consolation" (Romans 15:5), and "the Comforter of those that are cast down" (2 Corinthians 7:6). The Lord compares Himself to a father pitying his children (Psalm 103:13), and to a mother comforting with tenderest concern her afflicted infant (Isaiah 66:13). He charges His servants "to strengthen the weak hands, to confirm the feeble knees, and to say to them that are of a fearful heart, 'Be strong, fear not; behold, your God will come with vengeance, even God with a recompense; He will come and save you' " (Isaiah 35:3–4). He suffered His only and beloved Son to be in all points tempted as His people are that He might sympathize with and comfort them under all their temptations.

Comfort is administered to them by Jesus Christ, their Covenant-Head. The Lord Jesus is the trustee, the storehouse, of all spiritual comfort to the saints. From Him, as the hope set before them, they may daily derive strong consolation. Hence He is called "the Consolation of Israel" (Luke 2:25). He is the matter of His people's consolation, the Prince of peace, the true Noah "who comforteth them, concerning the work and toil of their hands" (Genesis 5:29) It is a part of His high office, to which He was anointed by the blessed

Spirit, "to comfort them who mourn in Zion, to give unto them beauty for ashes, the oil of joy for mourning, the garment of praise for the spirit of heaviness" (Isaiah 61:2–3). There is, therefore, "consolation *in* Christ" (Philippians 2:1), and the consolation of the saints abounds *by* Christ (2 Corinthians 1:5). They have it in Him and through Him, with Him and by Him. His person, righteousness, fullness, and love are the source and substance of abundant consolation to them against trouble of every kind. He it is who gives peace to His people, and "when He giveth quietness, who then can make trouble?" (Job 34:29).

Nothing can comfort the heart without Christ. He removes from the soul all that is dismal and bestows upon it all that is comfortable. He it is who makes even the darkness of trouble itself to be light before those who trust in Him. He is the Sun of righteousness whose light, warmth, and healing cheer their souls. When He vouchsafes His reviving presence to them, He leaves a delightful perfume of comfort behind Him. Indeed, a man can never know what true pleasure is till he knows Christ. The compassionate Redeemer, therefore, says to all who are weary, toiling in a fruitless pursuit of happiness, and also to all who are heavy laden, oppressed with the servitude of sin or bowed down under a load of misery, "Come unto Me, and I will give you rest" (Matthew 11:28).

Comfort is applied to the saints by the Holy Spirit. He is, therefore, called "the Comforter" (John 15:26). Being the inestimable gift of the Father through the mediation of the Son, He is "another Comforter" (John 14:16). The adorable Spirit discharges His office by testifying of Christ, or by taking of the things of

Christ and showing them to believers; by opening and applying the promises of the everlasting covenant to them, and by enabling them to believe these with application to themselves; by shedding abroad the love of the Father and the Son in their hearts; by witnessing to them their adoption, and their being heirs of God and joint-heirs with Christ; by abiding in them as the seal, the earnest, and the pledge of their eternal inheritance; and by dwelling in them as the Spirit of grace and of supplication. The Holy Spirit, like Noah's dove, flies with the olive leaf of peace to assure believers that the winter is past, and that the rain is over and gone. He not only brings words of comfort to their remembrance, but opens their hearts to receive them. Comforts may be so applied as to be brought close to the heart; but if the heart does not open for them, no consolation is experienced. The Spirit, therefore, not only opens and applies the promises to the heart, but opens the heart for the comfort of the promises, and then pours consolation into it. He comforts the saints also by enabling them to trust that in the Lord Jesus they have righteousness and strength, forgiveness of sins, and a title to eternal life, as well as by renewing them after the image of the Son of God, and so uniting their hearts to the holy will of God. The original word in the New Testament which we have translated "comforter" in John 14:16 signifies likewise an advocate. One special way in which the Holy Spirit comforts believers is the exercise of His advocacy or intercession in them (Romans 8:26). The more they are enabled to pray in faith, the more they walk in the fear of the Lord and in the comfort of the Holy Ghost (Acts 9:31).

 4. *The spiritual consolation which is given to believers*

is a part of eternal life. "Believing ye rejoice"
(1 Peter 1:8). "He that believeth on the Son hath everlasting life" (John 3:36). One part of the fruit of the
Spirit, when He imparts spiritual life to the soul, is joy
(Galatians 5:22). But spiritual life in the soul is eternal
life begun. When God, who cannot lie, promised before the world began eternal life to the second Adam
for His spiritual seed, He promised Him that, upon
condition of His bearing their griefs and carrying their
sorrows, they should become heirs of everlasting joy,
and heirs of Himself as their exceeding joy. As the saving knowledge of Christ in this world is the earnest and
beginning of the beatific vision of God and the Lamb
in the heavenly world, and as conformity to Christ in
holiness here is the beginning of perfect conformity to
Him there, so the consolation which the saints on
some occasions feel in this valley of tears is the first
fruits or beginning of that fullness of joy which will
constitute a part of their blessedness in that holy place
on high. The joy of the Holy Ghost which enters into
them here is the same in kind as the joy of their Lord
into which they will enter hereafter. It is called, therefore, by one apostle, "everlasting consolation" (2 Thessalonians 2:16), and by another, "joy unspeakable and
full of glory" (1 Peter 1:8). It is joy that is full of glory,
or glorious joy, the very dawning of the day of glory.

Holy consolation is glory begun in the soul, a bud
which will open in heaven and spread into ineffable
and endless glory; a dawn which will shine more and
more until the glorious Sun of righteousness brightens
it into perfect and eternal day. All the joy of the saints
below is but as a spark, a feeble spark, compared to
that blaze of rapture which will burn intensely in their

spirits above. It is but a slight foretaste, a small drop, of that immense ocean of unmingled joy which they are to inherit in the mansions of glory. Although they are not far from the heavenly Canaan, yet their hearts are often ready to faint under their sufferings from without, and their conflicts with corruption from within; but a taste of the grapes of Eshcol, the first fruits of heaven, revives their spirit, rouses their zeal, and quickens their desire for that endless rest which there remains for them. Consolation keeps the holy soul upon the wing and increases her strength. It is the very life of the soul. When Naomi would express the comfort that Boaz should afford to Ruth, she said to her, "He shall be unto thee a restorer of thy life" (Ruth 4:15). If the contentment and delight of the heart is taken away, it dies. The souls of the wicked have an existence in hell, yet, because it is an existence without comfort, their state is never said in Scripture to be a state of life but, on the contrary, a state of death. Accordingly, the restoring of comfort to mourners is called a reviving of them (Isaiah 57:15).

5. *The grounds and sources of holy consolation are especially the following:* God in Christ, with all His glorious perfections, as a God of love, grace, and mercy, and as the God and portions of the saints (Psalm 16:5); Christ, in His glorious Person (Philippians 3:3), righteousness (Isaiah 61:10 and 32:17), fullness, offices, and relations, or Christ living in them (Revelation 1:18); the Holy Spirit as inhabiting, quickening, sanctifying, and sealing them, and as the earnest of their eternal inheritance (2 Corinthians 1:22); the covenant of grace as well-ordered in all things and sure, according to which Jehovah—Father, Son, and Holy Ghost—

is their God and they are His people, His peculiar
people (Jeremiah 31:33); the infinite atonement
(Romans 5:11), the continual intercession (Romans
8:34), the supreme dominion, the inviolable faithfulness, and the gracious presence of the Lord Jesus, who
is given for a covenant of the people; and the ordinances, doctrines, promises, and offers, of His gospel
(Isaiah 12:3), with the peremptory commandment
given to sinners in common to believe on Him (Psalm
19:8; 1 John 3:23).

These are the leading and the immediate grounds
upon which the saints by faith build their comfort; and
they are, at the same time, the sources from which, by
the exercise of faith, they derive their consolation.
Besides these, their faith and sense of the pardon of
their sins, of the acceptance of their persons as righteous, of their adoption, their sanctification, and the
witnessing of the blessed Spirit are matters of consolation to them. And so is the lively exercise of all the
graces of the Holy Spirit, especially of faith, hope, and
love. The comfort of justification, because it is founded
upon a righteousness which is perfect and always the
same, is more stable and permanent than that of sanctification. The great things which believers have in possession, and the greater which they have in hope, are
the sustenance of their consolation (Hebrews 6:18).
The suitableness of those inestimable blessings to their
hearts (2 Samuel 23:5), together with their sense of
personal interest in them, affords them unspeakable
joy (Luke 1:47). As for their experiences and evidences
of grace, these are, strictly speaking, not grounds upon
which they build their comfort (Galatians 6:14;
Proverbs 13:12), but they are proofs of their saving in-

terest in those grounds of consolation mentioned above, as well as encouragements to build their comfort upon them. And so they are matter of consolation to their souls (2 Corinthians 1:12). The most comfortable of the saints are they who, trusting at all times in the second Adam as given for a covenant to them, can think of all dispensations, of all conditions, and of all duties with comfort (Isaiah 26:3). They who have the love of Christ displayed in the covenant of grace most constantly in their view, and most frequently warm on their heart, are of all believers the most free from perplexing doubts and fears.

6. *It is both the duty and the privilege of true believers to attain spiritual consolation.* It is their duty, for it is required of them in the law, and it is their privilege, for it is promised to them in the gospel.

It is the duty of all the saints to be of good comfort. Their God, the God of consolation, would not have them be, at any time, disconsolate or gloomy; and, therefore He expressly forbids them to fear, to be discouraged, to let their hearts be troubled, and to yield to oppressive grief. He says to them, "Fear ye not, neither be afraid" (Isaiah 44:8); "Fear thou not, for I am with thee; be not dismayed, for I am thy God" (Isaiah 41:10); "Fear not, for I have redeemed thee" (Isaiah 43:1). And, said the Lord Jesus, "Fear not them which kill the body" (Matthew 10:28). "Let not your heart be troubled, neither let it be afraid" (John 14:27). "Fear not; I am the First and the Last" (Revelation 1:17). "Fear none of those things which thou shalt suffer" (Revelation 2:10). The Apostle Paul forbids the believers in Thessalonica to sorrow for deceased saints, as others who have no hope (1 Thessalonians 4:13). The

Lord authorizes no sorrow but godly sorrow, which is consistent with holy joy and tends to the increase of it. He forbids His people all oppressive grief, all desponding fear, and all perplexing trouble of mind, as hindrances to the exercise of love and the practice of holiness. He is displeased when they suffer themselves to be uncomfortable in His service (Malachi 2:13), when they sit in sackcloth in His gate. He commands them, on the contrary, to rejoice before Him. He has made it their indispensable duty to cast all their care upon Him (1 Peter 5:7); "to eat their bread with joy, and to drink their wine with a cheerful heart; to have their garments always white, and to let their head lack no ointment" (Ecclesiastes 9:7–8). He delights to see them joyful, and to hear them singing in His righteous ways; and, therefore, His high command is to "rejoice in the Lord, O ye righteous; for praise is comely for the upright" (Psalm 33:1). "Be glad in the Lord, and rejoice, ye righteous; and shout for joy, all ye that are upright in heart" (Psalm 32:11). "Delight thyself also in the Lord" (Psalm 37:4). "Let all those that put their trust in Thee rejoice; let them ever shout for joy, because Thou defendest them; let them also that love Thy name be joyful in Thee" (Psalm 5:11). "Rejoice and be exceedingly glad; for great is your reward in heaven" (Matthew 5:12). "Finally, my brethren, rejoice in the Lord" (Philippians 3:1). "Rejoice evermore" (1 Thessalonians 5:16). "Rejoice in the Lord always; and again, I say, Rejoice" (Philippians 4:4).

It is as if the apostle had said, "I, in the most earnest and urgent manner, charge you to rejoice not at some times only, but at *all* times; not only when upon the mount with God, but when in the valley; not merely when the Lord shines upon you, but when He hides His face." Although no affliction is so hard to bear as the distress of the soul, which the believer, sometimes, when he is without comfort, endures, yet, that is but little, very little indeed, in comparison to the sin, of his disobeying God's authoritative command by refusing to be comforted. It is remarkable that, though Asaph had once and again offered reasons of comfort to his troubled mind, as appears from his soul's refusing to be comforted, yet, he still persisted in refusing consolation until he could say, "This is my infirmity," my sin, the distemper of unbelief in my heart; and *then* he ceased to refuse it any longer (Psalm 77:2–12).

It is also the privilege of the saints to have spiritual comfort. They have the beginnings of eternal life, and so have joy as a part of it. It is their inestimable privilege to have peace with God, to rejoice in hope of the glory of God, and to glory even in tribulation (Romans 5:1–3). They have joy with which a stranger does not intermeddle (Proverbs 14:10). To them, "wisdom's ways are ways of pleasantness, and all her paths are peace" (Proverbs 3:17). "My mouth," says the holy Psalmist, "shall praise Thee with joyful lips" (Psalm 63:5). "My lips shall greatly rejoice when I sing unto Thee; and my soul which Thou hast redeemed" (Psalm 71:23). The Apostle Paul speaks of his having been exceeding joyful in *all* his tribulation (2 Corinthians 7:4), and of his having been sorrowful yet *always* rejoicing (2 Corinthians 6:10). "Blessed be the God of all comfort," said he, "who comforteth us in all our tribulation" (2 Corinthians 1:3–4). He does not say, "who *has* comforted," or, "who *will*," or "who *can* comfort us if it pleases Him," but "who comforts, who *always* comforts

us." Neither does he say, "who comforteth us in some
or in many tribulations," but "who comforteth us in all
our tribulation, of whatever kind or degree." Indeed,
the Lord always comforts His people in a greater or
lesser measure. "He giveth them songs even in the
night" (Job 35:10).

7. *Believers have always the seed or principle of spiritual
comfort in them, but not always the sense or feeling of consolation.* As they have at all times ground of consolation,
and must have it so long as the everlasting covenant
continues to be established with Christ, and with them
in Him (Isaiah 54:8–10 and Ezekiel 37:26), so they
have always the seed and root of it in their hearts.
"Light is sown for the righteous, and gladness for the
upright in heart" (Psalm 97:11). Gladness is sown for
the upright in heart, and though, like seed sown in
winter which lies long under the clod, it seems to be
lost, yet it is preserved and it will, in due season, spring
up to view and yield a plentiful increase. Though the
seed of consolation appointed for the saints may lie
covered for a time, yet it is not destroyed.

Believers have, at all times, the seed or principle,
and also the habit, of spiritual joy in their hearts. Even
in their deepest dejection they have a seed of comfort
that will spring up. The fruit of the Spirit in them is joy
and peace, and the Spirit, as a Comforter, abides with
them forever. But although they always have the principle, yet they do not have at all times the sensible enjoyment of comfort. They do not continually exercise
the grace of joy, and, therefore, they do not always see
or feel in themselves the principle and habit of that
grace. It is when they are exercising any grace of the
Spirit that they commonly perceive it. Their sensible

enjoyment of consolation in this life is often interrupted by the remaining corruptions of their nature, by the fiery darts of the wicked one, and by God's hiding His countenance from them. In interrupting their sensible comfort, they themselves have a sinful hand (Jeremiah 2:17, 19). Satan and his instruments have a malicious hand (1 Peter 5:8), and the Lord, in order to manifest His sovereignty, to chasten them for their sins, to try and exercise their graces, to excite their more earnest prayers, and to teach them to improve for the future the sense of His favor, has a holy hand. Hence, though the believer is sometimes lively and, in his exercise of faith and love, feels in his heart a glow of heavenly joy, yet, at other times, he is languid, cold and, in a great degree, disconsolate. Like Hagar at the well, his eyes are so held that he cannot perceive as formerly his grounds of comfort; and then his day of gladness is turned into a night of heaviness.

8. The peculiar seasons in which actual and sensible comfort is commonly afforded to believers are the following:

The time of some special manifestation of redeeming love to the soul, after a dark night of desertion (Psalm 30:5); the season of God's appearing remarkably for His church (Exodus 15:1); when some heavy trial is approaching, in order to fortify their minds to endure it (Acts 27:24 and Isaiah 54:7–8); in, and especially after, a time of deep affliction (Isaiah 43:2; Psalm 94:19 and 112:4); the time of tribulation for the cause of Christ and His gospel; often, about the time of their first conversion (Acts 16:34 and 2 Corinthians 1:4–5); the season in which the ordinances of the gospel are administered to them, with uncommon liveliness (Isaiah 56:7); frequently, at the season of much humil-

iation, sorrow and melting of heart for sin; the time in
which they are more than ordinarily engaged in the
exercise of grace and practice of duty, and especially
when they are conflicting much with the corruptions
of their heart; after sharp conflicts with sin or temptation, from which they have come off victorious; the
season in which the Lord is calling them to some extraordinary service for which they need special encouragement; the time in which they see and find least
comfort in creatures, or in which they are destitute of
creature-comforts and are enabled more than usual to
despise them in comparison to Christ and God in Him;
the season in which the Lord confers upon them some
remarkable and unexpected favor; and the time in
which they employ themselves in fixed and deep meditation on the adorable Redeemer and His glorious
grace. These are, for the most part, the ordinary seasons of sensible comfort to the saints. But as the Lord
is infinitely sovereign, wise, and gracious in dispensing
His blessings to them, there are also some extraordinary seasons of rejoicing, some ineffable glances of
light upon their souls which penetrate, transform, and
fill them with rapturous and inexpressible joy.

9. *The comfort which the Lord bestows is, in every instance, the most suitable to the present necessity of the believer.*
"As thy days," said Moses, "so shall thy strength be"
(Deuteronomy 33:25). The Christian's comforts are
wisely and wonderfully adapted to the nature, degree,
and continuance of his grievances. When he has the
most discouragement without, he usually has the most
consolation within. When the Lord Jesus gives him
least of creature-comfort, He commonly affords him
most of Himself as "the consolation of Israel." He sel-

dom allows him much of the fatness of the earth and of refreshment from above at once, but when He shuts before him all doors of help from this world, He opens to him the doors of heaven. It was only when the martyr Stephen saw nothing but death for him in this world that he saw "the heavens opened, and the Son of Man standing on the right hand of God" (Acts 7:56). When the Lord brings His people into outward straits, He commonly favors them with inward enlargements. When He puts a cup of affliction into their hands, He usually gives them a cup of consolation. "Will He plead against me," said Job, "with His great power? No, but He would put strength in me" (Job 23:6). The Lord Jesus said to Paul, when he was afflicted by a thorn in the flesh, "My strength is made perfect in weakness" (2 Corinthians 12:9). The time in which believers are most sensible of their utter inability to resist and overcome their corruptions or temptations, and are most engaged in relying on their great Redeemer for strength, is the season in which, by supporting and strengthening them, He usually affords them the most illustrious displays of the perfection of His strength. In proportion as their weakness appears to them will His strength appear perfect in comforting or strengthening their souls under that weakness. Accordingly, the Apostle, in another place, said, "As the sufferings of Christ abound in us, so our consolation also aboundeth by Christ" (2 Corinthians 1:5). The comfort afforded to the saints is admirably fitted and proportioned to their sufferings in conformity to Christ and, especially, to their sufferings for Him. If the one abounds, so does the other, and that in the most suitable and exact proportion. If gall is dropped into their cup, a suitable proportion of sweetness will also be infused so that their affliction will be in measure (Isaiah 27:8). If they are under various troubles and trust in Christ, He has various comforts for them. If they labor under powerful evils, He has strong consolations; if under new afflictions, He has new comforts; if under small grievances, He has small degrees of support to bestow; if under great perplexities, He has great measures of consolation to impart; if in deep distresses, He has deep comforts, comforts that will sink to the very center of the soul; and if under continued trials, whether external or internal, He has continual, yea, everlasting consolations to give them. He will not suffer them to be tempted above what they are able, but will, with the temptation, also make a way to escape that they may be able to bear it. He will either bring down the trial to their strength or bring up their strength to the trial. If, accordingly, their holy consolation is at any time small, it is because they are then not exposed, as at other times, either to outward temptations or to inward conflicts.

As long as believers are liable to yield to the prevalence of unbelief, pride, indolence, an inordinate attachment to earthly things, and a legal temper, the Lord is pleased to bestow or suspend, to restore or increase, spiritual consolation at such seasons and in such degrees as He sees most suitable to prevent or control those evils, and to promote the increase of holiness in their souls (Ezekiel 34:16). Since true comfort is an inward strengthening of the soul against trouble felt or feared, it must, as was hinted above, be stronger than the trouble, else the act of comforting will not follow. If the comfort is not above the uneasiness, it is no longer comfort. No comforts, therefore, but such as are divine can refresh the holy soul under trouble because, in all other comforts, the disease is above the remedy. Believers should never be discouraged in the prospect even of the highest degree of affliction, for the spiritual comfort will be so adapted to the trouble as to rise above and prevail over it (Psalm 94:19). It is therefore better for them to have the consolation than to be exempted from the trouble and to lack the consolation. This is one special advantage of an afflicted condition to the saints, that the Lord Jesus pities them most and comforts them most in that condition. It is common, when Satan or the world or the flesh is most bitter to them, that He and His grace are most sweet. Indeed, His sharpest dispensations would often be His sweetest, if they but knew better how to improve them.

10. *The spiritual comfort of the saints is according to their faith.* "According to your faith," said the Lord Jesus, "be it unto you" (Matthew 9:29).

It is according to the strength of their faith. If a man's faith is weak, his consolation is weak and unstable. In some happy moment he may, indeed, feel a sudden transport of joy, but still he has very little solid or lasting consolation. Doubts, fears, and perplexities will often prevail against the peace of his mind. "Why are ye fearful, O ye of little faith?" (Matthew 8:26). That which usually stands between a Christian and the joy of God's salvation is his being unwilling to come anew as a sinner to Christ. So long as this is the case, any small degree of consolation that he may have will rise and fall according to his frames or feelings. But if his faith is strong, though he may not have rapturous joy, yet his consolation will usually be strong (Hebrews

6:18); if stable, his peace of conscience will also be stable. "He shall not be afraid of evil tidings: his heart is fixed trusting in the Lord. His heart is established, he shall not be afraid" (Psalm 112:7–8). Faith is not only a spiritual grace, but is the spirit of every other grace, and especially of joy. Spiritual joy is "the joy of faith" (Philippians 1:25), for it proceeds from faith as its principle. It is the office of faith to take and to hand comfort to the soul, to bring peace into the conscience and joy into the heart. If direct and firm reliance on the Savior increases, slavish fear subsides and settled comfort ensues. Sense looks upon the face, the external conduct of Jesus Christ; but faith, especially strong faith, looks upon His heart as revealing itself in the sure, unchangeable promise, and sees inward affections of love and mercy even under outward expressions of displeasure. Faith, when it is strong, can look through a thick cloud of desertion and discern the affection of a Father under the appearance of an enemy (Isaiah 8:17).

It is also according to the exercise of their faith that believers are comforted. If the Christian seldom exercises faith, his consolation is proportionably small; if he exercises it frequently, and rather because it is his duty than merely because he is impelled to it by a painful sense of need, his holy consolation is, in proportion, great. The more frequently and simply he acts out faith in Christ, the consolation of Israel, as the object thereof, and with the good tidings of great joy to all people as the ground of it, the more will he have the comfort of being conscious that he has the grace of faith. Besides, the more fervently and frequently he exercises faith, the more spiritual pleasure will he enjoy, for to trust earnestly that Jesus loves and saves me, and that He will save me with an everlasting salvation, is in itself a delightful and cheering persuasion. Moreover, faith is the instrument by which the believer received consolation at first, and by which he continues to receive it still. It is by trusting daily in the Lord Jesus for all his salvation, of which holy consolation is a part, that the Christian derives daily, renewed supplies of spiritual consolation from His fullness. The more frequent, simple, and lively his actings of confidence in his gracious Redeemer are, the more holy comfort will he in every time of need receive. To feel comfortable when he is conscious that he has clear evidences of his vital union with Christ is a duty, but to take his comfort fresh from the fountain, by the direct application and particular trust of faith, is still a greater duty, a duty by which he glorifies his faithful Redeemer more, and receives an increase of pure and solid consolation.

Hence are these cheering passages of Scripture: "I had fainted, unless I had believed to see the goodness of the Lord, in the land of the living" (Psalm 27:13). "I have trusted in Thy mercy; my heart shall rejoice in Thy salvation" (Psalm 13:5). "Let not your heart be troubled: ye believe in God, believe also in Me" (John 14:1). "Now the God of hope fill you with all joy and peace in believing" (Romans 15:13). "We who have believed do enter into rest" (Hebrews 4:3). Although the sight of His evidences of grace is indeed pleasant to a holy man, yet the sight of Christ in the offer and promise should be much more delightful to him. Unbelief and a legal spirit will always dispose a man to look for something in himself as his ground of comfort, but a holy faith will have to do with none but

Christ. Nothing is such a delight to the Lord Jesus, because nothing honors Him so much as direct and unsuspecting confidence in Him for salvation, whereas looking to Him, or looking upon Him, through one's own graces and frames reflects much dishonor upon Him. The man who so looks upon Him is like one who sees the sun reflected by water, which appears to move or waver as much as the surface of the water does.

11. The properties of spiritual consolation, by which it is distinguished from the joy of the hypocrite, are these:

True comfort comes by the Word of God, and that rightly understood (1 John 1:4), but delusive joy comes either by impressions without the Word or by a misunderstanding of the Word. True consolation is real and solid. The sadness of the believer is, as it were, but as seeming sadness, whereas his joy is real. "As sorrowful," said Paul, "yet always rejoicing" (2 Corinthians 6:10). The hypocrite, on the contrary, is only joyful in appearance while he is in reality gloomy and sorrowful (Proverbs 14:13). Spiritual comfort goes to the heart and inspires it with holy delight; it is solid, and dwells more in the heart than in the countenance. But delusive joy floats on the surface, makes a loud noise, and is, therefore, compared to "the crackling of thorns under a pot" (Ecclesiastes 7:6). True comfort, with regard to its object, is a rejoicing more in the amiableness and excellence of Christ manifested than in the manifestation of them (Philippians 3:3); but counterfeit joy is a rejoicing more in the manifestation itself than in the excellence of the divine object manifested. The true Christian rejoices most in the holy and amiable nature of the things of Christ; the formalist delights most in his own pretended interest in those things. That which delights him is not so much the beauty of the Lord as the beauty of his own experience. The delight which the believer takes in the Lord, and in His Word, is his chief delight, his exceeding joy (Psalm 43:4; 4:6–7; 19:10). The dearest delights of nature are, in his estimation, infinitely below Christ and God in Him. The presence and enjoyment of Christ will, in his esteem, supply the want of all other comforts. But the chief delight of the hypocrite is not in the Lord, but in some other object. True consolation usually accompanies or follows godly sorrow for sin (Matthew 5:4), but the joy of the empty formalist springs up quickly and without contrition of heart (Matthew 13:20 with Jeremiah 4:3). If the hypocrite but offers to mourn for sin, it will effectually hinder his rejoicing in God. But godly sorrow is matter of joy to the believer. He rejoices more, when his heart is melting for sin than he would do though he had all the carnal delights in the world. On the contrary, the delusive joy of the formalist will, either in time or in eternity, be matter of sorrow to him (Proverbs 14:13). True comfort is hidden from unregenerate men (Proverbs 14:10). It is as far out of the reach of worldly men to discern the spiritual joy of a saint as it is out of their power to prevent or remove it. The consolation of the sincere Christian is unspeakable (1 Peter 1:8), and no wonder, for the matter and importance of it are incomprehensible; but the greatest joy of the hypocrite and the worldling can easily be told. It can, without difficulty, be expressed to the utmost of its value. True consolation, is glorified or glorious joy (1 Peter 1:8). It has the highest and most glorious object, and it is the beginning as well as the earnest of glory in the soul.

Counterfeit joy, on the contrary, is base and inglorious. The consolation of the believer is holy. It has a holy, sanctifying influence upon his soul (2 Corinthians 3:18). It disposes him to practice willingly and cheerfully universal holiness. It strengthens, encourages, and enlivens his heart in holy obedience (Nehemiah 8:10). It invigorates him for it; it excites him to it. But the joy of the hypocrite is unholy: it leaves his heart as carnal and his life as unholy as ever; nay, it strengthens his lusts and encourages him in sloth and in the practice of some secret iniquity (Luke 11:21). True comfort humbles the sincere Christian and lays him in the dust at the footstool of a God of infinite holiness, and covering grace (Job 42:5–6; 1 Corinthians 15:10), but counterfeit joy puffs up the empty formalist with pride and self-conceit (Isaiah 58:2–3). Pure consolation is accompanied with a constant fear of displeasing the Lord (Genesis 39:9). Matthew 28:8), but delusive joy is connected with no fear except that of suffering from Him. Spiritual comfort cannot be maintained without a holy tenderness of conscience and a constant struggle against all manner of sin (1 John 3:3), but carnal and hypocritical joy is preserved without either the one or the other. True consolation renders every sin more and more hateful, but counterfeit joy leaves the hypocrite under the reigning love of all iniquity, and especially of some darling sin. Holy comfort disposes the believer to the frequent exercise of impartial self-examination (Psalm 26:1-3), but delusive joy inclines and encourages the hypocrite to neglect that exercise (John 3:20–21). In a word, true consolation is permanent (John 16:22). It is by the Holy Spirit so fixed in the heart that it can never be wholly removed, and it is so strong that it swallows up almost all matter of unwarrantable fear and grief. Indeed, when the believer has lost all sight of his personal interest in the Savior he cannot, as formerly, exercise his joy in God and cannot, in such a case, but lose the sense of that joy, even while the principle and habit of it still remain. But, though the hypocrite's persuasion of his pretended interest in the divine favor continues, yet his joy ceases; his sense of that interest becomes insipid to him (Job 15:5).

12. *In proportion to the degree of holy consolation that is afforded the believer, his duty is his delight.* Being renewed in the spirit of his mind, more clearly and spiritually, he discerns the loveliness of God in Christ, and the more cordially and firmly he believes His love for him, the more he loves God (1 John 4:19); and the more he loves God, the more he delights in Him. In proportion also, as he spiritually discerns the infinite amiableness of the holiness and the other perfections of God, and believes with application His redeeming love, he, in the same proportion, approves Him and the manifestations of His glory in the face of Jesus Christ; but the more he approves or is pleased with God as gloriously manifested in Christ, the more delight he takes in Him. Add to this that the more he is enabled to trust cordially that God in Christ loves him, and that He is not his enemy but his Friend and his Father, the more spiritual comfort he will have; and the more of that holy consolation he has (which is a rejoicing in the Lord), the more will he delight in Him as his own God and Father.

Now, in proportion as the believer is enabled to love, to be pleased with, and to rejoice in God through

the Lord Jesus Christ, he is, at the same time, enabled
to delight in the infinite holiness of God as his God in
Christ, and in all the illustrious displays of it which, especially in redemption, are afforded him (Psalm
138:5). And because the moral law in the hand of the
glorious Mediator is a fair transcript of God's holiness,
a declaration of His will, the believer also delights in
that law after the inward man (Romans 7:22). He loves
it because it is holy and just (Psalm 19:7–10 and
119:97), and he consents unto it that it is good
(Romans 7:1).

In the same degree, then, in which a holy man is
delighted or comforted by a spiritual discovery of the
transcendent loveliness of Jehovah, and by a firm belief
of His infinite love for him, delighting in the holy
commandments of the Lord, the more pleasure he
takes in spiritual and universal obedience to them
(Psalm 19:11). His heart is united to the will and to the
glory of his redeeming God; and the more he is refreshed by the holy consolations of the gospel, or enabled to rejoice in Christ Jesus and His great salvation,
so much the more does he delight in evangelical obedience to His will, and in holy activity for His glory.
The more his heart is comforted, the more will it be a
comfort to him to mortify sin and to practice holiness;
the more uniformly will he rejoice in all opportunities
of doing good and the more ardently will he seize
them (Proverbs 3:17). Beholding the transcendent
beauty of the Lord, and trusting that, in Christ, this
God is his God, and that He loves him with an everlasting love, the believer delights to think and speak of
Him, to adore and serve Him and in all things, to resign himself to His blessed will. Anointed with the oil

of gladness and refreshed with the sweetness of redeeming mercy, he delights, in imitation of his great Redeemer, to do the will of God, and accounts no pleasure under the sun equal to that of doing good. Could he be more holy and spiritually minded, it would please him better than if he possessed all the riches, honors, and pleasures of this world. The more his holy soul is invigorated with spiritual consolation, the more active and cheerful he is in all his duties, for, in proportion as he delights in them, they are easy to him (Psalm 25:13; Matthew 11:30). Indeed, holy living usually begins with comfort, and is maintained by it. The method of grace, as revealed by the gospel, is to comfort our hearts, and thereby to establish us in every good word and work (2 Thessalonians 2:17).

13. Finally, the Lord usually dispenses consolation and affliction alternately to His people in order that they may neither be too depressed nor too elated. The Apostle Paul informs us that, "lest I should be exalted above measure through the abundance of the revelations," which had, in an extraordinary manner, been afforded him, "there was given to me a thorn in the flesh, a messenger of Satan to buffet me" (2 Corinthians 12:7). In order that he might not, through the vanity and deceitfulness of his heart, be elated with an unbecoming conceit of himself, as if he were better than other apostles because of the abundance of the revelations with which he had been favored, the Lord employed the most effectual means to keep him humble. He permitted Satan and his instruments to afflict him, either in his soul or body, or perhaps in both, and that in a manner very abasing and grievous to him. But that the holy apostle might not be too much cast down by this

painful affliction, the Redeemer, in answer to his
prayer, comforted him with this gracious promise: "My
grace is sufficient for thee" (2 Corinthians 12:9). We
read also that the Lord gave David sore troubles, but
enabled him to trust that He would, at another time,
quicken him and comfort him on every side (Psalm
71:20–21). A prophet, representing the ancient church
in her captivity, says, "Thou hast lifted me up and cast
me down" (Psalm 102:10).

The believer, then, while he is in this world, has
cloudy and clear days, tempestuous and calm seasons.
He is at one time in the valley of tears, and at another
on the mountain of joy. His gifts, his prosperity, and,
in consequence of these, his danger of carnal security
are sometimes so great that the Lord, in order to prevent his being intoxicated, sees it necessary to mingle
water with his wine. He sees, it may be, that when the
outward path of the Christian is smooth he is not, in
such a case, fit to be trusted with inward consolation
except in a small measure. He, therefore, in His infinite wisdom and love, varies His dispensations to the
believer. By a wise interchange of adversity and prosperity, He sets trouble and comfort over against each
other (Ecclesiastes 7:14) so that the one may be a foil
to the other; so that the Christian may find a short,
easy, and safe passage between them; so that in adversity "he may weep as though he wept not," and in prosperity "rejoice as though he rejoiced not" (1 Corinthians 7:30). Indeed, as long as sin remains in the believer, he must, in order to grow in grace, have distress
and comfort either alternately or both together, to the
end that when he is sorrowful he may not be cast down
too low, and that when he is rejoicing he may not be

lifted up too high.

Are Christ and God in Christ, together with His grace, mercy, and truth, as has been said above, the primary grounds of a saint's comfort and hope? I hence infer that his manifold infirmities and deficiencies, in his exercise of grace and performance of duty, should at no time discourage him. Believer, your remaining darkness, deadness, carnality, weakness, and indisposition of spirit for holy exercises should indeed occasion in your soul much godly sorrow and self-loathing; but they should never discourage you in your holy endeavors, nor cause you to despond. They should not make you distrust your faithful Redeemer, or doubt any promised blessing, because the title to grace and glory is not founded on our own performances, but on the consummate righteousness of the Lord Jesus; and your exercise of hope should be suitable to the grounds of your hope. Be not disquieted, then, though you feel the corruption of your nature strong and active, while you find, at the same time, your renewed nature striving in opposition to it, and mourning under a painful sense of it. Unbelieving discouragement, arising from a sense either of sins or of wants, of desertions or of temptations, will weaken your hands and indispose your heart for spiritual obedience (1 Samuel 12:20; Hebrews 12:12–13). It was when Peter began to fear that he began to sink in the water.

Does the Lord Jesus usually afford inward and sensible comfort to His children about the time of their first conversion? They may see in this an illustrious display of His manifold wisdom, as well as of His redeeming love for them. One thing He designs by this is that they may perceive as early as possible the inexpressible advantages that they have gained by the gracious change which His Holy Spirit has produced in them, and thereby be encouraged, as well as inclined, so to run the race that is set before them as to attain the prize of inexpressible and endless joy in His immediate presence. For, having marrow and fatness in their Father's house instead of husks in a far country, spiritual and substantial delights instead of pleasures that are carnal and empty, they cannot, even at the beginning of their Christian course, but acknowledge themselves already unspeakable gainers.

Is spiritual joy required of believers in the law, and promised to them in the gospel? And is the Lord displeased when they appear uncomfortable in His service? Let them hence learn that it is their duty, at all times and in all conditions, to be of good comfort, and that it is their sin to neglect this part of their duty at any time or on any account. Consider, believer, that you are commanded to "be of good courage," yea, to "Rejoice in the Lord *always*" (Philippians 4:4). Rely, then, upon the promise of the gospel in order to obey this precept of the law. Trust firmly that Jesus, the consolation of Israel, will, according to His promise, comfort you in every time of need; and in the faith of the promise, as well as in obedience to the precept, endeavor frequently to rejoice in Him and in God as your God through Him. Exercise daily, in dependence on the promise, the grace of holy joy—not so much because it will afford pleasure to yourself, as because it is a duty which you are commanded by your God and Redeemer always to perform. If you allow yourself to neglect for a season any duty, and especially *this* one, you must not be surprised if you soon lose your present comfort.

Is spiritual consolation of joy a part of life, of eternal life? Hence I may justly infer that it is a slandering of true religion to say or insinuate that it deprives persons of the comfort of life. Nothing can be more false. None in the world has such good reason to rejoice as the true Christian. If a holy man appears at any time to be sad, it is not because he is religious, but because he is not more religious. The more holiness he attains, the more pure consolation he enjoys. It is true that he will take no more pleasure in sin, but instead of that will have peace with God and the joy of his salvation. It is far from being Christ's design to deprive him of pleasure, but only to determine and enable him so to consult his own happiness, in subservience to the glory of God, as to exchange sinful and mean for spiritual and noble pleasures (Proverbs 3:17). He accordingly experiences such delight in the ways of holiness as he never enjoyed, nor could enjoy, in the ways of sin. "A stranger doth not intermeddle with his joy" (Proverbs 14:10). The believer knows by experience that there is more joy even in penitential mourning for sin than in all the mirth of the most prosperous sinner. He finds such a secret sweetness in his godly sorrow that, instead of desiring, he rather fears the removal of that sorrow.

Is the comfort with which the saints are favored spiritual and holy comfort? Let no man then conclude that he is a true Christian merely because he has felt on some occasions natural and sensible consolation. Natural, outward, and sensible consolation is one thing; spiritual, inward, and holy comfort is another, and a very different thing. The former is natural, and is common both to saints and sinners; the latter is spiritual, and is peculiar only to the saints. One is outward and sensitive, proceeding, under common providential influence, from a man's natural constitution of body; the other is inward and holy, and is effected by the Holy Spirit, the Comforter, dwelling in the soul.

Spiritual consolation is sometimes sensible as well as that which is natural; or, rather, the former might (as it sometimes is) be called "sensible consolation" and the latter "sensory delight." Spiritual comfort delights chiefly the rational and inward faculties of the soul; natural comfort pleases only the outward and sensitive faculties of it, namely, the imagination, the natural spirits, and even the external senses. The former is wrought in the heart by the Holy Spirit, according to the Word spiritually understood and believed; the latter is often produced by the external manner of the reader or preacher of the Word, such as his elocution, tone, and action. Persons of a soft natural constitution of body have this sensory delight more often, and in greater measure, than they of a contrary temperament. When the one is enjoyed by the saints, they commonly can assign some reason for it; when the other is felt by persons of any description, they usually can give no reason for the delightful sensation, but only that something, they know not what, has made a pleasing impression upon them.

Spiritual comfort is the opposite of trouble of mind on spiritual accounts; natural comfort is the opposite of melancholy, which is a bodily disease. The former, as I already observed, is the special work of the Holy Spirit in the hearts of sincere believers; the latter proceeds from natural and external causes and is often raised by Satan in order to confirm sinners in their delusion and hypocrisy. The hypocrites in Zion mentioned by Isaiah (Isaiah 58:2) "took delight in approaching to God," and the hearers compared by our Lord to the stony ground "immediately received the word with gladness" (Mark 4:16). Thus it appears that thousands of men and women, whose unholy lives demonstrate them to be utter strangers to spiritual and holy consolation, have, nevertheless, on some occasions, much natural and sensible delight. Let no man therefore conclude that he is a true Christian merely because he has felt much sensible and even transporting joy, for his joy may be nothing but a natural sensation.

Once more, is holy consolation peculiar to holy persons? Then it does *not* belong to unholy men. The same spiritual comfort that the saints have received is, in the gospel, offered freely to you who live in the love and practice of some known sin; and the authentic offer affords you a warrant to receive it, but no warrant to receive it separate from Christ, or otherwise than by receiving Him with His righteousness and salvation. It, indeed, affords you a right to trust in the Lord Jesus for all His salvation, and for holy consolation as a part of it, but no right to trust that He will give you comfort apart from salvation; no warrant to trust that He will afford you spiritual consolation in the love and practice of any iniquity. You cannot rejoice as believers do, for you have no personal interest in Jesus, the consolation of Israel. Alas! there is not, and there never was, the smallest drop of spiritual consolation in your heart. You have comfort from the creature, but none from the Redeemer. You cannot have it from Him, for you delight in sinning against Him. The Lord says to you, and to all the other servants of sin, "Behold, My servants shall eat, but ye shall be hungry; behold, My servants shall drink, but ye shall be thirsty; behold, My servants shall rejoice, but ye shall be ashamed; behold, My servants shall sing for joy of heart, but ye shall cry for sorrow of heart, and shall howl for vexation of spirit" (Isaiah 65:13–14).

You now love vanity and rejoice in iniquity; but the day is coming when, if sovereign grace does not prevent it, your laughter shall be turned to mourning, and your joy to heaviness (James 4:9). Ah! how depraved is your heart when it can take pleasure in sin, but no pleasure in Christ or in holiness! What a reproach is it to your understanding and will to love darkness rather than light, to choose death rather than life! How deep is the corruption of your nature when you can love sin, which is altogether hateful, infinitely hateful, and hate Christ and holiness, which are altogether lovely; when you can take delight in the worst of things, but none in the best! What ignorance and enmity against God have you hitherto shown by standing aloof from holiness, lest it should deprive you of your delight in sin! You now say of the holy exercises of private and public worship, in which the saints enjoy delightful communion with their God and Savior, "Behold, what a weariness is it!" But take heed, lest you provoke the holy majesty of heaven to cast you into that place of eternal torment where you will have sufficient cause to be weary.

O sinner, the Lord Jesus, who is infinitely excellent and amiable, immensely full of grace and consolation, now offers Himself, and all that He is and has, to you as an undone sinner of mankind; and with inexpressible tenderness He invites you to accept Him, and to trust and delight in Him. He says to sinners in general, who read and hear His blessed gospel, "Come ye, buy and eat; yea, come, buy with wine and milk, without money, and without price. Hearken diligently unto Me, and eat ye that which is good, and let your soul delight itself in fatness. Incline your ear, and come unto Me; hear, and your soul shall live; and I will make an everlasting covenant with you, even the sure mercies of David" (Isaiah 55:1–3). It will be impossible for you to experience true consolation until you comply with this gracious, cheering invitation.

2

The Great Importance and Usefulness of Spiritual Comfort to the Saints

The high importance and utility of spiritual consolation, in qualifying believers for the lively exercise of their graces and the spiritual performance of their duties, will appear if the following particulars are considered:

1. It is of such unspeakable consequence to them that the eternal Father has, in the greatness of His love, sent His only begotten Son into the world with a commission to purchase it for them. The Father, according to His eternal covenant with the Son as last Adam, sent Him in order that He might bear their griefs and carry their sorrows, and so might, at the infinite expense of His unparalleled anguish, agony, and death, purchase for them the comfort which they, in the first Adam, had forfeited. He sent His only Son, His dear Son, to endure the pains of eternal death for them that they might enjoy, in union with Him, the comfort of eternal life; that they might enter into Zion with songs of triumph in their lips and everlasting joy on their heads. The Lord Jesus Himself has declared that the comforting of mourners in Zion was a principal object of His mission into the world. "The Spirit of the Lord God," said He, "is upon Me, because the Lord hath anointed Me to preach good tidings unto the meek. He hath sent Me to bind up the brokenhearted . . . to comfort all that mourn; to give unto them that mourn in Zion the beauty of ashes, the oil of joy for mourning, and the garment of praise for the spirit of heaviness" (Isaiah 61:1–3). The Father has also exalted Him in the human nature to universal dominion, with the purpose that He might dispense the comfort of salvation to all who should believe in Him. Accordingly, when He was about to leave the world, the legacy which He left to His disciples was comfort (John 14:27). He promised that their sorrow should be turned into joy, and that, in Him, they should have peace when in the world they should have tribulation (John 16:20, 33).

So great is the importance of divine consolation to the saints, and to the glory of God in their salvation, that the Father and the Son send the Holy Spirit to apply it to their souls. The Spirit, accordingly, testifies of Christ (John 15:26), witnesses their adoption into the family of God, and seals them to the day of redemption. In performing these offices, He invigorates and cheers their hearts. Nay, so important, so excellent, is spiritual comfort in the estimation of God that God the Father assumes these titles: "the God of consolation" (Romans 15:5) and "the God of all comfort" (2 Corinthians 1:3). God the Son is called "The Consolation of Israel" (Luke 2:25)," and God the adorable Spirit is distinguished by this cheering title: "the Comforter" (John 16:7). In few words, so high is the value which the Lord sets upon holy comfort that He gives this solemn

charge to the ministers of His Word: "Strengthen ye
the weak hands, and confirm the feeble knees. Say
to them that are of a fearful heart, 'Be strong, fear
not' " (Isaiah 35:3–4). Do men set such a high value
upon earthly comforts as to pursue with unwearied
diligence the enjoyment of them? With what in-
comparably higher esteem should believers regard
heavenly consolations, in which the infinite excellence of redeeming grace is displayed with transcendent luster (Job 15:11)!

2. *Spiritual consolation is of such high importance as to
form an essential part of that eternal life which God, who
cannot lie, promised before the world began.* That it is a part
of eternal life was evinced above. Comfort or joy is so
essential a part of life eternal in heaven that heaven
itself is in Scripture called "joy" (Matthew 25:21). To
enter into heaven is to enter into joy, the joy of the
Lord Jesus. If, then, fullness of joy is a necessary part
of eternal life as consummated in heaven, doubtless
joy, though in an inferior degree, is a part of the
same eternal life as begun upon earth. Now, does
spiritual consolation form a part even of life eternal? Is it necessary to holiness and happiness, not
only as a means to the end but, by a nobler kind of
necessity, as a part of the end itself? How unspeakably important, then, how divinely excellent must it
be! It is supernatural, spiritual, and divine, and,
therefore, is of a nature inconceivably more pure,
sublime, and ennobling than any natural delight,
any earthly joy. Instead of corrupting and debasing
the soul, as carnal joys frequently do, it beautifies
and dignifies it.

So highly important, in our view, is even earthly

comfort or joy that, as Chrysostom says, "We do all in order that we may joy." But creature-comforts, even though enjoyed in the utmost variety and in the highest degree, are, in comparison to divine consolation, and that in the lowest degree, but as the glimmering taper before the meridian sun. Holy consolation is a commodity of heaven, that distant country, not to be imported but by faith and prayer. It makes a man inexpressibly more happy than any earthly comforts can do. One smile of the Redeemer, one glance of heaven as the sure portion of the holy soul, yields more contentment and comfort than all the delights of this world. What are any, what are all earthly joys compared with the joy of him who rejoices in the Lord! Indeed, as Luther says, to comfort the heart is more than to create a world. How inexpressibly powerful and grateful is heavenly consolation to the distressed soul! When David had been under great trouble, when a flood of bitter waters had overflowed his soul, the Lord let fall a drop or two of heavenly comfort, and all was turned unto sweetness (Psalm 94:19). Oh, the inconceivable excellence, the unparalleled sweetness of divine consolation!

3. *The high importance of spiritual comfort will also appear if we consider that it is the pure delight which saints have in common with holy angels.* The pleasures of sense are such as believers have in common with irrational creatures, and the pleasures merely of reason are such as they attain equally with other men, but the delights of communion with God are such as they enjoy in common with the angels of light. They are not, indeed, the same in degree as the joys of angels,

but they are the same in kind. They are the pleasures of a soul and not of bodily sense, the delights of a holy soul and not of a carnal mind. The pleasures of true religion do immediately affect the soul, that part of a holy man by which he is allied to the world of spirits; and therefore they are to be regarded as the only sublime, the only true pleasures of a man. When holy souls are comforted, they are entertained as with angels' food. Their consolation is not only spiritual, and therefore suitable to a holy and immortal spirit, but it is substantial and satisfying, heavenly and glorious (1 Peter 1:8). Their joy is, in its own nature, unspeakably glorious, and is accompanied with glorying in the cross of the Lord Jesus Christ. It is truly honorable, and is the earnest of glory in their souls. When sinners have "come to Jesus, the Mediator of the new covenant, and to the blood of sprinkling," they so "come to an innumerable company of angels" as, in some measure, to participate with them in that sublime, that celestial delight which they always enjoy in the presence of God and the Lamb. They then begin to imitate the holy and blessed angels in delighting in objects of the greatest worth, and especially in the will and the glory of God in Christ.

4. *Spiritual consolation is of such consequence to believers, and to the glory of God in their salvation, that every part of sacred Scripture contributes to promote it, and is intended to do so.* "Whatsoever things were written aforetime," says the Apostle Paul, "were written for our learning, that we through patience and comfort of the Scriptures might have hope" (Romans 15:4). It is as if he had said, "Whatever things were, by the inspiration

of the Holy Spirit, written in the Old Testament were left on record not only for the instruction of our ancestors, but for ours likewise, in order that we, by means of them, might be excited and encouraged to exercise patience under all our afflictions, and might be partakers of the joy of faith and comfort of the Holy Spirit, so as to attain the sure hope of grace to bear them, and of glory to crown them." All the types and prophecies, histories and examples, laws and doctrines recorded in the Scriptures were designed to increase the consolation of believers under their various troubles. Accordingly, they all, in the hand of the adorable Spirit, serve either directly or indirectly to advance their comfort. For this end were the Old and New Testaments written, that they might, like breasts of consolation, be sucked by the children of God (Isaiah 66:11). The blessed Word is, in all its parts, a magazine of comfort to the saints. Even those parts of it which seem least adapted to afford them comfort do, notwithstanding, promote their consolation and their delight. The strictest of its commands prescribe to them delightful work (Psalm 119:140; Romans 7:12). The severest of its threatenings deter them from wandering out of such ways as are ways of pleasantness and paths of peace. The law as a covenant is subservient to the gospel, and both serve to bring the believing soul to holy comfort (1 Corinthians 14:3). One commendation of the statutes of God is that "they rejoice the heart" (Psalm 19:8). The holy Word of God is, in all its parts, inexpressibly sweet to the exercised Christian; it is "the joy and rejoicing of his heart" (Jeremiah 15:16). The most delicious honey is not so gracious to the palate as the holy Scriptures are to the spiritual taste (Psalm 19:10). How unspeakably important and useful, then, must spiritual consolation be when it is the great design of every part of sacred Scripture to advance it in the souls of believers!

5. *So important is this comfort that all the dispensations of divine grace and providence are continually concurring to increase it in the saints.* "We know," says the apostle, "that all things work together for good to them who love God, to them who are called according to His purpose" (Romans 8:28). By the "good" mentioned here is meant the spiritual and eternal happiness or welfare of the saints in spiritual joy as well as in spiritual knowledge and true holiness. All things, then, all dispensations and occurrences of providence, however diversified, however afflictive, do, even now, under the special influence of the overruling wisdom and grace of God, cooperate in all their diversified connections and consequences, one with another, to promote the spiritual joy, the holy consolation of those who sincerely love Him. All hands in heaven, earth, and hell are presently and continually at work in order to increase, either directly or indirectly, the comfort to those who delight in the Lord. And if all things continually work together for their consolation, nothing remains to work against it. How important, then, how useful to subserve the purposes of the divine glory in their salvation must the consolation of believers be when all things in the universe are continually employed in advancing it; when all persons, all dispensations, all events are incessantly concurring to promote it! Prosperity and

adversity, whether in things internal or external, work together, and under gracious and providential influence they form a curious quilt, which afterwards will, in the light of glory, be contemplated with unceasing admiration. If the Lord brings His people to His holy mountain, it is that He may make them joyful in His house of prayer (Isaiah 61:7); if He brings them into the wilderness, it is with a view to speak comfortably to them (Hosea 2:14); if their sufferings at any time abound, it is in order that their consolation may also abound (2 Corinthians 1:5). The sufferings of others are conducive to the increase of their consolation, and the comforts of others are also for their consolation and salvation (2 Corinthians 1:6). The Lord, by afflictions, empties, humbles, and melts them that they may be vessels fitted to receive a larger measure of grace and comfort (Psalm 119:71). Their loss of other comforts commonly issues in their being favored with more spiritual comfort, and therefore it is profitable for them.

The Lord Jesus wounds in order to heal. He casts down when He designs to raise them up; and He brings death, as it were, upon their feelings, wishes, and prospects when He is about to grant them the desire of their souls. When He had told His disciples that He was soon to depart from them, and so to remove from them the greatest earthly comfort that ever they enjoyed (which was His bodily presence), sorrow filled their hearts. But He assured them that this loss would be expedient, or, as the original word also signifies, profitable for them inasmuch as it would make way for a still greater mercy, the coming of the Comforter, to abide with them forever (John 16:6–7). Believers, then, may assure themselves that the all-compassionate Savior will, at no time and on no account, take away any of their comforts from them but with a view to give them better comforts. He will usually be sweetest to them when their lot in the world is most bitter; for the sharper their trials are, the more will they serve to prepare them for His sweetest consolations. If ever thick clouds intercept, for a season, the cheering light of His countenance from them, those very clouds will occasion this light to break forth again upon them with the brighter splendor. Whether their troubles are external or internal, they, in the hand of the Holy Spirit, serve to show them how much they need to trust constantly and solely in the Lord Jesus for sanctifying and supporting grace. And the more they trust in Him, the more comfort—as well as holiness—they receive from His fullness.

6. *Spiritual comfort is of much consequence to believers, for it serves, in a very high degree, to heighten and sweeten all their temporal comforts.* It renders every outward blessing a real, a substantial comfort to them. Spiritual consolation is that which makes them capable of relishing and enjoying their external comforts (Ecclesiastes 9:7). Were a man to possess everything under the sun that is delightful and splendid, everything that could please his eye or gratify his taste, if he did not enjoy the favor of God with it he would still be poor and wretched. To think that the almighty Jehovah is an infinite enemy to him, that his temporal comforts may be followed by endless torments, and that by all that he eats and drinks he

may be but fattening himself for the day of slaughter, will be as wormwood and gall mingled with all his delights. What can it avail him, though all the world smiles upon him, if he is under the infinite, the tremendous frowns of almighty God? They cannot for a moment screen him from the impending storm, nor secure him from the consuming fire. Trouble of conscience renders every comfort of life insipid and unpleasing, while, on the contrary, peace of conscience makes even the meanest morsel sweet (Proverbs 15:15–16). It infuses an additional sweetness into every other comfort. When a man is enabled cordially to trust that the Lord Jesus loves and saves him, and that He will perfect that which concerns him, his joy and peace in believing cannot fail to impart a heavenly sweetness to all his earthly joys. By trusting in the blessed Redeemer, he tastes that He is good to him, and so he enjoys Him in all his inferior enjoyments. He who places all his confidence and delight in the Lord will have a double relish for every earthly comfort, because he will see the hand of his gracious Redeemer providing and bestowing it. He will possess Christ in everything while he has it, and everything in Christ after it is taken from him (2 Corinthians 6:10). As it is the absence of his blessed Redeemer that embitters all his temporal blessings to the believer, so it is His presence, cheering his heart, that improves and sweetens them all. Thus we see that spiritual consolation is of high importance because, while it is in itself the greatest of all comforts, it is that which serves to heighten all other delights.

7. *This comfort is of unspeakable importance to the saints,*

for it not only heightens all their other comforts, but it alleviates all their calamities. It makes their heaviest afflictions light (2 Corinthians 4:17). When the spirit of the believer is without comfort, the smallest trial becomes a burden; but when his heart is glad, the greatest appears light and easy (Acts 16:25; Romans 5:2–3). The weight of an affliction is to be estimated rather by the impression which it makes upon the spirit than by anything in its outward appearance. The smallest will be so heavy as to overwhelm a holy man if he is left to struggle with it in his own strength, and without the presence of Christ to comfort him; but if Christ is graciously pleased to pour consolation into his soul, it will be so exhilarated and strengthened as to induce him to count even the greatest affliction as light, and the longest as but for a moment. A sweet and lively impression of the love of Christ in redeeming him, accompanied with a true sense of the sin and misery from which he is redeemed, will render him not only submissive, but even joyful in his affliction. And while he is rejoicing in hope, though the flesh may still have its uneasy feelings, the spirit shall triumph over them; though a sense of pain may not be taken away, it shall be overcome by the faith and sense of redeeming love. Paul and Silas, in the prison at Philippi, felt more pleasure than pain, more joy than sorrow.

It was the sweetness of divine consolation that caused one of the martyrs, when the flame first reached his ear, to say, "What a small pain is this, compared with the glory to come!" What is a drop of vinegar when put into an ocean of wine? It was this that, as another of them said, made their prisons their delectable orchards. Favored with heavenly consolation, many of the saints in ancient times not only took patiently, but joyfully the spoiling of their goods (Hebrews 10:34). When the Lord Jesus speaks peace to the holy soul, He so refreshes and consoles it that no afflictions, however painful, have any real bitterness in them. One drop of that consolation which He dispenses from heaven shall suffice to sweeten a whole sea of external trouble, and to fill the believing soul with inexpressible joy (Psalm 94:19). He has graciously promised to be, in a special manner, present with His people in their afflictions, and to administer such comfort to their souls as will greatly alleviate them. "When thou passest through the waters," said He, "I will be with thee, and through the rivers, they shall not overflow thee; when thou walkest through the fire, thou shalt not be burnt; neither shall the flame kindle upon thee" (Isaiah 43:2). And again, "In Me ye shall have peace, while in the world ye shall have tribulation" (John 16:33). When He comforts them with a lively sense of His love for them, it turns their wormwood into sweetness, their sorrow into joy. So comforted, they can rejoice, and even glory, in tribulation (Romans 5:3). This is a plain evidence of the high importance and excellence of spiritual consolation, that it overcomes the pains of sense, takes out their sting, and takes away their terror.

Holy comfort makes believers delight so in all the will of God as to take pleasure even in the hardest things, considered as His doing (2 Corinthians 12:10). How sweet, then, must that be which can sweeten even the wormwood and the gall! Of what consequence must that be which can make the heaviest burden light! The delights of sense forsake us when we are in trouble and have the greatest need of them (Job 33:19–20), but it is then that the comforts of the Spirit have the sweetest relish and the strongest influence (Psalm 119:50). They are like the tree cast into the waters of Marah, which made them sweet (Exodus 15:25). How much then are they to be pitied who are drinking deep of the bitter waters of affliction, and have nothing of divine consolation to sweeten them!

8. *It is spiritual consolation only which can effectively remove that greatest of all afflictions, trouble of spirit.* The delights of sense to one who is deeply wounded and dejected in spirit are "like the singing of songs to a heavy heart" (Proverbs 25:20). They, instead of yielding the smallest relief, become quite insipid, and even nauseous, for, notwithstanding the possession of them, and that even in the highest degree, "a wounded spirit who can bear?" But spiritual consolation, especially when it is strong, not only alleviates, but effectually removes that most intolerable of all afflictions. When after a dark night of desertion the Lord graciously returns to the disconsolate believer, and lifts up the light of His countenance upon him, He thereby puts gladness in his heart, far surpassing that of worldly men when their corn and their wine increase (Psalm 4:6–7). By so doing, He puts off the sackcloth of the exercised Christian and girds him with gladness (Psalm 30:11). No sooner does Christ comfort those who mourn in Zion than "He giveth unto them beauty for ashes, the oil of joy for mourning, the garment of praise for the spirit of

heaviness" (Isaiah 61:2–3). If they "have gone forth and wept, bearing precious seed," yet no sooner does He impart consolation to them than they "come again with rejoicing, bringing their sheaves with them" (Psalm 126:6). "In His favor is life; weeping may endure for a night, but joy or shouting cometh in the morning" (Psalm 30:5). How valuable, then, how unspeakably important, must divine consolation be to exercised Christians, when they consider that it is the only, the sovereign cure for dejection and anguish of spirit!

9. *The great importance of spiritual comfort also appears in that it serves to overbalance everything in true religion which seems difficult and unpleasing.* Not regarding here either the misrepresentations of some men or the misapprehensions of others concerning the way of holiness, I shall only advert to the chief difficulties and grievances which the Scripture itself represents as occurring in that way. The Lord Jesus, that faithful and true witness, informs us that the way to heaven "is a narrow way," or, as the words might be rendered, a strait or distressful way, a way in which the saints have to pass through much tribulation into the kingdom of God. Beside the multitude of imaginary difficulties which appears to the slothful man (when he says, "There is a lion in the way; a lion is in the streets," Proverbs 26:13), there are some real difficulties in the way to the heavenly felicity. Believers, as well as other men, are commanded to exercise repentance daily, and so to weep and mourn and loathe themselves for their iniquities; to crucify the flesh, and so to mortify the members of the body of sin in them, which is as painful

as cutting off a right hand or plucking out a right eye; to deny themselves, to renounce the world as a portion, and so to abandon forever all the pleasures of sin; to take up their cross and lay their account with manifold afflictions, and, at the same time, to fight the good fight of faith, to wrestle against the principalities and powers of darkness, to endure hardship, to run with patience the race that is set before them, and to be fervent in spirit, serving the Lord.

Now, though these, and others which might be mentioned, are in themselves real difficulties, which seem very unpleasant, and from which even eminent believers are often ready to shrink, yet holy comfort is more, much more than sufficient to overbalance them. It serves, in the hand of the blessed Spirit, to render wisdom's ways, notwithstanding all the difficulties and grievances which occur in them, "ways of pleasantness, and paths of peace" to the saints. Nay, so sweet and so powerful is spiritual consolation that, in proportion to the degree in which it is bestowed, it makes even those painful exercises themselves pleasant, those difficult duties easy (Matthew 11:30). It renders it very pleasant to the Christian to be without the pleasures of sin. It adds much more to the pleasantness of a holy life than it is possible for any sufferings or grievances in this world ever to take from it. The sufferings are but human; the comfort is divine. Believers know by experience that, in proportion as they trust in Christ, the times of their greatest affliction are usually the seasons of their strongest consolation (2 Corinthians 1:5); and, therefore, even the most dejected and sorrowful of

them would not, for a thousand worlds, change conditions or pleasures with the most prosperous of
those who are the servants of sin.

   *10. Holy consolation removes, in proportion to the degree
of it, the terror of death and judgment.* Spiritual consolation is that which, in the hand of the blessed Spirit,
takes away the terrors and alleviates the pains of
death. Though death is the friend of grace, it is still
the enemy of nature. A dislike and fear of death,
therefore, does in no way prove that one is not a true
believer. We are not in general fond of handling a
serpent, even though we know that its sting is
plucked out. But when the faith of a Christian is
strong, and his hope of salvation lively, the joy of his
faith and the rejoicing of his hope take away, in his
view, the frightful appearance of death and bestow
upon it an amiable, an inviting aspect. Living comforts in his dying moments make him even "desire
to depart and to be with Christ," the blessed Fountain of everlasting consolation (Philippians 1:23).

   It is the joyful hope of a blessed resurrection that
makes the saints think without fear of resigning
their bodies to the gloomy grave. It is the cheering
prospect of a house not made with hands that makes
them willing, without dismay, to leave their earthly
tabernacle. When the Lord Jesus would comfort His
disciples in the prospect of His departure from
them, He said, "I go to prepare a place for you: and if
I go and prepare a place for you, I will come again,
and receive you to Myself, that where I am, there ye
may be also" (John 14:2–3). If death were to come
alone to the saints, its ghastly countenance could
not but be terrible to them; but when they believe

and rejoice in the assurance that their living Redeemer will, according to His faithful promise, come along with it, to sweeten it to them and to conduct them safely through the dark valley of the shadow of it (Psalm 23:4), to the heavenly mountain of their Father's house, the prospect is no longer dreadful, but delightful.

How consoling are these words of the great Redeemer! He does not say that comfort merely will come in that time of need, but that He Himself, the glorious Fountain of consolation, will then come and receive them to Himself. It is the comfort of such a promise, when believed with application, that relieves them against the dread of endless torment, and so raises them above the slavish fear of dying. When the Apostle Paul says that Jesus died, he, speaking at the same time of believers, says that they only sleep, and sleep in Him (1 Thessalonians 4:14). One reason why he varies the term is this: Jesus endured death in all its terrors in order that it might become a quiet and sweet sleep to them who believe in Him. "It is Christ that died" (Romans 8:34). The suffering of death was bitter to Christ that the sleep of death might be sweet to them. When they, then, are enabled to rejoice in the well-grounded hope that death to them will only be a dissolution, a departure, a falling asleep in the arms of their dear Redeemer, the dread of it is thereby removed. People in general are not afraid to lie down in bed to sleep. Ah! how contemptible is that pleasure which is dampened at the view of death and chased away at the prospect of judgment! But how important, how excellent that joy which, instead of being itself abated, lessens and even removes the terror of that last enemy!

11. The high importance and excellence of it will further appear if it is compared with the delights of sense. Earthly and sensual joy is easily sold, and utterly void of glory; but the joy which is in believing is "unspeakable, and full of glory" (1 Peter 1:8). The greatest of worldly joys are mean and empty, and their highest amount may easily be expressed. Much more is frequently thought and said of their value than they deserve. They are never, from experience, found equal to the notion which worldly men have of them, nor to the expectation which they form from them. But spiritual joy is far above the highest conceptions that either men or angels can form of it, and the loftiest descriptions that they can give of it. Earthly joys are empty and vainglorious; even the most plausible of them can never fill or satisfy the soul. They are far below the excellence, as well as the high capacity, of the immortal soul. But the joy of faith, the comfort of communion with Christ, as it is substantial and satisfying, so it is excellent and honorable; it is that of which none needs to be ashamed, and is heavenly glory begun in the soul.

Spiritual joy is pure and sublime; sensual and sinful pleasure is sordid and mean. The one is ennobling to the soul; the other is debasing. The former is elevating and enlarging; the latter is degrading and enslaving. That is satisfying; this is surfeiting. The one increases and improves when used; the other fades with use, and leaves to them who place their happiness in it a piercing sting behind it. The former is pleasing to the Lord; the latter is offensive

to Him. That will issue in perfect and everlasting joy;
this will end in dire and eternal anguish. As it was
with the Israelites in the desert, who could not form
a right estimate of the milk or honey of Canaan,
who doted upon the onions and garlic of Egypt, so it
is with the carnal mind, that knows not and loves
not spiritual delights, that relishes and prefers before them the sordid pleasures of sense. In proportion as a man has experience of the sweetness of
spiritual pleasures, those that are sensual and ensnaring become insipid to him; they have now no
sweetness in comparison to the sweetness which ex-
ceeds them. Indeed, it is impossible to express how
low and contemptible the joys of sense, and especially of sin, appear to them who are rejoicing in
Christ Jesus.

*12. Finally, the inexpressible importance of spiritual com-
fort appears chiefly in that it promotes, in an eminent degree,
universal holiness of heart and life.*

It revives and invigorates the graces of the
Christian. It excites and encourages a holy man to
trust cordially and constantly in Christ for sanctification, to love Him, and God in Him, with ardent affection, and so to love His manifested glory as to
perform every duty in faith, from love, and for the
glory of His holy name. He cannot love God
supremely, nor delight in doing His will, unless he
himself is delighted and cheered by trusting that
God loves him (1 John 4:19). No arguments will persuade a man to commit his way to the Lord or cast
his care upon Him. It is a sense of redeeming love,
warm on the heart, that captivates the soul, concili-
ates the will, and engages the affections (2 Corinthi-

ans 5:14–15).

A comfortable persuasion of the love of Jesus for the soul will be operative in it as a torch in a sheaf: it will gradually destroy its remaining enmity against Him. It will enlarge the heart with ardent love for Him, and elevate the affections above the world. The soul, in order to be kept from lusting after earthly and carnal pleasures, must, by an appropriating faith, take pleasure in the Savior and in His love. Holy comfort embitters sin to a man, and disposes him, with deep abhorrence of it, to strive against it. It tends greatly to melt and humble the heart for sin (1 Corinthians 15:9–10). The firmer a holy man's comfort is, the softer his heart is. The more "his heart is fixed, trusting in the Lord, so as not to be afraid of evil tidings" (Psalm 112:7), the more disposed he is to fear the evil of sinning against Him (Acts 9:31).

Spiritual comfort also inclines and encourages the saints ardently to follow after universal holiness of life, and constantly to long for the perfection of it. "The Spirit of the Lord God," said the Messiah, "is upon Me, because the Lord hath anointed Me . . . to comfort all that mourn; to appoint unto them that mourn in Zion, to give unto them beauty for ashes, the oil of joy for mourning, the garment of praise for the spirit of heaviness; that they might be called trees of righteousness, the planting of the Lord; that He might be glorified" (Isaiah 61:1–3). It disposes believers to frequency and impartiality in self-examination (Psalm 26:1–3), and excites them to diligent endeavors after increasing communion with God in every duty (Psalm 63:1–8). It is employed by the Holy

Spirit to render them active, resolute, and cheerful in the spiritual performance of all their various duties (Psalm 119:32, 166). Godly sorrow, indeed, disposes them to be serious; but it is holy joy that renders them active. It is "the oil of gladness" that makes the wheels of their voluntary obedience move forward with ease and speed. Some measure of holy comfort is necessary to the practice of evangelical holiness. Summer, in the natural world, is necessary as well as winter.

The very nature of the duties and exercises of the true Christian is such that they require comfort of heart for the acceptable performance of them. A holy life commonly begins with comfort, and is maintained by it (Psalm 26:3; 2 Thessalonians 2:17). The way to be kept from carelessness and formality in spiritual exercises is so to trust in Christ for salvation as to cease to despond; for the soul grows careless by desponding. The sorrow of the world and the fear of hell enervate and numb all the faculties of the soul. A man can perform no spiritual obedience without some degree of spiritual joy, as well as of true love. The former is as much the fruit of the Spirit as the latter (Galatians 5:22). The Christian cannot be encouraged to pray to God unless he is consoled with the hope that God, for Christ's sake, will graciously hear and answer his prayer (Psalm 86:7). He cannot cordially praise God unless he is enabled to trust that God will glorify the perfections of His nature and magnify the promises of His covenant in his eternal salvation. It is in proportion as his heart is comforted that he will be truly thankful to the Lord for the smallest favor. It is holy con-

solation that makes every act of grace, every instance
of duty, and every part of spiritual service, however
secret it is, pleasant to a good man. In a word, it is
this that so exhilarates and so constrains him as to
make all his affection run out to the Lord Jesus, and
all his strength run out for Him.

So much for the importance and usefulness of
spiritual comfort to every believer.

From what has been here advanced, we may infer
that no comforts are so excellent, so sweet, and so
desirable as spiritual comforts. While these form a
part of eternal life and promote, in an eminent degree, the love and practice of holiness, they are the
same in kind as the delights of holy angels, and of
ransomed spirits in the holy place on high. They are
the pleasures of a holy soul, and they heighten the
relish of every outward comfort. The light of God's
gracious countenance, shining upon the soul, is
better than life and all its most valued enjoyments. If
an Israelite was to be cut off from his people who
had in his house a perfume like that of the
Tabernacle (Exodus 30:38), surely the Lord will not
hold him guiltless who persuades himself that any
other perfume can be so fragrant, so delightful as
that of the house of God; that any other joy can be so
excellent, so ennobling, so cheering as the joy of
God's salvation.

Is spiritual joy of such high importance to the
holiness and happiness of the saints in this world,
where it is far from being perfect? How highly, then,
will it contribute to their felicity in the heavenly
world, where it shall, through all eternity, be full

and ever-flowing! Oh, how transcendently great,
how inexpressibly glorious will the holiness and
blessedness of the redeemed, in the immediate
presence of God and of the Lamb, be, where they
shall attain fullness of joy, and, perhaps, an eternal
increase of rapturous delight! If spiritual consolation, even when it is small, impels believers to unwearied efforts in holy worship and spiritual obedience, we need not wonder that the four living creatures round about the throne are represented in the
visions of John as not resting day and night, as
never ceasing to thank and praise the Lord, "saying,
'Holy, holy, holy, Lord God Almighty, who was, and
is, and is to come' " (Revelation 4:8). If even a small
measure of pure consolation is of such advantage to
a holy man now as to encourage his heart, to invigorate his grace, to excite his holy activity, and to
heighten all his outward comforts, of what unspeakable gain to him hereafter shall the fullness of joy,
the perfection of endless delight be!

Is holy consolation of such inestimable value to
the spiritual seed of Christ that He, in the immen-
sity of His love, came down from the realms of light
to purchase it for them? Believers may learn from
this what infinite obligations they are under to their
incarnate Redeemer. Christian, your dear Savior has,
at the infinite expense of His own unparalleled obedience, anguish, and death, purchased and secured
everlasting consolation for you. He was troubled in
spirit that you might be comforted. He was encom-
passed with the sorrows of eternal death that you
might enter into the joys of everlasting life. He was
arrayed in the spirit of heaviness that you might be

clothed with the garments of praise. He who was, from eternity, the delight of His Father, rejoicing always before Him, endured for you the hiding of His countenance and the sense of His infinite wrath that you might, to eternity, joy in God through Him. Has He not done and suffered enough to show you that He is willing to enrich you with consolation, that He cares for your comfort, and that He gives you sufficient cause to be always of good comfort? Were it not that there is something in your heart which requires the discipline of His covenant, He takes such pleasure in comforting you that you could, at no time, be disconsolate. You are therefore infinitely bound to love Him ardently and supremely, to glory in His cross, and to delight in doing His will.

From what has been said, we may also learn that, in proportion as a man makes Christ and holiness his choice, he will find them to be his delight. The more communion with Jesus Christ, and the more conformity to Him, he desires and attains, the more delight in Him, and in God through Him, shall he experience. The more his heart is set upon growing in holiness, and the more willingly and resolutely he performs all his duties for the glory of his God and Redeemer, the more shall he know by experience that the comforts of religion overbalance the difficulties of it. In proportion as he takes pleasure in spiritual exercises and holy performances, and that from love for Christ and for the glory of God, the most laborious exercises of religion shall become pleasant to him, and the most difficult duties shall become easy. Holy consolation, in the hand of the blessed Spirit, makes everything in holiness a pleasure to him; and the closer he walks with God, the God of all comfort, the stronger and sweeter is his consolation.

If spiritual comfort is of such importance and utility to believers as has been shown, surely it is the duty of every believer to use diligently the appointed means of attaining a gradual increase of it. The Apostle Paul exhorted the believers in Corinth to "be of good comfort" (2 Corinthians 13:11); that is, to be so diligent in receiving, by the frequent exercise of faith, the comfort offered and promised to them in the gospel as to attain more and more of the joy of faith, and of a good conscience. Nothing will carry a Christian through the inward and outward difficulties of religion but the inward supports and delights of it. Every believer, therefore, should constantly endeavor to attain, as early as possible, much of the comfort of the Holy Spirit, that he may the more easily and cheerfully surmount every difficulty, and be the more resolute in the practice of universal holiness. The hypocrite will not "always call upon God," because he will not "delight himself in the Almighty" (Job 27:10). Were he to delight himself in the Almighty, especially as a God infinitely holy, he would no longer be a hypocrite, and would always call upon Him. If the true believer would at all times persevere in spiritual and cheerful obedience to the commandments of Christ, he must, in the strength of promised grace, labor to attain more and more of the comfort of communion with Him in His righteousness and fullness; for the more his heart is comforted, the word and work" (2 Thessalonians 2:17). He has always need of spiritual comfort in this valley of tears to strengthen him for his spiritual conflicts and holy performances; and therefore, under an abiding sense of his need of it, he should daily employ the means of receiving fresh supplies.

Once more, is holy consolation of such consequence to the saints? Hence it is evident that their loss of it must be a very great and grievous loss to them. The loss, indeed, of lively and pleasant feelings, though grievous, yet is not usually a very great loss to the exercised Christian; but the loss of that ordinary comfort or tranquility of mind which he has hitherto enjoyed is a very grievous loss to him. He may for a season be without sensible and lively impressions, and yet not be deserted of God, in respect of habitual comfort or serenity of mind. For as it is not a cloud intervening, nor even a partial eclipse of the sun, but the absence of the sun that occasions night, so it is not the want of a lively impression or a pleasant frame, but the loss of that peaceful tranquility of spirit which the believer was wont to enjoy that causes darkness to cover his soul. The loss of this is an unspeakably great and grievous loss to him.

If Christ the Sun of righteousness is graciously pleased to shine upon him, all is well; but if He hides His countenance, the smiles of the whole creation can afford him no solid comfort. Believer, take heed that you do not provoke the Lord to withhold influences of holy comfort from your soul. Do not, by carnal security, self-confidence, earthly-mindedness, or any other iniquity, provoke Him to turn the reviving smiles of His countenance, which you now enjoy, into killing frowns. Your soul is no more self-sufficient than self-existent. If the Lord ceases to refresh it with His cheering smiles, it cannot but languish and faint.

3

The Ways in Which Believers Lose Their Spiritual Comfort

Although a holy man cannot, so much as for a moment, lose that principle of comfort or joy which the Holy Spirit in regeneration has implanted in his heart, nor yet that entire habit of joy which He has in sanctification implanted there, yet he sometimes loses the sense or feeling of it. He is at times deprived of sensible comfort or of the joy of God's salvation. By his losing spiritual consolation I do not mean his falling merely for an hour or a day from a pleasant into an unpleasant frame of spirit (for his frames are almost perpetually changing), but his being more or less deprived of the sense of God's peculiar favor toward him, or of the sensible possession of spiritual comfort, and that for a considerable time. When the God of all comfort continues, for a season, to withhold the cheering light of His gracious countenance from his soul, it cannot but be disquieted and disconsolate (Psalm 30:7).

Though the Lord purposely—to display His wisdom and sovereignty, to try the graces of believers, to mortify their pride, and to teach them the necessity of venturing as sinners to trust simply in Christ for all the grace of the promise—withholds for a

time sensible comfort from them, yet, for the most
part, He does it in order to chasten them for their
sins against Him as their God and Father (Isaiah
59:2). At the same time, it is not for every sin of infirmity that He suspends consoling influences from
their souls; otherwise, as they can never so much as
think a thought without polluting it by some degree
of sin, He would at all times be afflicting them with
want of comfort. But it is for some peculiarly aggravated transgressions or for relapsing often into the
same sin. It is their iniquities and backslidings that
procure trouble of mind for them (Jeremiah 2:19).
Such is God's love for them and care of them, and
such is His abhorrence of their sin, that He cannot
but make even His dear children themselves feel
that He is displeased with them when they backslide
from Him (Hebrews 12:6; Amos 3:2). His faithfulness
also to His Word, in which He threatens trouble as a
fatherly chastisement, and even promises it as a
blessing in disguise to them, moves Him to do so
(Psalm 119:75). And though the sins of some particular believers (as in the case of Job) may not in every
instance be the procuring cause of their loss of comfort, yet they are at least the occasion of it (Jeremiah
31:18).

All that in this chapter I further propose to do is
to point out some of the leading sins and ways of
sinning by which believers provoke their heavenly
Father to suspend for a time that degree of holy
consolation from them which they have formerly
enjoyed.

   *1. In the first place, they provoke Him to do this by allow-
ing themselves to continue, in a culpable degree, ignorant of*

His countenance of grace, and of their warrant to come as sinners and to trust in the Lord Jesus for their own particular salvation. These are objects in which the comfort of true believers, is at all times intimately concerned, the spiritual and distinct knowledge of which is necessary to qualify them for deriving continual supplies of grace and consolation from the fullness of Christ (2 Samuel 23:5; John 17:3 and 6:40; Romans 15:13).

If believers then suffer themselves, surrounded as they are by the clear light of the blessed gospel, to retain ignorance or cherish mistakes respecting the covenant of Jehovah's peace (Isaiah 54:10), and the infinite fullness and freeness of His grace treasured up in Christ, the glorious Trustee of that covenant, they thereby undervalue the only doctrine on which all true comfort depends, and so provoke their heavenly Father to suspend the consolations of His holy covenant from their souls. The gospel is an exhibition of God's covenant of grace to lost sinners of mankind, and therefore it is "good tidings of great joy to all people" (Luke 2:10). To be willingly ignorant, then, of that gracious contract is the same as to be willingly ignorant of the glorious gospel; and to retain mistaken notions of the former is the same as to err concerning the latter. When true Christians satisfy themselves with superficial and indistinct views of the covenant of grace, or with knowing little more than the first principles of the doctrine of that august contract, they so far despise the doctrine of redeeming grace, the joyful tidings of a free salvation, and so lose the joy of that salvation.

Moreover, in the administration of that everlasting covenant, Christ, with His righteousness and fullness, is freely and fully offered to sinners of mankind in general; and sinners, as such, are graciously invited, yea, and are peremptorily commanded, to believe on His name (John 6:32; Revelation 22:17; 1 John 3:23). The authentic offer, call, and command, founded upon the infinite intrinsic value of the righteousness of Christ, and addressed to every sinner who hears the gospel, afford to everyone a full warrant to trust in Christ for all the salvation promised in the covenant. If Christians then allow themselves to remain in a great measure ignorant of their warrant as sinners in themselves to place direct confidence in Christ for all their salvation, or if they cherish mistakes concerning it, they provoke the Lord, who is jealous for the honor of His covenant and of His word of grace, to withhold from them that peace and joy which are in believing. And, at the same time, they indirectly invite Satan to tempt them to conclude that they have no warrant whatsoever to trust that Christ will save them.

Were believers to attain a more spiritual and clear understanding of the eternal covenant, and of the authentic offer of it, than they commonly do, they would see that they have, in the word of grace presented to them, a full and unchangeable warrant to trust at all times in the Lord Jesus for their own particular salvation; and then they would live a more holy and comfortable life than they commonly do. They would, in that case, clearly see that it is warrantable for them, and therefore lawful and reasonable, to trust, even with full assurance of faith, in their faithful Redeemer. Ah, how sinful, how displeasing to the God of all comfort is it to treat with neglect His holy covenant, and the warrant which He graciously affords sinners of mankind as such to take hold of it! And how effectually will it mar the comfort of one's own soul!

2. *They provoke the Lord to suspend influences of consolation from them by their yielding often to disbelief and distrust of Jesus Christ.* An Apostle says, "We which have believed do enter into rest" (Hebrews 4:3). "Thou wilt keep him," said the prophet Isaiah, "in perfect peace, whose mind is stayed on Thee, because he trusteth in Thee" (Isaiah 26:3). And again, "If ye will not believe, surely ye shall not be established" (Isaiah 7:9). If a Christian frequently neglects the exercise of trusting in Christ for fresh supplies of grace and comfort; if, instead of trusting with all his heart, and at all times, in his infinitely faithful Redeemer for the grace which is in Him, and is brought near in the promise, he often trusts to the grace that is in himself—then his heart, by so doing, departs from the Lord Jesus (Jeremiah 17:5), the only Fountain of consolation, and he places that confidence in his own renewed nature which he is commanded to place in his divine Redeemer. By so doing, he idolizes the new creature; he trusts in his own heart; he leans to his own understanding; he makes a savior of his own created grace. Thus he provokes his heavenly Father, who is a jealous God, to hide His face from him, and to eclipse His evidences of grace from his view. It is now necessary that the Lord, who "will ever be mindful of His covenant," should perform to him, in a higher de-

gree than formerly, this promise: "From all your idols will I cleanse you" (Ezekiel 36:25). Accordingly God, in order to chasten him for his idolatry, and to teach him the necessity of living continually by faith, withholds consolation from his soul and ceases to shine upon his evidences of grace. The consequence is that the believer now not only discerns no grace in his heart to trust, but begins to doubt if ever he had any. He formerly looked for comfort to the principle of grace which he discerned in himself rather than to the fullness of grace which is in Christ, contrary to this high command: "Thou therefore, my son, be strong in the grace that is in Jesus Christ" (2 Timothy 2:1). But now that he can see and feel nothing in his heart but deep and strong corruption, nothing but a body of sin and death, he becomes at once discouraged and disconsolate.

Christian, you never have greater need to trust simply and firmly in your divine Savior than when your graces are most lively and most discernible; for then self-confidence is most ready so to prevail against you as to provoke a jealous God to withhold spiritual comfort from your soul. If you desire to retain holy consolation, repose the unsuspecting confidence of your heart solely and constantly in your faithful Redeemer. Apply and trust and plead His promises. If you distrust Him, if you yield to suspicious and hard thoughts of Him, you transgress against Him without cause. The Lord Jesus has never dealt so, in His ways of grace and providence, with any soul as to give it cause to be suspicious of Him. Ah, what dishonor do you reflect upon the glorious Immanuel by refusing to trust solely in Him! Be not grieved that you have nothing to trust for your salvation besides Christ and the promise; but rather rejoice that you *need* nothing besides (Psalm 62:2, 5–6). Pray often and earnestly that the Holy Spirit may convince you more deeply of the exceeding sinfulness of sin, and especially of the greatest of all sins, unbelief (John 16:8–9).

3. Believers lose their holy comfort by making their graces, duties, or lively frames their warrant or ground of right to trust in Jesus Christ for salvation. These, indeed, are great encouragements to continue trusting in the Savior; but they form no part of a man's warrant to renew his actings of trust in Him. They are fruits and evidences of saving faith, but are no part of the ground of it. To make them the ground, or even a part of the ground, of our right to confide in Jesus for salvation would be as preposterous as it would be, when transplanting a young tree, to set the top branches of it in the ground instead of the roots. The faith of a believer must be grounded on faithfulness in the Word, and not on feelings in the heart. If the Christian, then, instead of making the authentic offer, call, and commandment to believe everything addressed in the gospel to him as a sinner of mankind in to his warrant to renew his exercise of trusting in Christ for all his salvation, thinks so highly of his experiences or evidences as to make them his ground or right to do so, he is guilty of presumption. He sets aside the warrant which the Holy Spirit in the Word affords him, and presumes to trust in Christ upon the ground of that in himself which is indeed the fruit, but not the root—the evidence, but not the ground, of faith.

Thus, instead of a true confidence, he places an unwarrantable confidence in his Redeemer, and hereby he discovers the pride and self-righteous propensity that remain in him (1 Corinthians 4:7). Sensible that his holy qualities and performances can give him no right to salvation itself, his legal spirit prompts him to conclude that they will afford him at least a right to the Savior, a right to exercise particular trust in Him for salvation. Hence, when he discerns his evidences of personal interest in Christ, he can freely trust Him; but when these are eclipsed and cannot be seen he counts it unwarrantable and presumptuous to confide in Him. Now, seeing it is pride or a legal spirit that disposes the Christian to think that his graces and evidences can give him a right to apply to and confide in Christ, and since the immutable design of God is to exalt the Savior and humble the sinner, He withholds the comfortable sense of His favor from the believer (Psalm 138:6). He ceases to shine upon his graces and evidences. He not only leaves him, it may be, to fall repeatedly into some known sin, but He permits Satan, and the man's own proud and unbelieving heart, to persuade him that he has now no right at all to trust that the holy Jesus will save such a sinner as he is. Thus he has procured for himself the loss of his comfort.

But even this loss, however great and grievous it may be, is almost less than nothing in comparison to the infinite dishonor which he has reflected upon the Lord Jesus by presuming to substitute his own graces and attainments in place of the authori-

tative offers and calls of the gospel as his warrant to
trust in Him, and by not venturing to rely upon Him
for grace, unless he sees grace already in himself, to
give him a right to place confidence in Him.
Believer, if you would retain spiritual consolation,
take heed that you never build your faith upon the
reports of sense; build it only upon the sure, the unchangeable record of God who cannot lie. Do not
substitute sense in place of His true and holy Word.
Build your faith and your comfort upon Christ in
the Word, and not upon your experiences. Do not
live upon Christ as felt in the heart, but upon Christ
as offered in the gospel.

4. *Believers procure for themselves the loss of spiritual comfort by discontent and impatience, arising from the inordinate
love of some earthly comfort.* When a good man—instead
of placing all his happiness and hope in Christ and
in God as his God and portion—places much of
them in some external comfort, so as to be disposed
often to say, "What would become of me?" or "How
uncomfortable should I be were it not for this comfort!" he thereby provokes the Lord, who is always
more ready to profit than to please His children, to
tear the idol from his embrace (Ezekiel 36:25). If he
begins to "make gold his hope, and to say to the fine
gold, 'Thou art my confidence' " (Job 31:24); or, if
"he trusteth in man, and maketh flesh his arm, so
that his heart departeth from the Lord, he shall,"
under the chastening of his heavenly Father, be for
a season "like the heath in the desert, and shall not
see when good cometh, but shall inhabit the
parched places in the wilderness, in a salt land and
not inhabited" (Jeremiah 17:5–6). "The broken reed

on which he leaneth" will not only fail him, "but will go into his hand and pierce it" (Isaiah 36:6). His comforts will be diminished; his hopes will be disappointed; his schemes will one after another be frustrated. His idol, whatever it is, will either be torn from him or be turned into a source of daily vexation to him. The Lord will break his cisterns and send a worm to his gourds. "For the iniquity of his covetousness," said Jehovah, "was I wroth and smote him. I hid Me and was wroth, and he went on frowardly in the way of his heart" (Isaiah 57:17). The inordinate and immoderate love of any temporal benefit does, upon the loss of that benefit, commonly produce discontent, impatience, and fretfulness, which have a natural tendency to wear down the spirit.

Were the Christian to bear his loss of outward comforts in the exercise of faith and of resignation to the holy will of God, he should still continue to experience inward consolation. But when he presumes to fret and murmur as if the Lord had wronged him or been unkind to him, saying, "Alas! My afflictions are very uncommon and peculiarly severe," thereby he procures for himself, in addition to his outward losses, the loss of inward consolation. Such a behavior as this forms a combination of various sins, all of which are inconceivably heinous and exceedingly sinful. Discontent inclines a man to be impatient under affliction. Discontent and impatience set his mind as on the rack, and torment it with distracting cares how to be delivered, or how to have his loss retrieved.

The secret root of these is an inordinate love of

the body and of worldly enjoyments (James 4:4). This again arises from a want of due resignation to the holy will of God, and of satisfaction with Him alone as an all-sufficient portion for the whole man (Psalm 142:5), and it is usually attended with much disbelief and distrust of His promise. The Lord, in His gracious promise, says to every believer, "There shall no evil befall thee" (Psalm 91:10). "No," says the fretful Christian, "this which has befallen me is evil, otherwise I should not have been disquieted by it."

But should it not, on the contrary, even delight the Christian to find that, the Lord is drawing him off from his worldly lusts? Knowing that he must surely die, why is he so fond of temporal and transitory enjoyments? Why is he so anxious to acquire them, so eager to embrace them, so disquieted by the loss of them?

Believer, your covenant-God is all-sufficient for you, and He allows you to call Him yours. Why, then, do you go begging creatures for your supply? Consider that it is a much greater felicity to desire nothing earthly but what you have than to have all that you desire. Do not any more provoke the Lord by obstinate or sullen grief for any outward loss, "lest a worse thing come upon thee." Then only are you in a right frame when God in Christ is enough for you. Know that it is in the absence or contempt of earthly comforts that the Holy Spirit is most a Comforter. Remember that God is never to be blamed for depriving you of things which would carry away your heart from Himself as your sure and all-sufficient portion. Let not your life, even for a

moment, be bound up in any worldly enjoyment. O
"take heed and beware of covetousness" (Luke
12:15)—it is idolatry—and "their sorrows shall be
multiplied that hasten after another god" (Psalm
16:4).

5. *Believers lose their spiritual comfort by entertaining vain
thoughts.* By vain thoughts, I mean empty, frivolous,
foolish, unprofitable, groundless, proud, ostenta-
tious, deceitful, impure, and vengeful thoughts; also,
wandering thoughts in prayer and in other religious
exercises (Ephesians 6:18; James 5:16). These
thoughts are vain; they are contrary to the holy law
of God, and they exalt themselves against it. "I hate
vain thoughts," says the holy Psalmist, "but Thy law
do I love" (Psalm 119:113). Now when a believer, instead of hating and repelling vain thoughts, suffers
them to lodge within him (Jeremiah 4:14), when he
entertains them and allows them to continue unre-
sisted in his heart, he thereby provokes the displeasure of his heavenly Father. The mind of the
Christian should always be well-furnished with
proper subjects of thought, and should habitually
exercise itself upon them.

Thus, under the influences of the Holy Spirit, it
will be secured against the frequent incursion of a
multitude of vain thoughts, which otherwise will
consume much of his precious time, defile his conscience, and expose him sooner or later to a multitude of perplexing, solicitous, and sorrowful
thoughts (Psalm 94:19). Nothing but the frequent
exercise of true faith and repentance will commonly
prevent, in such cases, his sin from being inscribed
in legible characters on his chastisement. His vain

thoughts, if entertained, will procure for him perplexing and uncomfortable thoughts. David experienced much perplexity of conscience in consequence of his vain thoughts, and prayed earnestly
that the Lord would "cleanse him from secret faults"
(Psalm 19:12). The Christian, if he would retain his
holy comfort, must "keep his heart with all diligence" (Proverbs 4:23). He must watch his thoughts
strictly and constantly, as well as his words and actions. It will be necessary that he walk circumspectly
in secret as well as in public. If he suffers himself to
indulge empty and proud thoughts, he will grieve
the Holy Spirit of God (Ephesians 4:30), and provoke
Him to withhold influences of consolation from his
soul.

Believer, if you would keep up the comfort of
communion with a holy God, trust in the Lord Jesus
at all times for sanctifying grace to enable you daily
to mortify the members of the body of sin in your
heart. Suffer not your thoughts to wander in prayer
or any other act of devotion. When you are about to
pray, consider on the one hand the greatness and
variety of your wants, and on the other the omni-
science and holiness of Jehovah, to whom you arc to
send up your supplications—who has said that He
will be sanctified in those who come near Him.
Guard especially in secret prayer against coldness
and indifference. If vain thoughts, intruding in acts
of divine worship, are not entertained, but on the
contrary are hated, resisted, and lamented by you,
they will seldom be permitted to rob you of your
spiritual comfort. But if you love them, yield to
them, or suffer them quietly to lodge within you,

they will soon occasion such a mist of darkness in your soul that you shall not be able to discern the graces which dwell there.

6. *Believers procure for themselves the loss of holy comfort by mistaking blasphemous and other evil thoughts injected by Satan for sins of their own.* Satan sometimes, in a way of furious assault, throws in suddenly and swiftly, upon the souls of many of the saints, temptations to blasphemous, atheistic, impure, vengeful, and despairing thoughts. Such horrible injections are, by the Apostle Paul, termed "the fiery darts of the wicked one" (Ephesians 6:16) because, like the sharp and venomous darts of a cruel enemy, flying swiftly and invisibly, they penetrate the soul before it is aware, and hurry it on to hard and blasphemous thoughts of God and of the Savior. These violent and sudden temptations, like poisoned darts, pierce and inflame the holy soul with anguish and horror; and they not only fill it with the greatest uneasiness, but, if they for a moment are yielded to, they produce the most unbecoming suspicions of the grace and Word of God (Psalm 77:7–9). Blasphemous and atheistic thoughts indeed arise often from the depravity that remains in believers themselves; for our Lord said, "Out of the heart proceed evil thoughts . . . blasphemies" (Matthew 15:19). When exercised Christians do not resist, but, on the contrary, yield to blasphemous and other evil thoughts, they ought, in that case, to consider them as arising out of their own hearts, and to charge themselves with them as sins of their own. But if such thoughts strike their minds violently and suddenly (Matthew 16:22–23); if their being assaulted with them vexes and grieves

them (Psalm 73:21–22); and if their souls tremble at them, and, with deep abhorrence, resist them (Psalm 73:15), they ought, then, not to charge them upon themselves as their sins, but upon Satan as his.

Now it is because believers do not, as they ought, distinguish between those blasphemous and evil thoughts which are injected by the devil and those which proceed from their own hearts that they are often so imposed on by Satan as to mistake the former for sins of their own, and so to be deprived of the consolation which in the gospel is allowed them. There is a great difference, indeed, between a man's being tempted to blasphemy, or to doubt the truth of the divine testimony, and his being actually guilty of blasphemy or of doubting the truth of Scripture. It is only by his complying with temptation that he becomes guilty.

Believer, you have much reason to be thankful if you have not been left to take pleasure in those suggestions, or to frame arguments in support of them. Satan may be permitted to overpower for a moment the apparent exercise of every grace in you by a torrent of blasphemous imaginations, but "resist him, and he will flee from thee" (James 4:7). Take the shield of faith. Trust that the Lord Jesus, your Savior and your shield (Psalm 28:7), will graciously enable you to quench all the fiery darts of the wicked one, and according to your faith it will be unto you. All Satan's attempts to hurry you into sin shall be as effectually disarmed of their force by that shield as fire is of its strength by being quenched. To distrust your almighty Redeemer, or to doubt that you are not a true believer because you are thus harassed by

Satan, is a much greater sin than all his suggestions put together, however numerous.

7. *Believers diminish their comfort much by not watching habitually against corruption within and temptation from without.* A good man loses much of his holy comfort by not observing cautiously and constantly the motions of sin in his heart. When he does not accustom himself strictly to watch these, in order to detect, resist, and mortify them as early as they begin to appear, they will speedily acquire such force as will urge him on violently and irresistibly to thoughts, words, and acts of sin. If he would retain comfortable fellowship with an infinitely holy God, he must watch diligently the first motions and sallies of depravity in his heart in order that, by the lively exercise of the contrary graces, he may resist them without delay; for if he does not in such a case instantly try to exercise his graces, and especially his faith, Satan, who is always envious and watchful, will seize that opportunity to exercise his corruptions. And if, by being negligent to watch and resist the first motions of corruption in his heart, he suffers them often to obtain such force as to gain the consent of his will to actual transgression, he can have none to blame but himself for the loss of his holy consolation (Jeremiah 2:19).

Since the remaining depravity of the heart is not only itself a source of temptation to actual sin (James 1:14), but is the inlet for all temptations from Satan and the world (Jeremiah 17:9), the believer, if he would retain spiritual consolation, must likewise be ever upon his guard against temptations from without. If he ceases for a short while to watch against those temptations of Satan which that deceitful adversary manages in a way of subtlety and stratagem, he will soon be so ensnared by one or more of them as to fall into sin. Alas, spiritual wickednesses in high places, which are every moment watching for opportunities to ensnare his soul, are so many, so powerful, and so subtle that it is in vain for the exercised Christian to hope that he shall be able to retain his comfort only if he can shut Satan wholly out of his imagination. He should, however, be very cautious that he does not, even in the smallest measure, provide fuel for his flame.

He should, for this purpose, often pray in faith that the Lord would so set a watch upon his eyes and his ears as to enable him constantly to reject and repel every appearance of temptation to sin. And if he would not be tempted by the men of the world who are also the inveterate enemies of his comfort, he must always keep himself at a due distance from them. Christian, the snares of Satan and his emissaries are continually set for you. "Be sober therefore and vigilant" (1 Peter 5:8). "Watch thou in all things" (2 Timothy 4:5), and "watch unto prayer and supplication in the Spirit, with all perseverance" (Ephesians 6:18). If you would retain your comfort, shake off carnal security and take good heed, lest your spiritual enemies surprise and overcome you. Be continually solicitous to spot temptations while they are yet at a distance, in order to prevent them from surprising you. And that you may be enabled to do so, "be strong in the Lord, and in the power of His might" (Ephesians 6:10). Trust that the Lord

Jesus will, and pray that He may, "strengthen thee
with all might, according to His glorious power, by
His Spirit in the inner man" (Colossians 1:11;
Ephesians 3:16).

8. *Believers likewise forfeit their spiritual comfort by presuming, without necessity, to omit repeatedly some known
duty.* The Lord declares in Psalm 89:32 that He will
"visit the transgression (of the spiritual seed of
Messiah) with the rod, and their iniquity with
stripes." By these phrases He expresses the sins or
modes of sinning which would procure for them
His paternal chastisements, which are four; and it is
remarkable that He employs three of them to express the omission of duties, and but one to express
the direct commission of sins: "If his children forsake My law, and walk not in My judgments; if they
break or profane My statutes, and keep not My
commandments; then will I visit their transgression
with the rod, and their iniquity with stripes" (Psalm
89:30–32). Though sins of commission do, indeed,
expose believers to fatherly chastisements, yet I believe it will be found that sins of omission do it
much more frequently because they are more often
guilty of these, and they yield to them with less
struggle and remorse than they do to sins of commission. The spiritual declension of a Christian, especially at its beginning, discovers itself, for the
most part, more by the customary omission of some
duties than by the positive commission of crimes
(Isaiah 43:22–24). For although the omission of a
present duty is indeed a sin, yet it does not usually
appear to a declining Christian at first view to be so
horrible as the direct commission of a known trans-

gression. And therefore nothing commonly but some violent and strong temptation can, at first, impel him to the downright perpetration of a crime, whereas a very small temptation will often suffice to move him to the neglect of an ordinance or the omission of a duty. If he should happen to be, at any time, fatigued more than usual, to be under a very slight bodily distemper, to have less time or less accommodation than usual, to be disturbed and ruffled in his temper, or to be receiving or paying visits, any one of these will probably suffice as a temptation to prevail with him to shift off, at such a time, secret prayer, family worship, or even public worship, or some other present duty—or at least to perform them in a cold and superficial manner. And having once begun to admit such frivolous excuses, he may, perhaps, be permitted for a season to offer to his conscience almost any sort of occurrence as an excuse for omitting the stated performance of one or another of these duties.

On such occasions, he commonly neglects likewise the exercise of his graces, especially of his faith and repentance, and, it may be, takes occasion, either from his sins or from his duties, to do so. Or perhaps he suffers himself to neglect for a season some relative duty (Ephesians 6:2–3), or at least to perform it not "heartily, as unto the Lord" (Colossians 3:23). Now, inasmuch as every omission of known duty is a sin against God (James 4:17), the Christian, by allowing himself for a season often to neglect some known duty, or not to perform it cheerfully (Malachi 1:13–14), grieves the Holy Spirit of God and provokes Him to suspend consolation

from his soul. When he thus presumes to make the
Spirit sad, he must not expect that the Spirit will
continue, as formerly, to make him glad. The moment his heart withdraws and hangs off from any
present duty, as if it were an unpleasant or irksome
task, it does in the same proportion withdraw from
the Lord; and so it loses the comfort of serving Him
as well as of communion with Him (John 14:21). To
resolve to omit a present duty is even more sinful
than actually to omit it without intending so to do
(Revelation 2:4). Ah, how heinous a sin is it to be
disposed, and without necessity to be resolved, either to omit or to curtail a single religious or moral
duty! It shows how little regard a man has for the
glorious Majesty of heaven when he can put Him off
with slight and curtailed service (Malachi 1:6–8).
Such behavior as this will soon, very soon, raise such
a thick and dark cloud as will intercept the cheering
beams of the Sun of righteousness from the soul.
Alas, the omission or slight performance of many
duties is far from being considered and lamented by
true Christians as it ought to be.

I have already said that a believer loses his comfort by omitting repeatedly, and without necessity,
some known duty. I must now go further and add
that if he lives for a long time in the omission of
some duty (which he does not yet know to be a duty,
but which he might have known to have been required of him if he had diligently availed himself of
his opportunities to know it), this instance of neglect may lie concealed, as a gnawing worm, at the
root of his comfort. His neglecting the study of the
moral law in its spirituality and great extent as his

rule of duty, so as to continue ignorant of his duty in any one point, is, when opportunity is graciously afforded him for attaining this knowledge, a greater sin than it ever will be possible for him, or even for the highest angel, to comprehend. It is not enough, in order to retain spiritual comfort, that a holy man study well the promises of the gospel; he must likewise study diligently the precepts of the law, in order to obey them (Psalm 119:92, 165).

9. *Believers procure for themselves the loss of comfort by sitting down content with their spiritual attainments.* When a good man so far forgets himself as to rest satisfied for a time with his present degree of knowledge, faith, or holiness, and to become remiss in his efforts to attain more and more of these; when he begins and continues to be so well pleased with his degree of knowledge as to read and hear the gospel with less relish and less diligence than formerly; when he is so delighted with his measure of faith and experience as neither to complain so much of his unbelief, nor to be so diligent and frequent in his actings of faith as in times past; and when he is so fond of his attainments in holiness as to be less diligent than formerly in pressing toward perfection, he may assure himself that he shall thereby lose the comfort of communion with a holy and a jealous God. If he accustoms himself for a season not only so to rest in his religious attainments as to be less eager in pursuing after higher degrees of holiness, but to rest on them or place his confidence in them, he adopts hereby the surest method of losing at once the sight and the comfort of them (Ezekiel 36:25; Psalm 30:6–7). In proportion as he

trusts in his own knowledge, faith, holiness, or
pleasant frames in the prospect of any duty which he
may be about to perform instead of trusting only in
Christ, or in proportion as he looks to them for
comfort instead of looking solely to Him, he prefers
them before Him. He idolizes them; he makes a savior and a comforter of them instead of Jesus Christ;
or at least, he suffers them to share with Him in that
honor. He relies on grace received, and so trusts in
his own heart. This is one sure way in which he provokes the Lord to hide His gracious countenance
from him, and to cover his evidences with a cloud in
His anger (Luke 9:33–34).

Spiritual comforts, if they are rested on, shall as
effectually as earthly ones keep a man from comfortable communion with Christ. When the Lord
Jesus vouchsafes to him the comfort of spiritual attainments, it is not that he may live upon it, but that
he may be incited and encouraged by it to persevere
in holy faith and evangelical obedience. But if he,
on the contrary, allows himself to be elated with his
attainments or comforts, and, like Hezekiah, invites
others to see his treasures, then it will be time for
the Lord to send the messengers of His anger to
carry away from his view these idols which steal away
his heart from Him. When his heart is swelling with
self-importance and self-confidence, all that is then
poured on it runs over into the gulf of self-conceit
and self-sufficiency. If he relies upon his own wisdom and strength in the prospect, especially of difficult duties, he must not think it strange if he
should soon become discouraged and disconsolate.
When he presumes to rest on the acting of his faith

rather than upon the glorious Object of it, and to draw consolation from that rather than from this, he so far prefers the act before the Object and becomes guilty of idolatry (Psalm 16:4). But when he at length begins, in his practical judgment, habitually to prefer receiving all his strength and comfort directly from Christ to having them in and of himself, even if he might, his consolation by Christ will continue, and even abound (2 Corinthians 1:5; 1 Peter 1:8).

10. Christians deprive themselves of holy consolation by their indolence in the exercise of graces and performance of duties. We read in Song of Solomon 5:2–6 that the Church lost the comfort of a gracious visit from Christ by her sluggishness, which disposed her to neglect entertaining Him so kindly as she ought, and as the kindness of His manifestation of Himself required. When any of the saints have, by joy and peace in believing, and by rejoicing in hope, found that "in keeping His commandments, there is great reward" (Psalm 19:11), and yet afterwards become slothful in the service of Christ, counting His yoke uneasy and His burden heavy, shall He not visit for these things? They need not wonder that they lose their sense of His favor when they are conscious that they often pray for His grace as if they prayed not; when by their criminal indifference and the coldness of their petitions they show that they do not care much whether these are granted or not. Were they duly concerned for the welfare of their souls, they would frequently refresh them by exercising holy meditation and faith, as they do their bodies by receiving food three or more times a day.

Diligence in holy exercises and moral duties is not only a debt to the Lord, but a privilege to believers themselves; and therefore, by being slothful, you reveal at once injustice and unkindness, a contempt of the glorious Majesty of heaven and a neglect of His redeeming mercy. When a Savior draws near and they regard it not, when He knocks and they open not, it is indeed high time that, by withholding the comfort of His gracious visits from them, He should chastise their negligence and rouse them to diligence (Proverbs 10:4; Hebrews 11:6). It is equitable as well as reasonable that the consequence of spiritual sloth should be a loss of sensible consolation. Accordingly, in the administration of the covenant of grace, an intimate connection is established between diligence in holy duties and the fruition of spiritual comforts. The indolent Christian cannot retain tranquility of mind (Hebrews 6:11). What heavenly consolation must he lose, for instance, by his criminal inattention to the precious promises of God, and even to the daily dispensations of His holy providence to him! If his love, which was once an ascending flame, becomes a feeble spark; if his penitential sorrow, which once, like Jordan, overflowed all its banks, becomes like a brook in summer; if his zeal, which formerly ate him up, is devoured by leanness or declension; if he who, in times past, could not "give sleep to his eyes nor slumber to his eyelids" (Psalm 132:4) till Jesus gave rest to his soul can lie down securely with contracted guilt in his conscience; and if he, who formerly was diligent in spiritual exercise and holy obedience, becomes remiss and regardless, he thereby makes a wide breach for the entrance of spiritual trouble (Proverbs 19:15; Hosea 5:15). It is indeed mercifully, as well as wisely, appointed that when he becomes indolent, his comfort should decline, in order that he may perceive in time that he is in a languishing condition, and may, without delay, entreat the Lord Jesus to restore his soul. Besides, if the Lord did not, on such occasions, withdraw Himself, the Christian would not prize His gracious presence highly, nor think it so comfortable as it is.

Believer, "be not then slothful in business, but be fervent in spirit, serving the Lord" (Romans 12:11). See that, by grace received daily from the fullness of Christ, your soul is vigorous and active in His holy service (Ecclesiastes 9:10). Be always diligent in attempting the exercise of grace, in using the means of grace, and in doing every good work in the strength of promised grace. If persons linger on a journey, they are sometimes benighted; if you become slothful in exercising your graces or performing your duties, wonder not if you begin to walk in darkness. Be continually on your guard, then, against every appearance of inward declension, and especially against slothfulness in the exercise of direct confidence in Christ and of secret prayer.

11. Believers suffer a diminution of their spiritual comfort by having and entertaining a low estimation of the counsels and comforts of the Holy Spirit of Christ. When they allow themselves, for a season, to entertain a light esteem of the counsels, ordinances, promises, influences, or comforts of the blessed Spirit; when they receive these, but not gratefully, or keep them, but not diligently, they thereby dishonor and grieve the Holy

Spirit Himself, who is the glorious Author of them.
An earthly sovereign would account himself dishonored if his proclamations, pardons, or favors
should not be entertained with high regard, especially if those who are not only the subjects of his
dominion, but the objects of his peculiar favor, do
not account his word their treasure, his promises
their joy, his Sabbaths their delight, and his consolations their felicity. They so far treat him with indignity. And the more exalted and glorious the
adorable Spirit is, the more sinful the indignity is
which is thereby offered Him. Besides, if in their
practical judgment they prefer mean and even sinful
objects before the great things of the Spirit, such as
the wisdom and the maxims of the world before His
counsels, the comforts and the pleasures of the
world, before His consolations, or the riches and
the honors of the world before the honor of holy
conformity to Him and of intimate communion
with Him, they do thereby offer an infinite affront to
His glorious Majesty. For what greater dishonor can
they reflect upon the holy and blessed Spirit than
practically to show greater regard to a creature, to a
vain creature, yea, to an enemy, than to Him!

Ah, when a Christian's desire for the food of his
soul is almost gone; when he appears as if he had
been surfeited with the gospel; when divine ordinances, instead of being highly esteemed, are basely
slighted by him; and when his heart is more set
upon his farm or merchandise than upon seasons of
communion with God in Christ, he must not be
surprised if he should, for a season, be taught the
worth of these inestimable blessings by the want of

them. Or when, by poring constantly upon the sins of his heart and of his life, and by setting the demerit of these, as it were, in battle array against the merit of the great Redeemer's consummate righteousness, he makes little account of the offers and promises of the blessed gospel, he must blame none but himself for his loss of comfort.

O Christian, consider well these words of the Apostle Paul: "To be spiritually minded is life and peace" (Romans 8:6). Endeavor to attain without delay a more spiritual and clear discernment of the things of the Spirit. Pray frequently and fervently for more acquaintance with them, and for more complacency in them. Learn to form such a low estimate of the creature as to expect nothing from it, and such a high esteem of the Lord Jesus as to expect all from Him. So shall you be exempted from those frequent and galling disappointments which cannot but render the life of a believer uncomfortable (Psalm 146:5). Were you to love your redeeming God so much as habitually to come before Him in His ordinances with delight in Him, and to go away with desire for Him, you would always retain the comfort of communion with Him (Psalm 37:4 and 71:21).

12. True Christians deprive themselves of comfort by presuming to pray for things which are not suitable to their condition, and which it would not be consistent with the scheme of their salvation to grant them at present, nor indeed at any time. When they venture repeatedly to ask in prayer something which the Lord sees to be improper for them, and not necessary to subserve the wise purposes of His glory in their sanctification, "They ask, and receive not, because they ask amiss" (James 4:3).

If, for instance, they pray that as much grace might be given them at once as would be sufficient for them all their lifetime (John 4:15); if they peremptorily ask sensible manifestations, great enlargements, and high ecstasies of joy; if they pray for any comfort whatsoever, without resolving to use diligently all the other appointed means of attaining it; if they entreat the removal of any affliction before they have been rightly exercised under it (2 Corinthians 7:8); and if they pray absolutely for a certain measure of the good things of this life, the Lord will not, and indeed *cannot,* in mercy to them, grant such petitions. The consequence often is that after having, it may be, waited long for answers without receiving any, they become discouraged and disconsolate. Moreover, when they venture in prayer to prescribe to the Lord a way and a time of appearing for their help, and when the Lord, as He will surely do, refuses to come for their salvation in that particular way, and at that very time (2 Kings 5:11), they take occasion from that refusal to yield to disquietude and discouragement. Or, when they venture to propose the Lord's particular way of treating some other believers as the way in which they desire that He would deal with them, and find that they are not gratified likewise in this, they sometimes begin to yield to discouraging and desponding thoughts. Thus, they presume to limit the Holy One of Israel, who has resolved to act as an infinite Sovereign in His manner of bringing all His saints to glory.

Believers, if they would retain spiritual consolation, would do well to consider that it is only such petitions as are for things unnecessary, and even hurtful to them, that the Lord refuses to grant. He never denies any of them without a sufficient reason, and He sometimes condescends to show them the reason (2 Corinthians 12:8–10). He never refuses but when they ask what is not good, or rather what is not best for them at the time referred to. And although they do not receive what they come for, yet He allows them that which is sufficient to bear their charges in coming and going, and invites them to come again. They ought also to consider that those are not the holiest, nor the greatest of believers whose sense is the most indulged. Believing Mary is forbidden to touch Jesus, and disbelieving Thomas is commanded to thrust his hand into His side.

Christian, if you would, from time to time, be comforted with answers of peace to your prayers, offer up to the Lord no unwarrantable desires; no desires but for things which are agreeable to His revealed will, and no desires but in the name of Christ and by the help of the Spirit. Ask nothing on purpose to consume it upon your pleasures (James 4:3). Regulate always your petitions by the promises of the everlasting covenant, which comprise all that is good for you, in time and through eternity, and infinitely more than you are able to ask or think (Ephesians 3:20).

13. Believers procure for themselves the loss of holy comfort by yielding for a season to such temptations as urge them to attempt things in religion that are impracticable. When Satan perceives that he cannot persuade the Christian— especially the young and inexperienced Christian— to live in the neglect of any known duty, he sometimes presses him vehemently to a rash and quick performance of some difficult duty. He suggests to him that the Lord is a hard Master, that He delights in requiring difficult duties, duties which must be performed speedily, and that on the pain of incurring His infinite displeasure; that like a tyrannical ruler who makes laws in order to ensnare His subjects, He commands duties which are oppressive, and does it with unrelenting rigor; and that He requires them to be done with the utmost degree of exactness or else he will not accept them. Now so far as a good man yields to this horrible temptation, he presumes to imagine that the commandments of God are grievous, that the yoke of Christ is hard. Apprehending the Lord Jesus to be a rigorous Master, he, under the prevalence of slavish fear (1 John 4:18), performs even the easiest of his duties without courage, without affection, and even with aversion. His comfort accordingly is destroyed; his heart is dejected; his hands are weakened.

Moreover, Satan sometimes urges him to attempt the doing of several things at once, which he well knows is impossible. And the moment he yields to this temptation his heart begins to be so divided, his thoughts to be so perplexed, and his attention to be so distracted between a multiplicity of objects which crowd into his view, that he becomes incapable of performing any duty well. Endeavoring to grasp too much, he lets all slip. Whatever he tries to perform, he does it superficially and unseasonably. When he is called to perform one duty, he is, perhaps, addressing himself to another, and, like Martha, he is "careful and troubled about many things" (Luke 10:41). The great rule of every duty is this: "Whatso-

ever thy hand findeth to do, do it with thy might"
(Ecclesiastes 9:10); that is, let your heart be wholly
intent upon, and occupied with, that one duty while
you are performing it. Indeed, it cannot otherwise
be performed, either acceptably or comfortably.

The tempter also will, sometimes, instigate those
of the saints who are called to perform a greater variety of duties than others to continue longer than
is required in doing some one duty, in order to put
it out of their power rightly to discharge some other
that is equally incumbent on them.

He will press them, for instance, either to employ
so much time in family worship, and especially in
that of the closet, as to have no opportunity for some
other duty equally necessary; or to spend so much
time in some duty respecting their secular affairs as
to have almost no opportunity for those holy and
necessary exercises. In proportion as a good man
yields for a time to this temptation, it is easy to see
that he thereby deprives himself of that comfort of
communion with a holy God which is enjoyed only
in a conscientious and seasonable discharge of
every known duty. Now in order to prevent his
falling into this destructive snare, he ought daily to
trust, as well as to pray, that the Lord Jesus, who is
given "for a leader to the people" (Isaiah 55:4),
would, according to His promise (Isaiah 58:11),
guide him continually to that which, in preference
over every other, is his present duty. And when he
discerns his present duty, he should resolutely, and
in the faith of the promise, dispatch that, and then
proceed in the same manner to his next duty. Let
him diligently perform every act of obedience in its

proper season; and, that he may have opportunity for every one, let him so redeem his time as to spend no time in idleness, or in doing anything but that which his conscience pronounces to be his present duty (Ephesians 5:15–16).

14. Believers forfeit the continuance of their spiritual comfort by the commission of gross and atrocious transgressions, of such sins as are contrary, not only to the light of revelation, but even to the light of nature. By doing so, they rebel against and "vex the Holy Spirit, so that He is turned," as it were, "to be their enemy, and to fight against them" (Isaiah 63:10). By such iniquities, they, at the same time, wound and waste their own consciences. When a holy man presumes to resemble the men of this world so much as to commit but one of the sins mentioned in 1 Corinthians 6:9–10, or any other heinous iniquity, he thereby pierces the Lord Jesus, grieves the Holy Spirit, inflicts a deep wound in his own conscience, and so procures for himself the loss of holy consolation. We see in some of the penitential Psalms of David that his adultery and murder not only deprived him of sensible comfort, but exposed him, and that for a long season, to divine desertion, in respect even of quickening and purifying influences. We know also that Peter's denial of his blessed Lord rendered him, for a time, very disconsolate.

If a good man, then, instigated either by corruption within or by temptation from without, suffers himself not only to contemplate with desire, but actually to fall into, any of those enormities which, by one apostle, are termed, "the works of the flesh" (Galatians 5:19–21), and by another "the pollutions of the world" (2 Peter 2:20), he exposes himself, in an uncommon degree, to the dreadful frowns of his heavenly Father. For such enormities, as they are directly opposite even to the light of nature, so they are most contrary to the influences of grace. The sin of a believer in falling into any one of them is deeply aggravated from all his manifold privileges, and more especially from this: that he usually has more strength afforded him against gross enormities than even against sins which are more spiritual and less obvious to his view.

The means of being kept from falling into gross iniquities, which the Christian ought diligently to use, are such as these: trusting in Christ at all times, for continual supplies of sanctifying grace; prayer without ceasing and without fainting; watchfulness unto prayer, and against his spiritual enemies, with all perseverance; and keeping a constant guard, more especially, against pride of heart, confidence in grace received, and the evil that is in the world.

15. Christians likewise destroy the peace and comfort of their minds by open sins of any kind which offend others around them, and cause many of them to stumble. When any of the saints commit such sins as are exposed to the view of others, and thereby grieve, offend, or cause them to stumble, the Lord is greatly dishonored and displeased, and His Holy Spirit is so grieved as to suspend for a time His cheering influences from their souls. He, in this way, frequently embitters those sins to His people by which they have offended others, and have given them occasion to reproach His blessed religion and to blaspheme His holy name. After David had sinned openly, in

the matter of Uriah, Nathan said to him, "Because
by this deed thou hast given great occasion to the
enemies of the Lord to blaspheme, the child also
that is born unto thee shall surely die" (2 Samuel
12:14). The Lord charged it as a deeply aggravated
sin upon His ancient people that, by the unholy and
offensive behavior of many of them, they occasioned
"His holy name to be profaned among the heathen"
(Ezekiel 36:20, 23; Romans 2:24).

If blasphemy is justly allowed to be a most atrocious crime, doubtless it must be a heinous iniquity,
especially in any of the children of God, to give occasion to it. When they at any time fall openly into
dishonesty, pride, passion, revenge, or unbecoming
discourse, and especially into covetousness, the enemies of the gospel never fail to take special notice
of it, and take occasion from it to become the more
confirmed in their inveterate prejudices against
faith and holiness. These sins therefore do, as much
as more enormous evils that are committed in secret, procure for believers the loss of spiritual comfort. "For the iniquity of his covetousness," said
Jehovah, "was I wroth, and smote him. I hid Me, and
was wroth" (Isaiah 57:17). When, after spiritual en-
largement and communion with God in holy exercises, Christians become negligent in glorifying
Him by good works before men; when, as soon as
they have come down from the mount, they, like
Moses, break the tables of the holy law, such un-
grateful and inconsistent behavior as this often provokes their heavenly Father to chasten them by the
infliction of inward as well as outward trouble. By
presuming to sin openly, they not only offend and

grieve the Holy Spirit, but trouble and discourage other saints around them. And therefore it is proper that they themselves should feel spiritual trouble, and should know by their own bitter experience that "it is an evil thing and bitter that they have forsaken the Lord their God" (Jeremiah 2:19).

16. *Last, believers procure for themselves the loss of holy comfort by relapsing often into the same sin.* Whatever sin it is, and however strong the temptation to it is, the repeated and, especially, frequent commission of it will provoke the Holy Spirit to withhold His consoling influences from the backsliding Christian. This will more especially be the case if, under the prevalence of corruption and the power of temptation, he suffers himself to resemble so much the secure hypocrite as to take the smallest encouragement from the riches of redeeming grace in Christ to repeat the same offense. By his daring to do so, he "maketh Christ the minister of sin" (Galatians 2:17). He practically represents the holy Jesus and His great salvation as leaving him still under the dominion of sin, yea, as affording him encouragement to practice iniquity. Besides, by relapsing often into the same transgression, the Christian practically declares that he still loves and has pleasure in that sin. Now by loving that which is inexpressibly hateful, and which the Lord hates with infinite abhorrence, and by counting that pleasant to his taste which is of all things the most bitter, and which tendered to the Savior's lips the vinegar and gall, the believer renders it indispensably necessary that the sweet and holy consolations of the Spirit be suspended from him in order that he may be made to see that his in-

iquity is most hateful, and to experience that it is most bitter.

Moreover, the repetition of a transgression heightens the crime. As in figures the addition of one figure, a zero, makes the number ten times greater, so the Christian's repetition of the same sin, of a sin which he has often confessed, lamented, and resolved against, renders it heinous in a tenfold degree, and calls aloud for paternal chastisement. In such a case, he must be taught not only by the anguish of the Redeemer's soul in the garden and on the cross, but by the trouble of his own spirit, that this sin is of all evils the greatest, and that his having fallen again and again into the same offense after he had received the forgiveness of sins renders his sin exceedingly sinful (Ezra 9:13–14; Malachi 2:13). And if, after he has, for his disobedience, been chastened with outward affliction, he, nevertheless, turns again to the same offense, this will, if infinite mercy prevents it not, inevitably expose him to inward distress, which is inexpressibly more dreadful and intolerable.

Ah, when a man who has believed through grace presumes to cast a propitious eye upon some easily besetting sin, and secretly to say, "Is it not a little one? My soul shall yet live," he is not aware how effectually he thereby robs his soul of holy comfort. If after having often complained to the Lord of his unbelief, pride, self-confidence, deadness, frowardness, censoriousness, and other evils, he still is ready on almost every occasion to gratify them, if not to excuse and vindicate them, does he not hereby resemble the hypocrite? And is it not proper that he should for a season be deprived of the comfort of seeing that he is a sincere believer, and also that he should be left under the prevalence of perplexing fears that he has hitherto been, and at present is, but a hypocrite? I do not say that a man's relapses again and again into the same transgression prove him to *be* a hypocrite, for God has nowhere promised such a degree of strength to His people during their state of imperfection as will set them beyond the possibility of relapsing for a season into the same offense; but I affirm that a true Christian's doing so makes him appear very much *like* a hypocrite, obscures his evidences of sincerity, renders his condition inexpressibly dreadful, and exposes him to a very severe chastisement.

Believer, if this is your present condition, oh, apply, and without delay plead, this gracious promise: "I will heal their backsliding, I will love them freely" (Hosea 14:4); and, in the faith of it, watch and strive with holy resolution especially against "the sin which doth so easily beset thee" (Hebrews 12:1). Know that your redeeming God has made an unalterable, an eternal separation between the love of sin and the joy of salvation. Oh, endeavor diligently to become eminent especially in that grace which is more immediately the opposite of your constitutional sin. Would you wish to keep down doubts and fears and keep up faith and comfort? Shun, oh, shun every occasion and every appearance, especially of *that* sin (1 Thessalonians 5:22). Be persuaded that the pleasure of overcoming even the most easily besetting sin is inconceivably greater than the pleasure of committing it.

From the foregoing particulars, the disconsolate believer may plainly see that he has none to blame but himself for his loss of holy consolation. When he is bewailing his want of peaceful tranquility or of holy joy, he must complain of none but himself. It is he himself who takes, and even forces away, his own comfort; for by his aggravated sins he has rendered it necessary that the Lord should hide His face from him. Indeed, he never sins against God without sinning, at the same time, against his own soul. We read in the Scriptures that we must forgive our enemies, but never in express terms that we must forgive our friends. The iniquities of God's own people are the most provoking to Him, and though He has forgiven them all, as to the guilt of eternal wrath, yet, as in the case of Moses, He may refuse to forgive some of them in respect of the guilt of paternal anger. The iniquity of others is marked before Him, but "the sin of Judah is written with a pen of iron, and with the point of a diamond" (Jeremiah 17:1). The friends of Christ, then, must be ever on their guard against sin, especially against willful sin. Sinning willfully will assuredly weaken their hands and bring trouble into their consciences.

Does a good man forfeit his holy comfort by making his graces, performances, or lively frames his ground of right to trust in Jesus for salvation? He should hence learn the need that he has to be daily exercising himself in mortifying the legal spirit which remains in him. It is this that prompts him to make his graces and duties his warrant to renew his actings of trust in the Savior, and thereby to forfeit the comfort of his soul. Next to unbelief itself, his legal temper is, perhaps, the worst enemy of his pure consolation. It is a secret and subtle foe that seems to intend him a kindness, while it is always putting him upon seeking for some good qualifications in himself, on the ground of which he may trust that God loves him and that Christ saves him. Let him, therefore, if he would retain spiritual comfort, be diligent in mortifying his self-righteous spirit, and know that the way to conquer and destroy it is, by faith, to bring daily into his conscience a better hope from a better righteousness than that of the law. All the spiritual distress of the exercised Christian may be traced to a legal spirit in him. He seldom wants comfort but by looking more to his own righteousness instead of looking off to the consummate righteousness of Jesus Christ. Believer, it is not sufficient, in order to maintain spiritual comfort, that you do not rely on your graces and performances for a title to eternal life. You must not presume to rely on them for even so much as a right to trust in Christ; you must not make them the smallest part of your warrant to renew your exercise of confidence in Him.

Again, do believers lose their holy consolation by living upon their comfort rather than upon the holy Comforter Himself, and by loving the former as much as or more than the latter? They may hence perceive that it is sinful and very displeasing to the Lord to rely upon the comfort already given them, or to love consolation in the streams more than, or even as much as, comfort in the Fountain. God takes away sensible comfort from such persons because they have loved it inordinately, or loved it too much, and because He would teach them effectually the necessity of loving the adorable Comforter Himself more than all the sweet consolation which they have received from Him. They must not expect that "the God of all comfort" will suffer them to let their love rest wastefully upon their pleasant feelings. He will elevate it all to Himself.

Because He loves them, He will so chasten them as to teach them to love Himself supremely, and to live upon Himself in the absence of sensible delights. He will teach them to love Him more for that boundless ocean which is in Himself than for the few drops which He had shed upon them; more for His own infinite benignity than for the grace or comfort which He has communicated to them. He will thereby, at the same time, show them how weak their love of Him is when they love Him chiefly for the comfort which they have received from Him, and how weak their faith is when they live upon the streams rather than upon the overflowing Fountain of consolation.

Further, do believers, by their aggravated offenses, provoke the Lord at any time so to hide His face from them as to leave them in the dark respecting the truth of grace in their hearts? It follows that, though grace is always in the heart of a holy man, yet he is not always able to discern it there. His heart is always the seat of the principles and habits of grace, and yet he does not continually enjoy the comfort of perceiving them. The figures of a sundial continue to be plainly marked upon it, and yet we cannot see by it what hour of the day it is unless the sun shines upon it. It is only when graces are in exercise, and when the glorious Sun of righteousness shines upon them, that they can be seen. Let not, then, any of the saints conclude that they never had, and that they now have not, a well-grounded assurance of their being in a state of grace because doubts of the truth of grace in them sometimes arise in their minds. Their assurance of personal interest in Christ is well-grounded and true, though it is far from being perfect. Their graces themselves are imperfect, and therefore that assurance of sense which arises from the perception of them must be imperfect likewise. Such believers as resolve never to rejoice till they attain perfect assurance must resolve never to rejoice while they are in this world. They should consider that there are many degrees of real certainty below a perfect degree of it, and that they injure themselves much as often as they do not perceive clearly their habits of grace.

Once more, is it only by sinning against the high and holy One that believers lose the comfort of communion with Him? They may hence discover what reason they have to abhor, and with holy detestation to turn from, all manner of sin. Their iniquity has not only pierced the incarnate Redeemer and grieved the Holy Spirit, but it pierces them through with man's sorrows. It is the worst enemy of their souls. It incessantly strives to rob them of their purest and sweetest joys. Let them therefore, without ceasing, strive against the motions and mortify the members of the body of sin that dwells in them. If they allow, even for a moment, sin to dwell at ease in them, it will assuredly deprive them of their holy tranquility.

4

The Grievous Consequences of a Believer's Having Lost His Spiritual Consolation

By withholding spiritual consolation from the souls of any of His people, the Lord, in proportion as He does it, is represented in the Scriptures as forsaking or deserting them. His forsaking of them, in respect of comforting influences, either in a lesser or greater degree, is the same as His withdrawing of the sensible influences and tokens of His special favor from their souls, or, as it is often expressed in the Scripture, His hiding His face from them. When He so forsakes them, or so hides the light of His gracious countenance from them, as to suspend in any measure His influences of comfort from their souls, they lose, in the same measure, that consoling sense of His special favor and love for them which hitherto they usually enjoyed.

The meaning of God's hiding of His face from believers may, in some degree, be understood from the opposite phrases: His "causing His face to shine upon them," and His "lifting up the light of His countenance upon them." These phrases appear to carry in them an allusion to the shining forth of the Shekinah in the ancient tabernacle and temple; that is, of the glorious luster which dwelt in the cloud as the visible token of Jehovah's favor to the Israelites, and of that gracious presence with them, which He was pleased on some solemn occasions peculiarly to manifest. There may also be in them an allusion to the pleasant appearance of the countenance of a friend in a superior station of life, when he converses familiarly with an inferior whom he regards with peculiar favor. Accordingly Job, when mentioning the regard shown him by his attendants, says, "If I laughed on them (or, jested with them) they believed it not, and the light of my countenance they cast not down" (Job 29:24). It is as if he had said, "They were, on an occasion so agreeable to them, solicitous to do nothing that would so displease me as to make me frown on them." And when the Jewish Church in captivity prayed to be restored to her former freedom, she said, "Cause Thy face to shine, and we shall be saved" (Psalm 80:3); that is, "Restore us to our former prosperity, and thereby manifest to us Thy mercy and Thy favor."

On the other hand, God is said in Scripture to hide His face from His children, or not to cause His countenance to shine upon them, when, as a mark of His paternal displeasure with their evil conduct, He suspended for a season the usual influences and tokens of His favor from their souls. Such forsaking, therefore, or suspension of spiritual comfort, though sometimes intended as a trial of their graces, yet is more often designed by their heavenly Father as a grievous chastisement for their sins.

Now the consequences of their loss of spiritual consolation are especially the following:

1. Trouble and sorrow of spirit are consequences of it. "Thou didst hide Thy face," said David, "and I was troubled" (Psalm 30:7). And when he was driven from the sanctuary of Jehovah, in which the visible symbol of His favor was placed, and where the manifestations of His favor were enjoyed, the soul of that holy man was cast down and disquieted in him (Psalm 42:5–6). Indeed, when a saint has (especially by his own aggravated folly) lost the sense of his peace with God, he cannot but be troubled; and when he hath forfeited the sense of his joy in God through the Lord Jesus Christ, he cannot but be sorrowful. "In the favor of God is life" (Psalm 30:5).

When, therefore, a holy man loses his perception of that favor, "the sorrows of death will compass him, and the pains of hell will get hold upon him: he shall find trouble and sorrow" (Psalm 116:3). And the more he is insensibly upheld by sustaining and quickening influences, the more troubled and grieved will he commonly be for his loss of comforting influences. A prevailing persuasion of the favor of God in Christ, and of acceptance with Him, is the ordinary attainment of the saints in this world. "The Lord will speak peace unto His people, and to His saints" (Psalm 85:8). But when a saint forfeits the light of God's gracious countenance and holy comfort, he ordinarily at such a time loses all sight of his evidences of grace; and when he cannot discern in himself the smallest evidence of grace, or of his being an object of divine favor, he cannot fail to be deeply dejected and troubled in spirit.

The sensible departure of a good and gracious God from the holy soul is like the departure of the soul from the body—painful and dreadful. In other losses, something still remains that is comfortable.

When a believer loses his earthly friends, he has still a heavenly Friend and Father who is unchanging in His goodwill to him, and to whom he may always look for comfort; but when this gracious, this matchless Friend Himself is apprehended to be lost, how perplexing, how grievous, how overwhelming is the loss! The heaviest of other losses is light and tolerable in comparison to this (Proverbs 18:14). No wonder if, in such a condition, the Christian takes up Jeremiah's mournful complaint: "When I would comfort myself against sorrow, my heart is faint in me" (Jeremiah 8:18). To lose the perception of the Savior's love for him is exceedingly distressing to a holy man. As all the candles in the world cannot make it day when the sun has set, so all the comforts in the universe cannot cheer the heart of such a man in the absence of the Sun of righteousness. A holy soul is like the flower that opens and shuts with the sun: if the Savior shines upon it, it opens; but if He withdraws the cheering light of His countenance, it closes itself and droops. It is, however, a comfort not to be forgotten that when the Lord Jesus leaves a believing soul He forsakes it not wholly, but always leaves something behind Him in it which makes it long for His return. Were He to desert it wholly, it would cease to long for Him.

2. *Piercing convictions and frightful views of their innumerable sins, in their heinousness and demerit, usually accompany this trouble of mind.* In the darkness of night, fire is more easily seen at a distance than in the light of day. When a holy man has lost the light of comfort and is walking in darkness, he has usually a more clear and disquieting sight of his great trans-

gressions than when he is walking in the light of consolation. The sin of his nature and the transgressions of his life are, in their deep malignity and dreadful demerit, then set in order before his eyes. The painful recollection of them, with their manifold aggravations, is revived in his mind; and they appear more horrible in his view than ever they did before. They are brought afresh to his painful remembrance as if they had been committed but yesterday. Being set in array before him, each of them gives to his disconsolate spirit a new and a deep wound, which increases the smart of his former wounds and makes them bleed afresh. They present themselves to his troubled mind with all their aggravations as having been committed against God and Christ, against redeeming love and grace, against the law and the gospel, against mercies and judgments, against the warnings of conscience and the motions of the Holy Spirit, and against the patience and forbearance of that gracious God who has so loved him as to give His only begotten Son to die for him. Holy Job, when in such a condition, said, "Thou writest bitter things against me, and makest me to possess the iniquities of my youth" (Job 13:26). David said, "My sin is ever before me. Against Thee, Thee only, have I sinned, and done this evil in Thy sight" (Psalm 51:3–4). "Mine iniquities have taken hold upon me, so that I am not able to look up: they are more than the hairs of mine head; therefore my heart faileth me" (Psalm 40:12). Thus the backsliding believer is sent back again to Mount Sinai, where he finds the devouring flames of the fiery law flashing in his face. His convictions

now are deeper, and his scorching hotter, than perhaps they ever were before. The Lord permits the
tremendous curse of the violated law to re-enter his
conscience; and thereby He shows him the awful
demerit of his innumerable offenses (Romans 5:20).
Perceiving that he has sinned in the midst of evangelical light, of frequent checks of conscience, of
manifold mercies, enjoyments, enlargements, and
experiences, he begins, it may be, to dread that he
may have committed even the unpardonable sin.

A sense of the horrible malignity and dreadful
demerit of his transgressions strikes a deep impression on his soul and makes his heart tremble. His
conscience upbraids him with his criminal folly and
base ingratitude in sinning against his gracious
God and Savior. Hence, cutting reflections, self-
condemning and galling thoughts often disquiet
his mind (Psalm 73:21–22). He can now think of almost nothing but the awful majesty, sovereignty, holiness, justice, and vengeance of the Lord. "I remembered God and was troubled" (Psalm 77:3). His
spirit is troubled, yea, overwhelmed, when he reflects that he has provoked the just, omnipotent,
great and terrible God to appear as an enemy
against him. Or, if he thinks at all of the mercy of
God, he will be disposed to argue: "Surely if my
transgressions had not been so heinous, or if I had
so much as a single spark of grace in me, an infinitely merciful God would not have thus forsaken
me."

Ah, sin committed against the high and holy
Majesty of heaven is a strange, horrible thing! If the
Lord should at once reveal fully to the exercised

Christian all the hideousness of this infernal monster, the discovery would be intolerable to him!

   3. *A distressing apprehension that some overwhelming
judgment will suddenly be inflicted upon them because of their
great offenses is often a consequence of their loss of holy comfort.* The writer of Psalm 88:5 apprehended that such
judgments were to come upon him as would cut him
off. The disconsolate Christian, under a deep sense
of accumulated guilt, is frequently struck with fear
that an offended God will inflict upon him some
sudden and terrible punishment. A filial and holy
fear of divine judgments, arising from the consideration of the great evil of sin, and of Jehovah's infinite righteousness and abhorrence of iniquity, as
well as of His tremendous wrath revealed against it,
is indeed lawful, and should at all times be exercised
by the saints. "O Lord, I have heard Thy speech,"
said Habakkuk, "and was afraid" (Habakkuk 3:2).
And David said, "Thou puttest away all the wicked of
the earth like dross; therefore I love Thy testimonies. My flesh trembleth for fear of Thee; and I
am afraid of Thy judgments" (Psalm 119:119–120).
But when a holy man has deprived himself of comfort, he commonly yields to a slavish and excessive
dread of the judgments of God. When he hears that
a thousand have fallen at His right hand and ten
thousand at His left, he trembles like a leaf of the
forest. In such a condition, he is disposed to indulge
a disquieting, distracting, and tormenting fear, a
fear which unsettles his mind, suspends his exercise
of faith, disturbs his peace, destroys his hope, and
instigates him to impatience, and to the use of unlawful means in order to escape the danger that

threatens him.

A fear of this kind is very sinful, as well as unbecoming, in a true Christian. It alienates his heart from the Lord and disqualifies him for the spiritual performance of his duty. Since he is walking in darkness, a thousand imaginary fears disquiet and perplex his soul. He is now more ready than before to be imposed upon by imaginary dangers, and to be "in great fear, where no fear is" (Psalm 53:5). Although the Lord has promised him that "no evil shall befall him" (Psalm 91:10), that no affliction shall ever come upon him but what will issue from the greatest love and terminate in the greatest good to him, yet he can think of almost nothing but imminent danger on every side, and his groundless and gloomy fears of it render him inexpressibly uneasy. Such fears are as so many galling fetters to his imprisoned soul, and when he would at any time try to shake them off, his quick sense of total inability discourages him. From this, they take occasion to become still more oppressive to him. Hence is that mournful expression of Job: "If I say, 'I will forget my complaint, I will leave off my heaviness, and comfort myself,' I am afraid of all my sorrows; I know that thou wilt not hold me innocent" (Job 9:27–28).

4. *Great uncertainty of mind about their present and their future state is usually a consequence of the suspension of spiritual consolation from their souls.* Now that the Christian is walking in darkness, he cannot as formerly see either his warrant to trust as a sinner in Christ for his own salvation in particular, or any good evidence of his having ever yet trusted in Him. Having lost the light of God's gracious countenance and of holy

comfort, he has consequently, and in the same proportion, lost sight of his vital union with the Savior,
and of his personal interest in His righteousness
and salvation. Hence great and sad doubts as to what
will become of him for the future frequently disquiet
his mind. "He who walketh in darkness knoweth
not whither he goeth" (John 12:35). Unbelief prevails so much against him that he often questions
whether Jesus Christ can or will save such a great
sinner as he is, and whether God will have mercy
upon him or not. He is in perplexing and painful
uncertainty what the great and terrible God may be
about to do with him when he is to depart hence.

He often suspects the worst; yea, his doubts may
be suffered to prevail so much as to make him conclude that the Lord will be favorable to him no
more. Thus Asaph, in a similar case, expressed himself: "Will the Lord cast off forever? and will He be
favorable no more? Is His mercy clean gone forever?
Doth His promise fail forevermore? Hath God forgotten to be gracious? Hath He in anger shut up His
tender mercies?" (Psalm 77:7–9). And the Jewish
Church in her captivity said, "My strength and my
hope are perished from the Lord" (Lamentations
3:18). When the holy soul is in darkness, it will often
argue thus: "The Lord has departed from me, and, it
may be, He will never return to me. Oh! what will
become of me if I am never to enjoy communion
with Him any more! What if I shall have my portion,
through all eternity, with hypocrites and unbelievers
in the place of torment! I have now no cheering
light, no enlivening hope, and perhaps I am soon to
be cast into outer darkness!" The Christian, in this

perplexing condition, has, indeed, some lucid intervals now and then; but, as one expressed it, they are like the small breathings and refreshments of a person who is newly taken off the rack, and is about to be carried to the rack again. If it is accounted a bitter ingredient in the cup of outward affliction to be kept in suspense concerning any object which is deemed necessary and important to our temporal welfare, how distressing must it be to the spirit of a holy man to be held in suspense between hope and fear, respecting objects which are absolutely requisite, and infinitely important, to his eternal felicity!

As a natural man cannot be at ease without natural accommodations, or the possession of such things as are adapted to the comfort of natural life, so a spiritual man cannot be quieted without the enjoyment of spiritual blessings. The possession of ten thousand worlds could not afford him the smallest ease. Nothing but the faith of redeeming love offered to him, the view of his personal interest in the Redeemer, and the hope of his eternal enjoyment of God can put his soul to rest. Were he but to know that he is to be glorified together with Christ, and in due time to enter into His joy, he should soon come forth to the light of consolation.

5. *Another consequence of their having provoked their heavenly Father to withhold comfort from them is their uttering of heartless and useless complaints.* "Even today," said Job, "is my complaint bitter; my stroke is heavier than my groaning" (Job 23:2). And Asaph said, "I complained, and my spirit was overwhelmed" (Psalm 77:3). Some believers, after they have lost their wonted consolation, are not at first deeply sensible

of the greatness of their loss; and therefore, though
they mention with sorrow their want of former comfort, yet their sorrow is far from being very deep.
Their hearts are indeed affected by their loss, but
they are not so deeply afflicted by it as bitterly to bewail the sins which have procured it. They fill the
ears of some of their Christian friends with lamentable accounts of their doleful condition; but at the
same time they utter almost nothing but complaints
of that which they themselves are suffering. They do
not humble themselves deeply before the offended
Majesty of heaven; nor do they by faith, prayer, and
holy circumspection strive to recover that which
they have lost. They are, like Issachar, crouching
down under their burdens; or they may be compared
to a diseased man who frequently bemoans himself,
but does not seek to free himself from his distemper.

Sometimes they are very peevish and obstinate,
and they seem to take pleasure in complaining of
the trouble which they endure. But they are not
aware that by indulging a temper of this kind they
render it necessary that their wound should yet be
deeper, and that they should yet have more reason to
complain before comfort is restored to them. When
David was under a sense of guilt and paternal displeasure, doubtless he felt his loss of holy comfort;
but yet he did not strive ingenuously to confess and
bewail his iniquities, and fervently to supplicate for
spiritual consolation until, "day and night, the hand
of God was so heavy upon him that his moisture was
turned into the drought of summer" (Psalm 32:4).
They think too that they can never complain

enough, that their condition is inexpressibly miserable. Job exclaimed, "Oh, that my grief were thoroughly weighed, and my calamity laid in the balances together! For now it would be heavier than the sand of the sea; therefore my words are swallowed up" (Job 6:2–3).

But such thoughts and expressions as these are very unbecoming in the true believer who has, in every condition, a compassionate Savior to trust in, a consummate righteousness to rely on, and promises of grace and glory to apply and plead. The exercise of faith is certainly intermitted when he can allow himself to utter such clamors. He undoubtedly, at that time, forgets the infinite freeness, suitableness, fullness, and sufficiency of the grace which is in Christ Jesus. Besides, he thereby shows plainly that his grief and fear are, after all, far from being great. When sorrow and fear are shallow or superficial they are usually clamorous; but when they are great and deep they are commonly silent. They are so great that they cannot be expressed (Psalm 77:4); and, therefore, like the waters of a large and deep river, they move silently. The dejected Christian should complain to others around him only of an absent God and Savior (Lamentations 3:39); he should complain of himself rather, and should complain of himself chiefly to the Lord, who alone can relieve him.

6. *A deep and painful sense of God's paternal anger is also a consequence and a concomitant thereof.* Though believers are, in their justification, so entirely delivered from condemnation to vindictive and eternal wrath as to be no longer exposed to wrath of that kind

(Isaiah 54:9), yet by sinning (which after their justification they do) against the Lord not as their
avenging Judge, but as their gracious God and
Father, they incur the guilt of fatherly anger. By the
fatherly anger of God is meant His holy and righteous displeasure with His disobedient children,
which is manifested by His infliction of chastisement upon them. In this manner, the Lord was angry with Moses (Deuteronomy 1:37), and with His
ancient church, the members of which expostulate
with Him thus: "O God, why hast Thou cast us off
forever? Why doth Thine anger smoke against the
sheep of Thy pasture?" (Psalm 74:1).

When the Lord is so displeased with any of His
children as to withdraw from them the sense of His
special favor, He commonly, at the same time, impresses on their souls in place of it a sense of His paternal anger. Instead of cheering them with that delightful sense of His redeeming love for them which
they formerly enjoyed, He fixes deep in their souls a
painful feeling of His being angry with them. "For
the iniquity of his covetousness," said Jehovah, "was
I wroth, and smote him. I hid Me, and was wroth"
(Isaiah 57:17). When the Lord is wroth with any of
His people for their iniquities, He will not only hide
His face from them, or deprive them of the cheering
sense of His favor, but He will smite them likewise.
And this He will do not only by some external stroke
of His rod on their bodies or estates, but sometimes
by an internal and deep impression of His anger on
their souls. And, if depriving them of the cheering
sense of God's favor is connected with the feeling of
His hot displeasure, an inexpressibly bitter and

grievous conflict in their souls must ensue. Therefore the Lord has said, "I will not contend forever, neither will I be always wroth; for the spirit should fail before Me, and the souls which I have made" (Isaiah 57:16).

When God is wroth with His children, He makes them feel His displeasure either:

• By frowning so upon them that they shall for a season discern almost nothing in His countenance but a continual and dreadful frown; or,

• By "covering them with a cloud in His anger" (Lamentations 2:1, by seeming "to be angry even with their prayer" (Psalm 80:4), to shut it out (Lamentations 3:8), and to "cover Himself with a cloud, that it cannot pass through" (Lamentations 3:44); or,

• By leaving their souls to languish under the prevalence of unbelief, discouragement, and dread; or,

• By laying sore and long affliction upon their bodies, and rendering all the means which they employ for the removal of it unavailing; or, in a word,

• By threatening to destroy at once all their external comforts.

Indeed, when the Lord impresses on their spirits a deep and fixed sense of His anger, no creatures can afford themselves the smallest consolation. In vain will they seek for ease to their oppressed souls in business, amusements, or pleasant company. Friends may, indeed, mourn with them, but, as one expresses it, "They cannot wipe away their tears." Nor can they then find relief even in the ordinances of God. Every threatening of His holy law appears as an arrow aimed at their heart. Every promise of His blessed gospel, however full of consolation to others, seems empty to them. Every offer of a Savior, and of His great salvation, however unlimited, appears to be directed to other sinners, and not to them. The Lord Himself seems to them as if He were taking no notice of their distress, yea, as if He were an enemy to their souls. We are not to wonder, then, if, in such a case, they feel overwhelming trouble and anguish of spirit (Job 19:6, 8).

Indeed, it is because the Lord still loves them and resolves to save them that, when He sees them running on to sin and misery, His paternal anger thus overtakes them in order to stop and bring them back again to the comfort of holy conformity to the image of His Son Jesus Christ.

7. *A most distressing sense even of the vindictive wrath of God is sometimes a consequence of their loss of comfort.* True believers indeed can never be cast into hell, but the Lord may, as it were, cast hell into them. Some of them, accordingly, when God has hidden His face from them, have been permitted, rashly and falsely, to conclude that because they cannot see Him now they *never* saw Him; that because they cannot perceive their evidences of grace now, they *never* had true grace; that as they never had true grace formerly, they have no saving grace now; and that the anger of God which they now feel is not His fatherly displeasure, but His vindictive wrath (Psalm 88:14). Thus they unjustly, as well as rashly, conclude that what they now feel is an impression of avenging wrath. It is of this wrath that Heman seems to com-

plain when he said, "Thy wrath lieth hard upon me. Thy fierce wrath goeth over me" (Psalm 88:7, 16). In like manner one of the prophets said, "I have eaten ashes like bread, and mingled my drink with weeping, because of Thine indignation and Thy wrath" (Psalm 102:9–10).

The sense of vindictive wrath is much more doleful and intolerable than even that of paternal anger; and therefore the Psalmist prays that if he must be chastened the greatest of all chastisements may not be inflicted upon him: "O Lord, rebuke me not in Thy wrath; neither chasten me in Thy hot displeasure" (Psalm 38:1). He prays not merely that the Lord may not punish him in vindictive wrath, but that He may not so chasten him as to lay him under an overwhelming impression of that intolerable wrath.

When the soul of a holy man is, for a season, under that dire impression, he can see nothing, feel nothing but consuming wrath. Conscious as he is that he deserves the fierceness of eternal wrath, he is filled with dreadful apprehensions that the hand which presses him sorely is the hand not of a merciful Father, but of an avenging Judge, casting him down like a condemned criminal into a deep and horrible dungeon. Heman, under a sense of that wrath, complained to the Lord thus: "Thou hast laid me in the lowest pit, in darkness, in the deeps" (Psalm 88:6). When a saint is under terrible impressions of Jehovah's infinite wrath, he cannot but be under great horror of conscience and in perplexing depths of mental trouble. The sense which he has of avenging wrath occasions an inexpressibly agonizing and terrible conflict in his spirit. When his troubled conscience is inflamed by a sense of the fiery indignation of God Almighty, the more he thinks of Him as his infinite Enemy, the more he is dismayed (Psalm 77:3). Every thought of Him brings doleful tidings, and pours oil upon the raging flame.

Trouble of conscience for sin is indeed very disquieting, but a sense of the vindictive wrath of God, kindled in the conscience, is still more dreadful. No words can express the dire anguish which the disconsolate soul then feels (Psalm 116:3). The Christian cannot at that time think so much as one quieting or cheering thought. What he first thinks of is tormenting to his wounded spirit. He exchanges that thought for another, and that is still more tormenting. He finds himself entangled as in the midst of a thicket of thorns, so that whichever way he turns himself he is pierced and grieved afresh. The dismal thought often arises in his troubled mind that if death were, in his present condition, to surprise and cut him off, he should sink forever and ever under the intolerable wrath of the infinite Jehovah. The most exquisite torment of body is almost nothing in comparison to the anguish of his spirit at such times (Proverbs 18:14). Oh, how inconceivable is the anguish, the agony, especially of a holy soul when it is conflicting with the tremendous wrath of the eternal God! The bodily torture even of crucifixion could not extort from the holy Jesus the smallest sigh or complaint; but the sense of His Father's wrath in His soul wrung from Him that doleful outcry, "My God, My God, why hast Thou forsaken Me?" (Matthew 27:46).

8. *Another consequence of their having deprived themselves of spiritual comfort is overwhelming terror.* Terror is an excessive fear and trembling of heart. The troubled soul begins to dread that its present feeling of vindictive wrath is but the beginning of what it shall have to feel through an endless eternity. "The terrors of God," said Job, "do set themselves in array against me" (Job 6:4). "Destruction from God was a terror to me" (Job 31:23). And Heman said, "While I suffer Thy terrors, I am distracted. Thy fierce wrath goeth over me; Thy terrors have cut me off" (Psalm 88:15–16).

The Lord permits some of His children, when they are under the hiding of His face, not only to draw from that awful dispensation false conclusions, with regard to their past and present state, but to form rash and despondent conclusions concerning their future condition. They then conclude that it will never be better with them, as to their outward afflictions. Hezekiah, in a similar case, said, "I shall not see the Lord, even the Lord, in the land of the living. I shall behold man no more with the inhabitants of the world" (Isaiah 38:11). They likewise conclude that it will never be better with them in this world, with respect to their inward troubles. "I shall go softly all my years," said Hezekiah, "in the bitterness of my soul" (Isaiah 38:15). Nay, under the prevalence of unbelief and despondency, they peremptorily conclude that the Lord, whom they have greatly displeased, will cast them off and punish them with everlasting destruction in the world to come. They do not merely question, as Asaph did, if the Lord

will be favorable to them any more; but they rashly
and positively conclude that He never will. They say,
as the house of Israel did, "Our bones are dried, and
our hope is lost; we are cut off for our parts" (Ezekiel
37:11), and as the Israelitish Church did, "My
strength and my hope are perished from the Lord"
(Lamentations 3:18). This they do not during a
short fit of despondency, or in their haste, as David,
but for a long time. When neither sun nor stars of
consolation in many days appear, all hope that they
shall be saved seems to be taken away. Those awful
passages of Scripture, in which "the wrath of God is
revealed from heaven against all ungodliness and
unrighteousness of men, who hold the truth in unrighteousness" (Romans 1:18), continually present
themselves to their view. And by a strange kind of
belief, they apprehend that every part of the Word, as
well as every dispensation of the providence of God,
is the sword of an enemy; that promises as well as
threatenings, mercies as well as judgments, are
against them; and that by all, the Lord, as with a
flaming sword turning every way, hinders their access to the tree of life. Terrors, like fire, assimilate
everything to their own nature; and so they render
dejected souls unable to put a just or favorable construction upon any of the words or dispensations of
the Lord.

The terrors of God may indeed be felt, but they
cannot be expressed. They are inconceivably dreadful and overwhelming. They are "the arrows of the
Almighty within a man, the poison whereof drinketh up his spirit" (Job 6:4). Wounding him in the
most vital and tender part, they cause his spirit

within him to pine away and almost to die. "I shall doubtless perish," says the frightened soul. "I am undone, forever undone. I am already, as it were, in the place of torment, under inexpressible anguish and insupportable terror. The great and terrible God has cast me off, and I see nothing before me but horrible darkness, black darkness forever. The shadows of the evening are stretched out over me; and what will become of me if it shall prove an endless night! Oh, what will my eternal state be should death surprise me in my present condition! If I cannot now bear even a slight impression of the anger of God, how shall I be able to endure the full weight, the eternal fierceness of His avenging wrath! If I am so troubled, so terrified, so amazed now, what shall I do when my tremendous doom shall be pronounced, and the endless execution of it begun!" Oh, what overwhelming horror, what dire agony must an awakened and disconsolate soul feel in the awful prospect of suffering the vengeance of eternal fire! Oh, eternity, eternity! How, in the night of terror, does the prospect of eternity amaze and even absorb the spirit!

9. *Satan's being permitted to add to the trouble and terror of believers is usually a consequence of their having forfeited their spiritual comfort.* In that condition, they are commonly "in heaviness through manifold temptations" (1 Peter 1:6). When the Lord is chastening any of His children for being more ready to believe the lies of Satan than the truths of His holy Word, He often permits that crafty and cruel enemy to hold them down and terrify them. And so far as he is permitted, his constant work is to render them as uncomfort-

able in their way to heaven as possible. Thus he treated Job. The spiritual trouble and the dismal terror of that holy man were, for the most part, from the immediate hand of Satan.

When this enemy of souls perceives that believers constantly resist his temptations to presumption, he assaults them with furious and horrible temptations to despair. And when he observes any of them under a sense of divine anger, and a dread of eternal wrath, he commonly selects this as the fittest opportunity to enforce those temptations. He then, especially, labors to persuade them that when God is afflicting them with such great severity it is a sure evidence that He is not their God but their adversary, and that they are not His people but His enemies. He misrepresents both God and themselves to them, and so insults them in their misery.

When that cowardly enemy perceives that their spirit is already broken down, he makes his most furious assaults on them; for he knows that when they are cast down he can the more easily trample on and afflict them. No sooner does the Lord depart than Satan comes to triumph over their anguish and say, "Where now is your God? Remember that your iniquities have been peculiarly great and aggravated, and that you have thereby provoked the Lord finally to abandon you. You already feel His fiery indignation, and you have reason, good reason, to dread that you shall endure it forever." He takes occasion from their anguish of spirit to represent the Lord to them as a cruel tyrant, as one who has resolved to destroy them. And when they already fear and even feel that God has departed from them, what can they say in answer to him? Perceiving their distress, and knowing their weakness, he, with amazing dexterity and unwearied importunity, urges against them even passages of Scripture, and dispensations of providence in order to enforce his infernal suggestions. When he sees that their faith is very weak, and that their sense of divine displeasure is very deep, he then shoots his fiery darts, which penetrate and inflame their souls with additional anguish and horror (Ephesians 6:16). It is a pleasant sight to that wicked one to behold God afflicting His children, and to see but one of them wounded with griefs, broken with terrors, made "a brother to dragons, and a companion to owls" (Job 30:29). He, therefore, after they have been long disquieted and enfeebled by desponding fears, assaults them furiously in order that, when they are already pressed down, he may throw upon them additional weight.

It is his usual method so to impress terror on their minds that it frequently comes upon them by sudden fits. These fits or paroxysms commonly return whenever the troubled soul would promise itself some degree of ease. Accordingly, the usual times of refreshing the body with food and sleep are ordinarily the seasons which Satan watches for his renewed assaults (Job 3:24 and 7:13–14). He commonly injects at such times blasphemous and atheistic thoughts which fill them with horror; and when he has thereby prepared their hearts he seizes the opportunity to persuade them that such a heart must be wholly destitute of regenerating grace.

And when he perceives that any of them are afflicted with melancholy, he considers that as a dis-

temper which affords him advantages, peculiarly
suited to his design. The imagination is then disordered, and so is more fit than at any other time to receive impressions from him. It also affords him
much advantage if they have lately fallen into some
great and grievous sins, especially, as William
Perkins observes, into sins against the third, sixth,
or seventh commandment. Arguing from such
crimes, he labors to persuade them that they are
reprobate and doomed to eternal destruction. When
he perceives that they have been guilty of some atrocious iniquity, he will suggest that it is even the unpardonable sin. He argues likewise from their perturbation of spirit that their heart is so hardened by
the deceitfulness of sin as to be utterly incapable of
exercising repentance unto life. The more he dis-
tracts and amazes their minds with terrors, the more
unable they are to detect the fallacy of his arguments, and the more disposed they are to admit the
force of them. Excessive fear removes their souls to
such a distance from true comfort that they will not
be persuaded to trust in the Lord Jesus, either for
His salvation or for the joy of that salvation. Under
such perplexing fears they seem disposed so far to
take part with Satan as, with much eagerness and
wonderful subtlety, to plead against themselves.

Believer, when your transgressions are at any
time so exceedingly aggravated in your view as to exceed either the mercy of God, the blood of His Son,
the power of His Spirit, or the grace of His covenant,
you may be sure that it is one of the lies of the devil.
Oh, be henceforth so wise as no longer to expect
truth from a liar, sound argument from a deceiver,

or true comfort from an enemy.

10. *To be discountenanced or coldly treated by Christian friends is often a consequence of a believer's having forfeited his spiritual comfort.* When the Lord is angry with His rebellious child and is chastening him, He not only gives Satan leave to trouble him, but permits some of the saints who are acquainted with him to discountenance him, and by their cold treatment of him to add to his grief. When the father of a family resolves the more effectually to correct his obstinate child, he will say to the rest of his household, "Do not be familiar with him; show him no countenance; put him to shame." In like manner, when the Lord is smiting (especially with spiritual troubles) His disobedient child, He, as it were, says to others of His children, "Have for a season no familiarity with him; treat him with coldness and neglect in order that he may be ashamed and humbled for his iniquity." Job, under his grievous affliction, complained thus: "He hath put my brethren far from me, and mine acquaintances are utterly estranged from me" (Job 19:13). And likewise Heman, "Thou hast put away mine acquaintances far from me; Thou hast made me an abomination unto them. Lover and friend, hast Thou put far from me, and mine acquaintances into darkness" (Psalm 88:8, 18).

When the favor of God to the soul is clouded, the comfort of Christian society is also obscured. When He frowns on one, His children commonly appear to frown likewise; and when He makes Himself strange to one, so, for the most part, do they. If a holy man, then, under trouble of spirit, begins to be treated with disregard, and even with contempt, by some of his Christian brethren, he ought not to be surprised. Neither should he take occasion to be angry or quarrel with them; but he should look above them, and take the afflictive dispensation only out of the hand of the Lord as a necessary part of the chastisement intended for him. He ought to say with respect to them, as David said concerning Shimei, "The Lord hath bidden them"; or, as Heman did, "Thou hast put away mine acquaintances far from me."

11. *Hard thoughts of God, and jealous thoughts of Christ, often take occasion to arise from the want of comfort, especially if believers have remained long in that condition.* Hard thoughts of God proceed from their disconsolate hearts, such as that He is so greatly incensed against them as to be implacable; that He has so forsaken them as never any more to return; that He has passed such a sentence of condemnation upon them as shall never be reversed; that He has covered Himself with such a cloud in His anger as shall henceforth render it impossible for their prayer to pass through; that He has forgotten to be gracious to them; that His mercy has clean gone forever, and such like. When dejection and terror continue long, they obscure the mind and cause it to form and entertain gloomy, yea, monstrous apprehensions. Hence are these words of Job: "He performeth the thing that is appointed for me; and many such things are with Him. Therefore am I troubled at His presence; when I consider, I am afraid of Him. For God maketh my heart soft, and the Almighty troubleth me, because I was not cut off before the darkness" (Job 23:14–17).

Jealous thoughts of Christ, the glorious Head and husband of believing souls, likewise arise from the disconsolate heart. If souls have hard thoughts of God, they will quickly entertain jealous thoughts of Christ Jesus. And if they but begin to suspect that Christ does not love them, or that He is not faithful in performing His promises to them, they will be afraid to take His Word, and afraid to trust Him or commit themselves and their salvation to Him.

Christian, be continually on your guard against unbelieving and suspicious thoughts of the love of Christ for your soul. Trust firmly that He loves you, and cares for you, and that He will never leave you or forsake you. Your sensible comfort may leave you, but your faithful Redeemer, the husband of your soul, will never totally or finally forsake you. He may indeed for a season "cause grief; but He will have compassion, according to the multitude of His mercies" (Lamentations 3:32). Say not, then, when He hides His face from you, "He has utterly forsaken me," but rather, in the exercise of unsuspecting confidence in Him and His love for you, say, "He will turn again. He will have compassion upon me. He will subdue my iniquities and will cast all my sins into the depths of the sea" (Micah 7:19).

Oh, guard against jealous thoughts of your infinitely faithful Redeemer. Do not suspect Him without ground. The moment you are jealous of His love for you, you sin against Him without cause. The Lord Jesus at no time so conducts Himself in His ways of grace and providence toward you as to give you the smallest cause to suspect His faithfulness (Lamentations 3:23). And if you would never suspect

His kindness and faithfulness to your soul till you had a cause, it is all that He would desire. Remember that to be jealous of the holy Jesus is to sin not only against Him, but against yourself. "Jealousy is the rage of a man" (Proverbs 6:34). It will disquiet and torture your soul; it will waste your spirits and prey upon you like the grave. You, indeed, have been unfaithful, very unfaithful, to the Lord Jesus; but this, though a ground of deep humiliation, is no ground at all for suspecting His faithfulness to His own promise, upon which He has caused you to hope (Psalm 119:49).

12. Another consequence of their loss of spiritual consolation is their being usually so discomposed and dispirited thereby as to become at the time unfit for the spiritual performance of their duty. This will more especially be the case with them if, as is too common, they, in their disconsolate condition, forbear to trust in the Savior for present and eternal salvation. Though their obedience is not accepted on account of their faith, yet it is spiritually good and acceptable in proportion to the strength and the frequency of their actings of faith. If, then, they cease for a season to act in faith, they, in the same proportion, cease for that time to perform spiritual and acceptable obedience to the Lord, for "without faith, it is impossible to please Him" (Hebrews 11:6). It is not sufficient, in order to have acceptable obedience, that Christians have faith in principle, and even in habit: they must likewise have it in exercise, and that even when they walk in darkness and have no light of sensible comfort (Isaiah 50:10). But if, in the darkness of spiritual trouble, they forbear for a season to trust in the Lord

Jesus for complete salvation for themselves in particular, that trouble will so disquiet and dispirit them as to disqualify them either for doing or for suffering, according to the will of God. "I am," said Heman, "as a man that hath no strength" (Psalm 88:4). Nay, it has made some of them even think that it is to no purpose for them to endeavor spiritually to perform any duty. Indeed their souls, when in that doleful condition, are commonly so occupied with the fear of eternal wrath that sin as sin and duty as duty are but little considered by them. Moreover, that conscience by which they judge themselves to be still under the guilt of all their sins is in the Scripture called "an evil conscience" (Hebrews 10:22), a conscience which the blood of Christ must purge from dead works in order for them to be capable of serving the living God (Hebrews 9:14).

Love, which is the fulfilling of the law and the end of the commandment, must arise out of a good conscience, as well as out of a pure heart (1 Timothy 1:5). That evil or guilty conscience by which disquieted Christians judge that the Lord is still their enemy because of their sins greatly strengthens the remaining enmity of their hearts against Him; and so it indisposes them for affectionate and filial obedience to Him. For in proportion as they decline in their love for Him, they are hardly drawn to Him in any spiritual service, and are easily drawn from Him. They come slowly and depart readily. They approach with reluctance, and while they stand before Him it is with hesitation and dislike.

Besides, as spiritual joy raises and invigorates the spirit, so carnal and legal sorrow depresses and enfeebles it. All sorrow, except godly sorrow, lies like lead on the heart, cold and heavy, and presses it still downward. It likewise makes the soul contract itself, or shrink from that spiritual intercourse with God in Christ which it ought eagerly and incessantly to pursue. Under the pressure of sadness, especially when it is accompanied with terror, believers themselves find no heart to pray, and no life in praying. They bow their knees; they sigh and cry; but the Lord seems to regard them not, nor to return answers of peace to their prayers. Their thoughts are, for the most part, in a continual tumult; and so, in all their efforts to pray, wandering and perplexing thoughts sadly prevail against them. Their sadness greatly abates their vigor of spirit and destroys their freedom of speech. It dampens also their faith, hope, and love; and so it mars their prayers, as well as all their other spiritual exercises.

Finding that they are still as perplexed and disconsolate after prayer as before, and fearing that their prayer is an abomination to the Lord, they are almost at the point of giving it over. They are troubled when they do not pray; and when they would pray they find that they cannot. Sometimes, when their trouble of mind becomes great and violent, it suppresses their words and can itself find no vent. "I am so troubled," said Asaph, "that I cannot speak" (Psalm 77:4). The waters of their trouble and anguish so drown their cries that they either cannot pray at all, or can find no liberty, no pleasure, no relief in their prayers.

13. Last, the joint effect of those consequences mentioned above frequently is that their natural spirits begin to be disor-

dered and dejected. Trouble of mind, especially when it is great or of long continuance, commonly produces this effect. Such is the nature of the union between the soul and the body that there is almost never any vigorous exercise of any of the affections or passions of the soul without some corresponding effect thereby produced on the motion of the fluids, and, especially, of the natural spirits of the body. The motion of the animal spirits is thereby altered; whence often arises some bodily sensation, especially about the heart and other parts essential to life, which are the fountains of those fluids.

So much is the body subjected to the soul, and so much do the spirits of the body depend on the affections of the soul, that the exercise of any one of the affections has a direct tendency to produce an effect on the body. And if the exercise of any one of them is great or violent, it will produce an effect, proportionably great and violent. Accordingly, the holy Psalmist, expressing his vehement desire for communion with God in public ordinances, said, "My soul thirsteth for Thee, my flesh longeth for Thee" (Psalm 63:1). And again, "My heart and my flesh cry out for the living God" (Psalm 84:2). Now, the affections of grief and fear, in proportion to the degree of their exercise, contract the natural spirits and render their motions feeble and slow. The consequence is that the vigor of the body commonly declines; its motions become sluggish. The lamp of life burns dimly. The countenance grows dejected; the complexion waxes pale; and no liveliness or activity seems to remain. Hence are these complaints in Scripture: "On my eyelids is the shadow of death"

(Job 16:16). "I am become like dust and ashes" (Job 30:19). "My moisture is turned into the drought of summer" (Psalm 32:4). "There is no soundness in my flesh, because of Thine anger" (Psalm 38:3). "I am become like a bottle in the smoke" (Psalm 119:83). "My soul is full of troubles, and my life draweth nigh unto the grave" (Psalm 88:3).

As the motion of the spirits of the body is re-tarded and altered by the influence of the grief and fear of the soul, so this alteration, especially if it continues for a considerable time, will at length produce that disorder which is called "melancholy." Though melancholy, which is indeed a distemper of the body, is totally distinct from trouble of mind, strictly so called, yet the former often proceeds from, and is increased by, the latter; and the latter, again, is reciprocally augmented, and often prolonged, by the former. For as the soul can but feel with the body in its pain, so the body cannot be exempted from sharing with the soul in its trouble.

Having now considered the leading conse-quences of the loss of spiritual comfort, it will be proper to observe, in order to prevent mistakes, that in the case of some disconsolate Christians all these consequences concur, but in that of others, only some of them take place. It is seldom, unless when spiritual distress becomes very deep and continues long, that they are all felt by one and the same be-liever. Spiritual trouble usually consists either in the loss of comfort, together with all those conse-quences of it, or in the want of comfort, with some of them only, and that in a greater or lesser degree.

Accordingly, it is either total or partial. Some believers have been afflicted with total distress of soul so that they have, in a certain degree, even despaired of mercy. It may possibly, to some, appear harsh to charge so horrible a sin as despair upon true believers, even in their deepest perturbation of spirit. But if it seems uncharitable to say that any of the saints ever fall into a degree of despair, it will surely be more harsh and uncharitable to affirm that none who ever fall into despair are saints. Indeed, it cannot be denied that some of the saints, under the deepest anguish of spirit, have for a time so despaired as to have been overwhelmed with terror in the dreadful prospect of eternal wrath.

Other believers, again, upon their loss of comfort, are afflicted only with partial trouble of mind and are soon delivered from it. They have, indeed, painful experiences of some, or even of most of those consequences mentioned above, but not all. They have, it may be, a painful sense of paternal anger; but, being enabled still to trust that the hand which afflicteth their souls is the hand of a Father, and not of an enemy, they are exempted from an overwhelming sense of avenging wrath. Or they may, perhaps, have some feeling even of vindictive wrath, and yet be under but a very small degree of despondency (Psalm 88:1). Those of the saints who have even all those doleful consequences of their having forfeited their holy consolation may have them in a greater or lesser degree; and those who have only some of them may likewise have these in various degrees. Trouble of mind in some believers is transient and short; in others it is fixed, of long continuance, and sometimes attended with very alarming symptoms. But still, however short and however low in degree it is, the very lowest degree of it is inconceivably more intolerable and dreadful than the highest degree of bodily affliction.

Now, from the foregoing details, the following remarks are obvious:

First, trouble of mind, especially when it is excessive, is not in itself good, but evil. It is sinful in true Christians to suffer themselves to be disquieted by, and to languish under, despondent fears, as if they had not a compassionate Savior to trust in. Deep dejection of spirit produces much aversion of heart from the spiritual performance of every duty. It is contrary to the great duty of believing. Faith is a resting; this trouble is a disquieting of the heart. Faith is the eye of the soul; such trouble is the blindness and darkness of the soul. Faith gives glory to God; this reflects dishonor upon Him. It is not only a sin, but a heinous sin to so yield to dejection of spirit as to refuse to be comforted. The troubled spirit of the Christian actually rises against redeeming grace. It is well for him in such a case that the covenant of grace, in which he is still instated, is well-ordered in all things; that it stands like a well-marshalled army on the field, ready to resist his attacks on whatever part of it he may choose to fall upon. Be deeply convinced, O disquieted believer, that your refusing to trust in the Savior and be comforted is your aggravated sin, and that it is inexpressibly dangerous, as well as sinful, to allow despondency and trouble to grow upon your spirit.

Next, the most tender compassion from all, and

especially from fellow Christians, is due to them who are under trouble of spirit. Such distress cries aloud for the tenderest sympathy. If it is a great sin to treat fellow creatures who are under exquisite pain of body with roughness or severity, it is a much more heinous iniquity so to treat fellow Christians, who are under anguish of soul (Obadiah 12; Galatians 6:2).

Again, it is the duty of the disconsolate believer to hope that he shall, in due time, be delivered from his trouble. "It is good that he should both hope, and quietly wait for the salvation of the Lord; for the Lord will not cast off forever" (Lamentations 3:26, 31). On these words of the Lord Jesus, "The very hairs of your head are all numbered" (Matthew 10:30), Augustine puts to a believer this pertinent question: "You who cannot lose a single hair, how comes it to pass that you are afraid of losing your soul?" Christian, cheer your troubled spirit with the hope that your compassionate Savior will deliver you, though you cannot tell how or when (Psalm 34:19). Let the consideration of His infinite mercy, and of His near relation to you, encourage you, in expectation of deliverance, to bear with patience your grievous trial (Micah 7:9; James 5:11). Consider what you have deserved at the hand of the Lord, and what has provoked Him to set yet a keener edge on your trouble. You have need of patience. "Let patience therefore have her perfect work" (James 1:4).

Moreover, it appears evident that it is also the duty of the disconsolate Christian never to give way to carnal reasoning against himself. When his faith is lively and his evidences are clear, he can refute carnal reasoning, and say with the Apostle Paul, "Who shall lay anything to the charge of God's elect? It is God that justifieth; who is he that condemneth? It is Christ that died, yea, rather, that is risen again" (Romans 8:33–34). But when his faith is languid, and his evidences are eclipsed, it is not only useless, but dangerous in the extreme to yield to carnal reasoning about the state of his soul. For then he is least qualified to take God's part against the cavils of Satan, and of an evil heart of unbelief.

Were a man, in order to try to confirm the validity of his title to an estate, to encourage a suit to commence against himself, he surely would not choose for that purpose the time in which he could not find his evidences of that title. Alas! The time which a good man chooses for giving ear to carnal reasoning is commonly the very time in which he has lost his evidences of grace. And it is grievous to see with what a weak piece of sophistry the devil will baffle him at such a time. It is inexpressibly dangerous for a child of light, especially when he is in the dark, to be reasoning with the prince of darkness. He cannot, in such circumstances, be safe, otherwise than by the resolute exercises of prayer and that faith which is above sight, as well as contrary to sense and carnal reason. He should not spend a moment in framing arguments against himself. Satan will be ready enough to suggest them. And, in particular, he ought never to conclude that he is a hypocrite from such things as are nowhere in the Scripture declared to be marks of reigning hypocrisy. Where, O disconsolate Christian, do you read in the Oracles of Truth that the want of legal terrors in conversion, wandering thoughts, resistance, dullness, and deadness of spirit in prayer, even though you bewail them and strive against them; the want of present evidences of sincerity, and of those degrees of peace and joy to which some have attained; or some iniquity for a time prevailing against you, notwithstanding your frequent efforts to resist it—where, I say, do you read that any of these is an evidence of reigning hypocrisy? Or where can you find that the presence of hypocrisy in the heart is the same as the predominance of it?

It is no less the duty of the disquieted believer to distinguish between the atheistic and blasphemous thoughts which are injected by Satan and those which proceed from his own heart. His doing so will, through grace, be a means of lessening, in no small degree, the anguish of his soul. Atheistic and blasphemous thoughts sometimes proceed from his own heart, for our Lord said, "Out of the heart proceed evil thoughts . . . blasphemies" (Matthew 15:19). And he may charge himself with such thoughts as having arisen from his own heart when, instead of resisting them instantly and with abhorrence, he for a while yields to them. But if, as is more frequently the case, they come in suddenly and violently upon his mind; if his heart trembles at them, and with holy abhorrence instantly opposes them (Psalm 73:15); and if his being assaulted with them is very grievous to him (Psalm 73:21–22), he ought, without hesitation, to charge them upon Satan and not upon himself. He should, for his comfort, never impute them to himself as his own transgressions, but to the tempter as his temptations.

It is likewise his duty to read diligently and frequently such passages of Scripture as are most suited to comfort him. It is no less true than strange that the believer, under mental trouble, is usually much disposed to read, remember, and apply to himself such passages of Scripture and of human writings as are most adapted to increase the trouble and terror of his soul. Such places of Scripture, and of other books, as are arousing and alarming are indeed very proper for a good man often to read and remember when he finds that carnal security is prevailing against him. But when his soul is already depressed with terror and dismay, so that he needs comfort to refresh his drooping spirit, he ought chiefly and frequently to read, meditate, and believe with application to himself such passages of Scripture as are most encouraging and consoling to his fainting soul, especially the following: Psalm 43:5 and 71:20-23; Isaiah 1:18 and 55:1-4; Ezekiel 33:11; Hosea 14:4-6; Isaiah 57:15-19, 66:13, and 40:27-31; Isaiah 49:8-16, 54:7-14, and 61:1-3; Isaiah 41:10-14 and 43:1-2; Lamentations 3:22-26; Matthew 11:28-29; Revelation 22:17; John 3:14-17 and 14:15-27; 1 Timothy 1:15; Matthew 9:13; and Psalm 138:3-8. Let him resolve firmly, in dependence on promised grace and in defiance of his disinclination, to read again and again these and similar passages, to believe them with regard to himself, and to convert them into matters of ejaculatory prayer.

As the dejected believer is chastened less than he deserves to be, and as it is of the Lord's mercies that he is not even consumed, let him readily acknowledge this, and see that he expresses his grateful

sense of it by glorifying the Lord even in the fires
(Isaiah 24:15). Let him endeavor to glorify the Lord
by being constantly upon his guard against all manner of sin, and especially against omitting any
known duty. He must never take occasion from the
uneasiness of his mind to neglect a single duty that
it is possible for him to perform. It is inexpressibly
dangerous for the Christian to be indolent at any
time, but especially when he is under depression of
spirit.

To conclude, does God afflict some of His own
dear saints with unutterable anguish and terror of
soul, when He is only chastening them for iniquity?
What exquisite torment, then, what dire anguish
awaits impenitent sinners in the place of torment
where they must lie throughout eternity under His
vindictive, infinite, tremendous wrath! Christ has
given infinite satisfaction to the offended justice of
God for all the iniquities of His children. They love
God supremely; they also love His commandments
and study to keep them. They are the objects of His
redeeming, immense, and everlasting love. And yet,
in chastening them for their iniquity, He sometimes
afflicts them with dreadful impressions of His displeasure. Now, if a sense only of His fatherly anger is
so terrible and intolerable to them, how will you, O
impenitent and careless sinner, be able to endure
the fierceness of His vindictive wrath, the heat of
His fiery indignation, which shall burn unto the
lowest hell? If the suffering of that, only for a short
season, for a small moment, is so inexpressibly
painful to them, oh, what dire agony, what overwhelming anguish must you endure when you shall

suffer this not for millions of ages merely, but through all the endless ages of eternity! Ah, secure sinner, if you do not flee speedily from the wrath to come to the great Redeemer offered to you in the gospel, "the smoke of thy torment, will ascend up forever and ever; and thou shalt have no rest, day nor night" (Revelation 14:11). We are informed by Him who cannot lie that "the wicked shall be turned into hell" (Psalm 9:17), that "they shall go away into everlasting punishment" (Matthew 25:46), and that they shall be "cast into a furnace of fire, of everlasting fire, prepared for the devil and his angels" (Matthew 13:42 and 25:41). Consider this, you who live in sin, and be afraid. Oh, do not continue any longer in the love and practice of iniquity. Do not, for the momentary and polluted pleasures of sin, persist in exposing yourself to endless wrath. Walk while you have the light, lest darkness come upon you. While you have light, believe in the light, that you may be one of the children of light (John 12:35–36).

5

*The Nature and Signs of Melancholy, with
Directions to Such Believers as
Are Afflicted with It*

Though melancholy so weakens and disorders
the mind as to render a person unable to enjoy the
comforts and perform the duties of life, it is, nevertheless, seated in the body. But the state of body
which accompanies this disease is acknowledged by
the best physicians to be in general beyond the
reach of their investigation. By this distemper, the
mind is so disordered that, like an inflamed eye, it
becomes disqualified for discerning its objects
clearly and justly. The disease is commonly attended
with gloomy thoughts, heaviness, sorrow, and fear,
without any apparent cause of them. Wicked men
arc as liable to be afflicted with it as good men. In
the case of some, melancholy, though a bodily distemper, produces dejection of mind; in others, it
produces trouble of mind on spiritual accounts, especially if it is great, or of long continuance.
Melancholy also increases trouble of mind, and
trouble of mind increases melancholy. Where they
both exist together, they mutually increase and confirm each other. However great a believer's grief
over sin and his dread of divine anger may be, he

ought not to be called "melancholy" so long as
these appear to be rational, and his imagination appears to be sound. But, on the other hand, however
small his measure of sadness and of fear may be, yet,
if his imagination and mind are so distempered or
impaired that he cannot assign a proper reason for
his sadness and fear, nor express them in a rational
manner, he is to be counted melancholy. Now,
when a good man is at any time afflicted with this
grievous distemper, it will usually reveal itself by
some of the following signs.

SECTION 1. Of the signs of melancholy, especially in a true Christian.

When a holy man is under this mournful disease,
he commonly gives himself up to excessive grief. He
often weeps without knowing why, and thinks that
he ought to do so; and if he but appears to smile at
any time, or to talk cheerfully, his heart smites him
for it, as if he had done amiss.

He is usually exceedingly timorous or full of
groundless fears. Almost everything that he sees or
hears serves to increase his dread, especially if fear,
as often is the case, has been the primary cause of
his melancholy.

If the distemper is not deep, sadness and fear
commonly seize him at intervals. He is seized with
fits of them for a part of a day, or for a whole day, or
even for several days together; and after some short
abatement of them they return upon him, and he
feels them again fastening on his spirit without
knowing why.

Through the distemper of his imagination, he is

disposed to aggravate his sin, misery, or danger. Of every common infirmity or fault he is ready to speak with horror, as if it were an atrocious crime; every ordinary affliction he considers as utterly destructive, every small danger as a great one, every possible danger as probable, and every probable danger as certain.

He often thinks that his day of grace is past, and that now it is too late for him to believe, repent, or expect mercy. Were anyone to declare to him that redeeming grace is infinitely free, or that the riches of saving mercy in Christ are always overflowing, or that the offers and calls of the gospel are directed to him in particular, he would still affirm that now it is too late, because his day of grace is undoubtedly past. No arguments will convince him that his day of grace is not past, or that God will again show mercy or give grace to him, while all the while God is continually beseeching him to accept His offers of grace, and so to be reconciled to Him. He has an unbelieving suspicion that the God of truth is not sincere in His offers, and most sinfully attempts to make Him a liar (1 John 5:10). The Christian, dejected as he is, ought seriously to consider how atrocious, how reproachful, and how dreadful the sin of unbelief is.

He is perpetually apprehensive that he is utterly forsaken by God, and is always prone to despair. Like one who is forlorn and desolate, his continual thought is that he is utterly undone. But he certainly ought to consider that sinners who are utterly forsaken of God are habitually willing to continue in their sinful state and frame; that they are lovers of sin, haters of holiness, and, so far as they have power and opportunity, persecutors of all who would reform them, as if they were enemies to them—which is far indeed from being his case.

He frequently takes occasion from the doctrine of predestination to despair of divine mercy, and so he abuses that great and fundamental doctrine. Perceiving every object through a colored and distorted medium, he thinks that if the Lord has not elected him it will be altogether in vain for him ever to attempt believing and repenting; and then he strongly imagines that he is not elected, and therefore that it cannot be his duty to hope for the mercy of God. But he would do well to recollect that all whom God has predestined to life, He has predestined to the means; in choosing sinners to salvation, He has chosen them to faith and repentance not only as means, but as necessary parts of salvation. And it is his present duty, upon the warrant of the unlimited offer of the gospel, to choose Christ for his Savior, and God for his God, and immediately to trust in them for all the parts of salvation. This would, in the meantime, be a comfortable evidence to him that God has chosen him (2 Thessalonians 2:13). To trust in the Lord Jesus for all his salvation, and, in the faith of offered and promised mercy, to repent of all his sins, are the ways to know that he has been elected to faith and repentance, as well as to every other part of salvation.

He always asserts that he cannot believe, and hence concludes that he cannot be saved. If any Christian friend exhorts him to come as a sinner to the compassionate Savior, and to trust in Him for salvation for himself in particular, he is ready to reply, "Alas! You seem to understand nothing of my doleful condition; otherwise you would not exhort such a vile and unworthy sinner as I am to trust that the Holy One of God would ever save him. Indeed, it would be daring presumption in one like me ever to attempt trusting in Him. I dare not, I will not, I cannot confide in Him against whom I have so heinously sinned." His distemper, so far as it prevails, will not permit him to exercise faith. This is a dreadful chastisement, for he has omitted the great duty of trusting at all times in the only Savior, when his imagination was sound!

He is, at the same time, utterly unable to exercise joy or take comfort in anything. He cannot comprehend, or so much as think of, anything which is suited to comfort him. When he reads or hears the dreadful threatenings of the violated law, he always applies them to himself; but when he reads or hears the precious promises of the blessed gospel, he either takes no notice of them, or says, "They do not belong to me; the greater the mercy of God and the riches of His grace are, the more miserable I am, who has no part in them."

He looks upon his wife, children, friends, house, wealth, and all, without the least comfort, as a man would do who is going to suffer the most tormenting death for his crimes. He is like a man in continual sickness or pain who cannot take pleasure in anything around him because the feeling of his incessant pain prevents him.

He never reads or hears of any dreadful example of divine judgment but he presently imagines that it

will soon be his own case. If he hears of Cain or
Pharaoh being given up to hardness of heart, or but
reads that some are vessels of wrath fitted to destruction, or that they have eyes and see not, ears and
hear not, hearts and understand not, he thinks that
this is his very case, or that it is all spoken of him. If
he hears of any tremendous judgment inflicted on
someone, he concludes that it will also be executed
on him. If he is told that some person has become
distracted, or has died suddenly, or died in despair,
he presently thinks that it will be so with himself.
The reading of Spira's dreadful condition has, I believe, increased melancholy in many; the ignorant
author described a case of the plainest and deepest
melancholy, contracted by means of mental trouble,
arising from sin committed against conscience, as if
it had been the rational despair of a sound understanding.

He persuades himself that none ever was in such
a dismal condition as that in which he is. Although
he is ever so often told that many of the saints have
been in this very case, yet he still persists in saying,
"Never was anyone's case like mine."

His conscience is usually quick in charging him
with sin, in presenting to his view the infinite punishment which he deserves for his sin, and in urging him on to still greater dejection of mind as his
duty. But he seems dead to all the duties which directly tend to his consolation, such as praising the
Lord, thanksgiving for manifold mercies, meditating on the glorious Redeemer, and on the love,
grace, and promises of God. Press these, and such as
these, ever so frequently upon him, and he will

make no conscience of them; he will regard them as duties for others, but not for him.

He is always displeased and discontented with himself, just as a peevish or froward person is apt to be with others. Is such a man hard to be pleased? Is he ready to find fault with everything which he sees or hears of? And is he offended with everyone who comes his way? Just so is a melancholy man, with respect to himself: he is always suspicious of himself, always finding fault, always displeased with himself.

His thoughts, for the most part, are turned inward upon himself. Like millstones which grind on themselves when they have no grain between them, his thoughts are usually employed upon himself. When he suspects that he has thought irregularly, he thinks again and again on that which he has already been thinking of. He does not usually meditate much on God (except on His terrible majesty, justice, and wrath), nor on Christ, nor heaven, nor the state of the church, nor, indeed, on anything outside himself. His thoughts are all abstract and turned inward upon himself, and are such as tend not to alleviate, but rather increase his perturbation. His musing on himself is chiefly that he may perceive the working of Satan in himself, that he may find, in the depravity or infirmity of his nature, as much of the hateful image of that wicked one as he can; but the holy image of God in him he frowardly overlooks and will not acknowledge. And so, as noble objects kindle love in one's soul; as cheering objects fill it with delight, and as God in Christ, who possesses every excellence, elevates, perfects, and makes it happy—so mean objects of thought debase it; loathsome objects fill it with disgust; and mournful objects impress it with sadness. To fix, therefore, his thoughts incessantly upon his depravity and misery cannot fail to increase the sadness of his spirit.

He commonly gives himself up to idleness: either lying in bed, or sitting unprofitably by himself. He is much averse to labor, especially to the work of his usual calling.

At the same time, he is daily harassed with fears of want, poverty and misery to himself and his family, and sometimes even of imprisonment or banishment. He is often afraid that somebody will murder him; and if he but perceives anyone whispering to another, or winking with the eye, he presently suspects that they are plotting to take away his life.

He is weary of company, for the most part, and is much addicted to solitude.

His thoughts are commonly all perplexed, like those of a man who is in a labyrinth or pathless wilderness, or who has lost his way in the dark. He is continually poring and groping about, and can make out nothing but is bewildered and entangled the more. He is full of perplexing fears, out of which he cannot find the way.

He is ordinarily endless in his scruples; afraid lest he sins in every thought, every word, every look, in all the food that he eats, and in all the clothing that he wears; and if he resolves to amend his ways, he is still scrupulous, with regard to his designed amendments. He dares neither speak nor be silent, neither travel nor stay at home, but considers everything as if his conscience were wholly enslaved by self-perplexing scruples.

Hence it comes to pass that he commonly addicts himself much to superstition. He makes laws for himself which God never made for him. He ensnares himself by unnecessary resolutions, vows, and austerities. He places much of his religion in outward, self-imposed tasks, such as to spend so many hours of every day in this or that act of devotion; to wear such and such clothes, and forbear others that are more fit for him; to forbear all sorts of food that please the taste, and such like.

He has lost the power of governing his thoughts by reason. If a Christian friend exhorts him ever so earnestly and frequently to forbear his unprofitable, self-perplexing thoughts, and to turn his mind to cheering objects, he is unable to comply. He seems to be under a necessity of thinking anxious and distracting thoughts; he cannot turn away his mind from gloomy and frightful ideas. He cannot meditate on redeeming love, grace, or mercy. He can no more cease to muse on that which is already the subject of his thoughts than a man afflicted with a violent toothache can forbear, at the time, to think of his pain.

Hence he usually becomes incapable of engaging in secret prayer or meditation. When he would try to pray or to meditate, his thoughts are presently thrown all into confusion. He cannot fix or keep them upon any object outside himself; for a distempered and confused imagination, with a weak reason which cannot govern it, is the very disease with which he is afflicted. Sometimes terror drives him from prayer. He dares not hope, and therefore dares

not pray; and usually he has not courage to receive
the Lord's Supper. If he is at any time prevailed on
to receive it, he is presently filled with dread, fearing
that by partaking unworthily he has eaten and
drunk judgment to himself.

The consequence is that he begins to feel an uncommon degree of averseness to religious exercises.
Hence he rashly concludes that he is a hater of God
and of holiness, imputing the effects of his bodily
distemper to his soul, while yet he would rather love
God and be holy than have all the riches, honors,
and pleasures in the universe. Strictly speaking, it is
to the renewed perplexity and terror which he experiences in those exercises that he is averse, rather
than to the duties themselves. For he still desires to
have that calmness of spirit, that confidence and delight in the Lord Jesus, which he would be glad to
express by prayer and praise.

Here we ought to distinguish between that degree of averseness which is so predominant as habitually and entirely to overcome holiness in the
soul, and that degree which indeed strives vehemently against it, but does not overcome it. Every
holy man has some degree of backwardness to spiritual exercises remaining in him; but if this had dominion over him he would willingly abandon them,
which he is far from being permitted ever to do.
Still, however, he may, when he is under melancholy, be so deterred from some external duties as to
give them over for a time. Many real believers have,
for a season, been deterred from receiving the Sacrament of the Supper. Some of them, when under deep
melancholy and strong temptation, have even given

up outward prayer, hearing, and reading the Word of God; and yet they have not lost their desire for holiness, which is inward prayer, nor their desire to believe, love, and obey the gospel.

The melancholy man is commonly occupied much with eager and conflicting thoughts. He now and then feels as if something were speaking within him, and as if all his own violent thoughts were the impulses and pleadings of another. He, therefore, frequently attributes his irregular fancies either to some extraordinary motions of the Holy Spirit, or even to some uncommon agency of Satan. He often uses such expressions as these: "It was impressed on my heart," or, "It was said to me that I must do thus and so." And soon afterwards, "I was told that I must not do this or that." He conceives that his imagination is something talking within him, and saying to him all that he is thinking of.

Hence he becomes intractable and very obstinate in adhering to his own conceits. It is with the utmost difficulty that he can be persuaded to relinquish any one of them, however irrational. He, at the same time, becomes peevish and froward; it is easy to offend him and difficult to please him.

It is seldom that the most convincing argument or the best advice, though pressed upon him in the most affectionate and attractive manner, does him any good. If a Christian friend tries to persuade him that he has some evidences of a work of grace begun in his soul, and so far succeeds as to lessen, in a small degree, the dejection of his mind, yet as soon as he again views his heart and life through the medium of his perturbing humors, every such argument and advice is forgotten, and he is as far from serenity of mind as ever. Any encouraging thought of his state to which one can be the means of helping him seldom continues above a day or two.

When his melancholy becomes deep, he is almost constantly troubled with hideous and blasphemous temptations against God, Christ, the Scripture, or the immortality of the soul. These arise partly from his own fears, which make him think most of that of which he is most afraid to think. The very uneasiness, occasioned by his fears, attracts and confines his thoughts to that which he dreads. As he who is overly desirous of sleeping, and is fearing that he shall not sleep, is likely to continue awake because his desire and fear keep him awake, so the fears and anxieties of him who is melancholy counteract themselves. But these temptations arise chiefly from Satan who, seizing the opportunity of the Christian's being under that disease, vexes him and tempts him to blasphemous thoughts. For as that crafty and malicious enemy of the saints knows that he can more easily and successfully tempt a melancholy saint to unbelieving, despairing, and blasphemous thoughts than any other saint, so, when permitted, he will be sure vehemently to instigate him to such thoughts.

Hence a good man, when he is under strong melancholy, often feels as if something within him was forcibly urging him to utter some blasphemous or sinful expression; and he can have no rest unless he yields to the temptation. But no sooner does he yield than he is tempted utterly to despair, because he has committed so heinous a sin. And when Satan has gained this advantage over him, he still, to increase his dejection of spirit, sets it before him. It is wonderful what extraordinary acuteness the Christian, under this grievous distemper, will discover in evading the force of the strongest arguments that can be urged for his comfort. But I believe that Satan is, on such occasions, permitted to suggest his answers to him, and to assist him in setting them in the strongest light possible.

Upon the tempter's gaining that advantage over him, he further prompts him to conclude that he has been guilty of the sin against the Holy Spirit, which will never be forgiven him. This increases his despair of mercy. The man who indeed commits that horrible sin must be a professed infidel, and that in opposition to confessed miracles. And yet the melancholy believer despairs because he dreads that he has committed that sin—though, perhaps, he neither understands what it is nor has any reason but his own groundless fear, or some blasphemous temptation which he abhors, for imagining that he has been guilty of it. Alas! He does not consider that a temptation is one thing and a sin another, and that no man has less cause to fear that he shall be condemned for his transgression than he who abhors sin most, and is least willing to commit it. For no man can be less willing to commit iniquity than the Christian afflicted with melancholy is to be guilty of those blasphemous and hideous thoughts of which he bitterly complains.

When a good man, under deep melancholy, has been long harassed with suggestions to blasphemy and despair, he at length begins to dread that he is possessed by Satan. A man may be said to be possessed by Satan when that enemy is at any time permitted to exercise, in a certain measure, his power on him, and that by a stated and effectual operation either on his soul or on his body. The devil thus possesses the souls of the ungodly (Ephesians 2:2), but he is never permitted for a single moment thus to possess those of the saints. But though he cannot possess the souls of any of the saints, yet he may, as in the case of Job, be suffered to possess for a season the bodies of some of them. He may, perhaps, in the hand of the Lord, be an instrument of inflicting, among other distempers, the disease of melancholy on them; and he may also, by harassing them with horrible and despairing suggestions, be an instrument of increasing that grievous disease. But let it still be remembered by the dejected believer that Satan's exercising, for a season, such power on the body as may be termed a possession of it is no sign at all of an unregenerate state, or of his having gained possession again of that soul from which he had, in the day of regeneration, been cast out. Still, however, as this malicious and cruel enemy often raises a storm of persecution against the Christian from without, so in proportion as the Lord permits him he likewise produces trouble within. It should also be regarded by the disconsolate saint as matter of unspeakable comfort that, of all men, none loves the sin under which he sighs less than he does, for it is the heaviest burden of his soul; and that no sin evinces Satan's possession of a soul but that which the man loves more than he hates, and which he would rather keep than forsake.

The melancholy Christian should likewise, for his encouragement, recollect that God will charge his temptations only upon Satan himself, and in no way upon him, so long as he receives them not by the consent of his will, but continues to abhor them; and that He will no more condemn him for those evil effects which, produced by the force of a bodily disease, are unavoidable than He will condemn a man for raving thoughts or words in a strong fever or delirium (Psalm 103:13–14). But so far as reason in the dejected Christian yet has power and his understanding has the government of his passions, it is doubtless his own fault if he does not exert himself in using that power, though the great difficulty of using it renders his fault the less.

If his melancholy becomes very deep, the dejected believer often imagines that he hears voices, and sees lights and apparitions, or that something meets him and says this or that to him, when all is but the error of a diseased imagination and an impaired intellect.

In consequence of the continued and harassing perplexity of his mind under strong melancholy, the dejected Christian becomes weary even of his life. Some, under deep melancholy, are strongly tempted to do away with themselves; and they are assaulted with the temptation so incessantly and so forcibly that they can go nowhere but they feel as if something within were instigating them vehemently, and saying, "Do it." For the grievous disease under which they labor will permit them to feel nothing but anguish and despair, and to say nothing but that they are forsaken, miserable, and undone. It not only makes them weary of their lives, even while they are sore afraid to die, but it affords Satan a special opportunity to urge them to destroy themselves. Thus, if they by themselves happen to be crossing a bridge, he urges them to leap into the water. If they, when alone, see a knife or any other destructive weapon, he instigates them to kill themselves with it; and they usually feel as if something within them were importunately urging them, saying, "Do it, do it instantly." Hence some of them begin secretly to contrive how they may accomplish it, yea, and so far yield to the importunity of the tempter as actually to destroy themselves. This undoubtedly would be self-murder, were it not that the doleful distemper under which they labor so impairs their understanding as to render them at the time incapable of resisting the horrible temptation.

Although the use of means for the preservation and recovery of Christians afflicted with melancholy belongs as much to others connected with them as to themselves, yet so far as it is possible for them to exercise their reason they must be warned:

1. To abhor all such temptations, and not for a moment to give place to them in their minds.

2. To avoid carefully all occasions of yielding to them, so as not to go near a river, or any instrument which Satan would instigate them to use for that purpose.

3. To make known their case without delay to some of their Christian friends in order that suitable means may be employed for their preservation, and restoration to health.

Finally, the dejected Christian, above all, will not believe that he is under the disease of melancholy, but will be displeased if he hears any friend so much as hint it to him, and will affirm that it is but the rational sense of his extreme misery, or of being utterly forsaken by God and lying under His terrible wrath. It is therefore with no small difficulty that he can be persuaded to observe the prescriptions and directions of a physician, or to employ any means whatsoever for the cure of his bodily disease, asserting that his body is in perfect health, and that it is only his soul that is troubled.

These are, for the most part, the signs of melancholy, especially when the true Christian is in that dismal case, a case to be pitied, but never to be scorned. Let no man despise or vilify such, for men of all descriptions are liable to that grievous malady: high and low, learned and unlearned, religious and irreligious, yea, and persons who have hitherto lived in the greatest jollity and luxury, all such have actually fallen under it as often as it has pleased the Lord to make them thus feel some of the dreadful effects of His hot displeasure for their aggravated transgressions of His holy law.

SECTION 2. Directions to Christians who are afflicted with melancholy.

If the disease has proceeded far or become strong, directions to those Christians themselves are commonly to little purpose because their minds are so weakened that they cannot comply with them. But, because in some, especially when the distemper has but lately begun to seize them, there is some power of understanding and of reason still remaining, I offer the following directions and advice:

1. *Endeavor to understand well the covenant of grace.* Study, without delay, to attain just and clear views of the infinite riches, suitableness, and freeness of the grace of that everlasting covenant. The better you understand, and the more you think of that wonderful contract in which complete salvation is purchased, promised, and sure to you, the more, under the consoling influences of the Spirit of grace, will your souls be sustained and your tempers be sweetened. Think as often of the righteousness of Jesus Christ as of your own sinfulness, as often of His fullness of grace as of your own emptiness of grace, and as frequently of the boundless love, grace, and mercy of your Covenant-God as of His majesty, holiness, and justice. The way to diminish and even overcome those terrors which arise from partial and false apprehensions of God is to attain spiritual, clear, and enlarged views of Him as a God whose glory it is to be merciful and gracious even to the chief of sinners, and who will certainly show mercy to those who unfeignedly desire to honor Him and to be eternal debtors to His redeeming grace for all their salvation. Let your thoughts also dwell on these cheering truths: The Lord Jesus has, according to that well-ordered and sure covenant, given such an infinite satisfaction to divine justice for your sins as secures you from eternal death; that He has performed such a perfect obedience to the divine law as merits eternal life for you; and that life eternal is to you the infinitely free gift of God (Romans 6:23).

2. Be firmly persuaded that the incarnate Redeemer, with His righteousness and fullness, is in the gospel offered to you as sinners of mankind. Constantly believe not only that He is able and willing to save you, but that by His eternal Father and Himself He is freely, wholly, and particularly offered to you (John 6:32; Isaiah 55:1; Revelation 22:17). Believe cordially the record "that God giveth to you eternal life, and that this life is in His Son" (1 John 5:11). Consider that it is not your sin but your duty, always to believe that, to you in particular, He gives His Son, with righteousness and life eternal in Him; and that it is not your sin but your duty likewise to believe that the Father's authentic offer of Him to you affords you a warrant presently to confide in Him for salvation for yourselves, or to trust that He saves, and will continue to save you.

It would be presumption in any of the fallen angels to trust in Him for their salvation, because He is not offered to them; but it is not presumption in you, but a duty, to confide in Him for all your salvation because the offer, the call, and the commandment to believe in Him are directed to you, in common with all other hearers of the gospel. And these afford you a right, at all times, to place the confidence of your hearts in Him for grace and glory. Believe, then, that, seeing you have an ample warrant to trust confidently in the Savior for the whole of your salvation, it cannot be your sin, but your duty, your principal duty to do so. Oh, if you but saw, in the light of His Word and Spirit, and believed your divine warrant to come as you are, to come at all times and confide in the Lord Jesus for complete salvation, how greatly would it alleviate the trouble of your minds (John 4:10; Psalm 28:7)!

3. *Be persuaded to trust accordingly in Jesus Christ for all the inestimable blessings and comforts of a free salvation to yourselves in particular.* Come as unworthy, lost sinners in yourselves; come not upon the ground of any qualifications in yourselves, but upon the warrant afforded you by the gospel offer, and entrust your whole salvation to the compassionate Savior. Rely with unsuspecting confidence on the faithful, dear Redeemer for the enjoyment of all that is offered to you in the glorious gospel. There all the love of His heart is, in and with Himself, offered to you; trust therefore that He loves you (1 John 4:16). His consummate righteousness is granted to you; rely upon it for all your title to eternal life. All His salvation is also presented to you for your acceptance; trust therefore that His right hand will save you (Psalm 138:7). Since it is all offered to you as a free gift of grace, trust, with the entire approbation and consent of your hearts, that He will save you in a way of boundless grace (Acts 15:11). Seeing all the good things of this life which are necessary for you are likewise offered, trust that He will give you these also in the kind and the measure that He sees good for you (Psalm 84:11). All the promises of His eternal covenant are, in the indefinite offer, left and directed toward you; trust therefore that He will perform them to you, and so save you with an everlasting salvation. The absolute promises of the Spirit and of faith especially are, in the offer, given to you; trust that He will give His Spirit to you, and thereby enable you yet more and more to believe in Him.

Oh, that you knew what a comfort it is that the great Redeemer has made it your duty to trust at all times in Him, and in God through Him. He commands you to trust in Him with all your heart (Proverbs 3:5); and therefore you may be assured that He will not deceive your confidence, nor disappoint your expectation. Ah! If a faithful and able friend but suggests that you may depend on him for relief in some external difficulty, you will most readily confide in him, and believe that he will not deceive you. And yet you cannot trust a faithful, almighty Redeemer, though He commands you to do it, and promises that He will not turn away from you, to do you good (Jeremiah 32:40).

4. *Love not the good things of this world so as to place either your happiness or your confidence in them.* No objects whatever can continue in your possession except Christ and God in Him. No mercies can either be satisfying or sure to you but "the sure mercies of David" (Isaiah 55:3). Set not, then, such a high value on any of the empty and transitory things of this world, so as to put it in their power ever to disquiet your souls. Reproaches, injuries, and losses are all without you; they cannot come into your souls to vex them unless you open the door to let them enter. The Lord sends affliction upon your bodies and, it may be, permits men to injure you in your good names and worldly estates; but it is you only who allow these, or any other outward calamities, to enter and to vex your souls. The things of this world are still so high in your estimation, and they lie so near to your heart, that you cannot suffer the loss of any of them without vexation of spirit. Ah! that the

world should seem so great, and that God in Christ should appear so small, in your view as not to satisfy you, except when you can have the world along with Him! Oh, watch diligently against the inordinate love of earthly things, for it will dispose you to indulge distracting care and repining opposition of spirit to the holy disposals of adorable providence. It is anxious care and peevish discontent that are often, at first, the occasions of melancholy. They usually so disturb a man's mind as to render it defenseless against those temptations, respecting the state of his soul, with which Satan will afterwards assail him.

The disquietness which has been occasioned by outward crosses is then removed to his conscience, and so inflames it that he begins to be for a long season oppressed with many fears about the salvation of his soul. Thus, as if the Lord had not afflicted him enough, he adds to his own affliction. Only consider how heinous a sin it is so to love the world as to set up your own wills in opposition to the holy will and providence of the Most High. By repining against Him, you secretly accuse Him; and by accusing Him, you blaspheme His worthy name. Consider that the resignation of your wills in everything to the will of God is a principal branch of holiness, and that it is in proportion as you take complacence in His blessed will that your hearts are comforted. Oh, be persuaded to trust firmly that God in Christ loves you and bestows Himself upon you as your everlasting portion, and that the Lord Jesus will give you that which is good, and withhold no good thing from you; for that is the way, through the

Spirit, to mortify the inordinate love of the world.

5. Be not solitary, except as little and as seldom as possible.
A time for retirement from company is, indeed, for
those Christians who are well, a season of the greatest value for meditation, self-examination, and
prayer; but for you it is a season of great danger. If
the devil, with his temptations, assaulted Christ
Himself when he found Him in a wilderness, remote
from company, much more will he assail you if he
finds you solitary. It is your duty, therefore, to be, as
often as attention to your other duties will permit, in
the company of humble, faithful, and cheerful
Christians, especially of those whose views of the
gospel are clear, whose faith is strong, and who can
speak from experience of deliverance from dejection
of spirit. It may also be of advantage to you if you
confer at some time even with Christians whose
cases are similar to your own, in order to be satisfied
that your condition is far from being singular.

*6. Recollect frequently that, although it is a sin to yield to a
temptation, yet it is not a sin to be tempted.* Jesus Christ
Himself "was in all points tempted like as we are, yet
without sin" (Hebrews 4:15). He was tempted to the
most atrocious and horrible sins, yea, even to fall
down and worship the devil, and yet, having with
perfect abhorrence resisted every temptation, He
still was without sin. You can at no time be tempted
to more horrible iniquities than those to which the
Holy One of God was tempted. Though you cannot
endure temptation without sin as He could, yet, as it
is not every sinful inclination in the heart of a believer that is to be considered as a compliance with a
temptation, you should not charge upon yourselves

that which is the sin only of the tempter.

7. *Consider how much it gratifies Satan to see you indulging gloomy and despondent thoughts.* It pleases that gloomy spirit exceedingly to perceive you sullen and melancholy like himself, to behold you distrusting your Savior and suspecting your God to be an enemy to you, and that under the pretense of being deeply humbled and grieved for your sins. That surely cannot be either your duty or your ornament which gratifies the devil and serves to promote the interests of his kingdom. That can be no honor to you which robs your gracious God and Father of the honor of His redeeming grace, and which disposes you to hate Him and flee from His presence, as if He were your implacable enemy.

8. *Meditate frequently on the promises and grace of the gospel, but let each of your meditations be short and easy.* A deep and continued meditation will but harass and perplex your minds, and render you the more unable to perform your other duties. Your imagination and mind are, at present, so weakened that you cannot employ them in a fixed and protracted meditation without increasing thereby your malady. Do not mistake my meaning. I am not directing you to neglect meditation, especially on consoling subjects, but to forbear deep and long meditation because, in your present condition, it will strengthen your painful distemper. A short meditation on some cheering subject may be a means of lessening, and even of removing, your dejection, whereas a deep and continued meditation will distract you, and by increasing your disease will render you the less able to perform the other duties incumbent on you.

When you are at any time meditating, do not look down into the gloomy dungeon of your own heart where, at present, nothing can be seen but darkness or confusion; but look away from yourselves to the compassionate Redeemer, and to God, as a God of infinite grace in Him. Instead of dwelling on your own hearts to discern if love for Christ is there, you ought rather to be thinking of the infinite loveliness of Christ, and of His love for you. This would be the means of exciting the exercise of your love toward Him, and of bringing it forth to your view. A sight of your own hearts will but render you the more melancholy, whereas a believing view of the glorious grace of the Redeemer will comfort you. Frequent thoughts of the Lamb of God, who loved you and gave Himself for you, and of the love and mercy of God in Him, would, through the Holy Spirit, produce sweetness and love in your hearts, when, on the contrary, fixed thoughts of sin and the wrath of God would beget bitterness and aversion of spirit to Him.

9. *Be frequently employed in ejaculatory prayer, and let your stated prayers be shorter than ordinary.* In your present case, you are not able to continue in these holy exercises so long as formerly. Since therefore you cannot do as you would, you should do as you can. If sickness or pain of body excuses a man for being short in devotional duties, because nature is then so debilitated that it cannot hold out long, the sickness of the natural spirits, which enfeebles not only the body but also the mind, may well excuse him. When you feel yourselves unable to continue long prayer, as you will most certainly do, struggle not too

hard in opposition to enfeebled nature; for this, by
increasing your distemper, will disable you the more
for every duty. Study at the same time to retain, as
much as possible, your relish for holy exercises, and
to guard against everything that would render them
troublesome or grievous to you. Let not your present
inability to continue so long in prayer as formerly
discourage you; for this also would increase your
malady. Endeavor, when you are praying, to employ
as much of the time in thankful acknowledgment of
mercies as in penitent confession of sins. Were you
to employ even more of the time in thanksgiving
and praise than in confession and complaint, it
might, under the influences of the blessed Comforter, be a means of lessening, or even removing,
the bitterness of your spirits.

   *10. Be not discouraged, though in your holy exercises you
have no lively feelings or elevating conceptions.* These, however desirable and useful they are, yet cannot, in
your present condition, be reasonably expected.
Although they are sometimes enjoyed by many holy
persons, yet they are not the essentials of true holiness. Lively feelings depend more on one's natural
constitution than many are willing to allow. Some
Christians have naturally a quicker sensibility than
others. A very small affair will make some of them
feel deeply. They who live nearest to God are commonly not those who have liveliest feelings and
emotions of joy or grief, but those who are most
conformed to the holy image of the Son of God, and
who, from principles of faith and love, are most de-
voted to Him, and most inclined, at all times, to do
His will. Many believers, especially when dejected in

spirit, have bewailed bitterly their want of deep feelings, who, if their feelings had been but in the smallest degree deeper or livelier than they already were, might have been disordered, and even distracted by them.

11. Be diligent, from principles of faith and love, in doing the work of your lawful calling. Be constantly occupied, as far as your bodily strength will permit, in doing seasonably your proper work; and consider that it is very sinful, as well as dangerous, to squander any part of your precious time in idleness. The Lord has commanded you to labor six days, and therefore you cannot neglect prosecuting your secular business without omitting your duty, and thereby incurring, in a still higher degree, the displeasure of your heavenly Father. Besides, if you allow yourselves but for a short season to be unemployed, Satan will be sure to find employment for you. By being idle, you invite him both to tempt and trouble you; and he will not fail instantly to seize an opportunity so very favorable to his design. Then you will have leisure to hearken to him, and to revolve in your minds every one of his infernal suggestions.

Your precious time is continually wasting away, and the Lord has allowed you none to consume in idleness. If, then, you, notwithstanding, allow yourselves to squander any part of it in sloth, you may thereby provoke the Lord to permit Satan to harass you in a very uncommon degree. No pretense of employing your time in exercises of devotion will excuse your idleness; for you are omitting that duty which the holy law of God requires (Proverbs 27:23; Romans 12:11). Besides, you should consider that to employ your time as formerly in the work of your lawful vocation, especially if it is in the open air, will probably be a most effectual means of curing you of your bodily distemper.

12. Represent your case to some skillful, cheerful, and humble minister or private Christian, and follow diligently his directions. Your imagination is so distempered, and your mind is so weakened, that you cannot judge rightly either your condition or your duty. Your diseased imagination will represent every object to your mind in dark and frightful colors. Relate your case, therefore, to some skillful and faithful counselor, especially to one who himself was once in your afflicted condition, and do not despise his judgment concerning either your dejection or the means to be used for the removal of it. Be directed by him with respect to the subjects of your thoughts, the objects of your fears, the scruples of your consciences, and the manner of your devotional exercises. Be not wise in your own conceits. Do not obstinately adhere to every fancy that strikes your minds, but, distrusting your own understandings, follow resolutely the directions of an experienced and cheerful Christian. This is prescribed by the Spirit of God, and He will bless His own ordinance (Job 33:23–25).

13. If you have reason to apprehend that your malady is increasing, you ought to consult a skillful physician and, in the hope that you shall in due time recover, to observe carefully his prescriptions. Since the body is afflicted as well as the mind, you should, in order to remove your dejection, follow the directions of this physician as well as of the divine Physician. This is one of the duties required of you in the sixth commandment of the moral law. Indeed, until the disease of the body is in some degree removed, it cannot be reasonably expected that the mind will be relieved.

14. Finally, trust that the Lord Jesus, whose infinite compassions fail not, will, as far as it shall be for His glory and your good, command deliverance for you. "Though," for a season, "He cause grief, yet will He have compassion, according to the multitude of His mercies" (Lamentations 3:32). Instead of trusting in the means, which it is still your duty diligently to use, trust in your infinitely compassionate Savior; and in the exercise of humble confidence in Him let each of you say, "He will turn again, He will have compassion upon me" (Micah 7:19). "Thou wilt compass me about with songs of deliverance" (Psalm 32:7).

SECTION 3. Advice to the relatives and friends of such Christians as are afflicted with melancholy.

It will now be proper to subjoin some advice to those relatives and friends of Christians under melancholy, who are often in their company, and to whom it belongs to take care of them.

1. I would counsel you to regard them, at all times, with the most tender compassion. Of all the maladies to which persons in this valley of tears are liable, melancholy is the most dismal and overwhelming. Other distempers seize the body only, but this fastens on both the body and the mind at once. It disquiets a man's mind, disorders his thoughts, and fills his soul with anguish and horror. Look then on such Christian friends as are under this dreadful distemper with the greatest pity and tenderness. Considering that you yourselves are also in the body, and are vulnerable to

the same overwhelming malady, regard them with
the most affectionate and tender sympathy. They are
deeply afflicted in body and sorely vexed in spirit.
Their minds are troubled; their spirits are dejected;
their consciences are inflamed; their sighs are deep.
The language of their doleful condition, especially
to you, is the same as that of Job to his friends: "Have
pity upon me, have pity upon me, O ye my friends;
for the hand of God hath touched me" (Job 19:21).

2. *Pray frequently and fervently to the Lord for them, and
request other Christians to pray for them likewise.* In presenting your supplications for them, you have strong arguments to plead. You may plead that the Lord Jesus
endured unparalleled anguish of soul as well as
torment of body for them; that their trouble is so
great and overwhelming that none but He can help
or deliver them; that the more insupportable their
anguish and terror are, the more illustriously will
His power and mercy be displayed in delivering
them; that the more dismal and formidable their
distress is, the more gloriously will the kindness of
His love be manifested in granting peace to their
troubled souls; and that the less others can do to relieve them, and the more unworthy of relief they are,
the more brightly will the glory of His redeeming
grace shine in saving them. And though they may,
under deep despondency and terror, even forbid you
to pray any more for them, yet persist still in send-
ing up your supplications to the Father of mercies
on their behalf, and in requesting others to do the
same. For if the Lord stirs you and His saints around
you to continue constant in prayer for them, He will,
in due season, "stir up His strength, and come and

save them" (Psalm 80:2). The Lord Jesus said to His disciples, "If two of you shall agree on earth, as touching anything that they shall ask, it shall be done for them of My Father which is in heaven" (Matthew 18:19). Accordingly, when many of the saints were gathered together and employed in praying for Peter, who was kept in prison, the Lord delivered him at the very time in which they were presenting their supplications for his deliverance (Acts 12:12).

3. Study frequently to suggest grounds of comfort to them by telling them, especially, that the Lord can, and that you trust He will, shortly deliver them. Endeavor often to revive their drooping spirits by reminding them that the Father of mercies can in a moment command deliverance for them, and that you hope "He will satisfy them early with His mercy, and make them glad, according to the days wherein He hath afflicted them, and the years wherein they have seen evil" (Psalm 90:14–15). Remind them frequently that the more bitter their anguish is, the more sweet will their deliverance be; and that the more deep and doleful their sadness is, the more delightful will their joy bc. Encourage them, likewise, by repeating daily to them that many others have been in as deep anguish as they are, and yet have afterwards been made to rejoice in the light of God's countenance. By encouraging discourse like this, you may, by the blessing of God, give the deliverance which will alleviate their doleful trouble and console their wounded spirit.

4. Often remind them of the infinitely rich and free grace of the Lord Jesus, of His being in the gospel freely and wholly offered to them, and of the ample warrant afforded them by the offer to trust in Him for all salvation for themselves in particular. Exhort them daily to come as they are, to come as sinners in themselves, and to entrust the whole of their salvation to Jesus Christ. Put them often in mind that this is their first, their principal duty, and that neglecting this is their greatest sin (1 John 3:23; John 3:18). Urge them daily to trust that the Lord Jesus loves them with a free, immense, and everlasting love, and that He will surely bestow upon them all the salvation that He offers to them. Remind them frequently that God in Christ is infinitely merciful and gracious; that as the heaven is higher than the earth, so His thoughts of mercy and grace are higher than their thoughts of guilt and unworthiness, of misery and despondency; and that the very chief of sinners have been, and still may be, pardoned and received into His favor. The greatest kindness that you can show them, next to praying for them, is to set the consoling truths of the gospel often before them. For these, in the hand of the adorable Comforter, are more fit than anything else to comfort them.

5. Do not relate in their hearing any mournful or frightful tale, for if they hear a doleful story their diseased imagination is prepared to fasten upon it, and thereby to increase the sadness of their spirit. The hearing of a melancholy tale will throw them into a still more violent perturbation of mind, and so will strengthen their doleful malady. They are commonly very acute in exaggerating every dismal story and in turning it to their own prejudice, so that when they read or hear any sad and shocking narrative, they will not fail to say

within themselves, "If it is so grievous, so terrible, to
be treated with such severity, such barbarity—how
miserable, how dismal, how dreadful, must our condition be, when we have a sin-avenging God for our
infinite enemy, and have no prospect but that of being tormented in fire and brimstone, forever and
ever!" Their hearts already meditate terror, and
therefore every sad account which they happen to
hear increases their terror. It pours oil into the
flame. Study, then, as much as possible, never to
mention before them anything that would add to
their mental trouble.

6. *When you converse with them upon religious subjects,
do not press upon their minds and consciences the law as a
covenant of works.* The law in its covenant form
should be set before believers as well as before others, but not before such believers as are afflicted
with deep melancholy. To bring the fiery law more
and more home to them, when they are already overwhelmed by a sense of contracted guilt and a dread
of eternal wrath, is indeed the way to inflame, but
not to heal, the wounds of their consciences. The
law as a rule, indeed, ought frequently to be urged
upon them, but not the law as a broken covenant.
They are already much cast down, and they should
rather be lifted up by the comforts of the gospel
than cast down still lower by the terrors of the violated law.

7. *Do not, at any time, speak to them in a harsh or pas-
sionate strain.* Bitter words will do them no good, but
will, on the contrary, inflame their wounds and so
increase their anguish. If you desire to be instrumental in alleviating their sorrows and removing

their sadness, do not, on any pretense whatsoever, irritate their minds by rugged speeches. To rebuke or upbraid them now, when they are least able to bear it, will but embitter their wounded spirits and so add to their dejection. Do not say to them that they complain without a cause, for they would not complain if their hearts were not perplexed by the terrors of the Almighty. Besides, if you are harsh in your speeches to them, they will begin to suspect that you have no kindness for them, no sympathy with them, and, consequently, they will disregard almost everything that you say to them. Job, in answer to the severe speeches of his three friends, said to them, "Miserable comforters are ye all. If your soul were in my soul's stead, I could heap up words against you, and shake my head at you. But I would strengthen you with my mouth, and the moving of my lips should assuage your grief" (Job 16:2, 4–5). The enemies of Messiah are, in ancient prophecy, thus characterized: "They talk to the grief of those whom Thou hast wounded" (Psalm 69:26). Let not the behavior of your dejected friends, then, provoke you at any time to anger against them; nor let any of their expressions ever make you speak passionately or harshly to them.

8. *Believe that their griefs and fears are such as they say that they are.* When you talk with them, believe that their words are a true expression of their thoughts and feelings, and do not contradict them. Be not so cruel as to say, in answer to any of their doleful complaints, as some have said, "It is but a mere whim, an odd freak, a strange fancy." If it is but a fancy, a distempered imagination is at least as real

and as grievous an affliction as any other calamity; and the persons afflicted with it require, at least, to be treated with as tender sympathy as they do who are under any other, however great it may be. Do not think that they attempt to be more sad than they really are. They are under such perturbation of spirit that they need not, and will not, and cannot, counterfeit any more sadness or anguish than that which they already feel. If you do not appear to them to credit what they say, it will not be in their power to believe that your concern for them, or sympathy with them, is real. And when they find that it is to no purpose to disclose the anguish of their souls to you, they will suppress it; and then it will overwhelm them, and so increase the disease of their natural spirits. If, then, you have the smallest desire to be instrumental in relieving your afflicted friends, do not disbelieve or contradict them, but show them invariably that you believe their doleful complaints to be true expressions of the anguish which they feel.

9. *Study as far as with a good conscience you can to please them in everything, and not to do or say anything that may displease them.* To irritate them will but disquiet and perplex them the more, and so will increase their distemper, whereas to please them in everything, and in every way possible, will be one of the most effectual means of curing them. If you know what it is that, in any degree, disgusts them, let it be removed without delay; and if you can conscientiously do, say, or afford anything which you know would gratify them, do not withhold it from them. This indeed will not be an easy task, for to be gloomy or apt frequently to be displeased forms no

small part of their distemper. But you ought carefully to study it, for if you could frequently please them, it might, by the divine blessing, be a means of arresting the progress of their doleful malady, if not of removing it in process of time altogether.

10. Do not press them to do anything which their grievous distemper renders them unable to do. They are under great depression and anguish of spirit, and are continually full of perplexing thoughts. It would then be very unkind, and even cruel, to urge them vehemently to do anything which requires exertion of mind or intenseness of thought. If you importune or press them to do that which, in their present condition, they are no more capable of performing than a man whose bones are broken is of running apace or of walking under a burden, you will thereby throw them into still deeper perturbation of spirit, and this will increase their malady. If the distemper has not yet advanced far, you may indeed, if necessary, often exhort them to do anything that can easily be done, and to engage in the exercises of social and public worship; but even this must be done not in a peremptory, but in a gentle and affectionate manner.

11. At the same time, do not, if possible, allow them to be habitually idle or to be long alone. Endeavor, with loving and mild importunity, to allure them to some agreeable and easy task—such as will exercise the body, but, in some degree, withdraw the attention of the mind from its disquieting thoughts. Do not permit them to remain for a long time alone, especially if their doleful malady appears to be increasing; but study to procure suitable company for them. Do also all that you can to prevent them from reading such books as may discourage, alarm, or terrify them, and from reading any book long at a time.

12. To conclude, choose such a physician for them as is eminently skilled in curing the disease of melancholy, and, at the same time, is prudent and cautious. If one can be found who has himself, in any degree, been afflicted with that grievous malady, and who has, by the blessing of God, cured some who have been under it, he should, in preference to any other, be consulted; and his prescriptions and directions ought to be so carefully observed as even in extreme cases to force, if it cannot be otherwise attained, the afflicted persons to comply.

From what has been advanced in this chapter, it will, I hope, be obvious to the intelligent and candid reader that true religion is neither the cause nor the effect of melancholy.

It cannot be the cause of melancholy, for many have been, and many are, truly religious who have never appeared, in the smallest degree, to be under the disease of melancholy. Were genuine religion the cause of melancholy, it would undoubtedly have been so in the case of all who have exhibited satisfactory evidences of their godly sincerity. Every religious man would inevitably be afflicted with that dreadful malady; yea, he would be oppressed with it, usually in the very degree to which he is religious. But so far is this from being the case that, on the contrary, not a few instances have been found of persons whom pure religion has most effectually cured even of deep melancholy. Peace with God and peace of conscience, together with the exercise of supreme love toward God, have in many instances removed deeply rooted melancholy, and that after it had resisted all the power of medicines. Joy and peace in believing have, by the divine blessing, often effected the cure without the help of medicines, especially in those cases in which the melancholy constitution of the body had been produced by trouble of mind. True religion, then, when it has its due effect upon the heart, is so far from being the cause that it is the best cure of melancholy.

As religion is not the cause, so neither is it the effect of melancholy. Were true religion the effect of melancholy, every melancholy man would become truly religious, and his degree of genuine religion would be in exact proportion to his degree of melancholy, so that the more afflicted with that dire malady he were, the more joy and peace in believing, and the more love of God and delight in Him, would he at the same time experience. But, instead of this, it appears in fact that the greater number of those who are under the disease of melancholy consists of persons who are entire strangers, yea, and some of them avowed enemies to true religion. Faith, holiness, and spiritual comfort, which constitute real religion, are so far from being the disease of melancholy that they are in themselves a great hindrance to them. It is true that the Lord may render this dreadful malady subservient to faith, holiness, and comfort, as He sometimes does legal terror; but both the one and the other are, in themselves, obstructions to them. Melancholy, indeed, effects slavish fears, legal terrors, and endless scruples; but these

constitute no part of pure religion. For in proportion as religion is increased in the heart and life of
the believer, these are diminished.

To say, then, either that genuine religion makes
persons melancholy, or that melancholy renders
people truly religious, is to utter an ignorant and
impudent slander against our holy religion. No
man who has the smallest experience of godliness
can deliberately reproach it in that manner. Some of
the saints, it is granted, are sometimes melancholy,
but this is not because they are religious. It is either
because they find that they have too little of religion, or because they fear that they have none at all.
Melancholy, therefore, instead of being called
"religious" should rather, I humbly apprehend, be
termed "superstitious" melancholy; for while this
distemper makes no man truly religious, it has a direct tendency to render all who are afflicted with it,
whether they are converted or unconverted, superstitious. See Matthew Henry on *The Pleasantness of a
Religious Life* [published by Soli Deo Gloria].

Hence, the devout reader may also learn that so
much does the dire disease of melancholy weaken
the mind of a holy man while he is under it that he
not only cannot, but will not be sensible of joy or
any other grace in himself. So far as that doleful
malady prevails, it renders him sullen and averse to
seeing, feeling, or attending to anything which
might afford him comfort. It makes him willing to
despond, and unwilling to hope or to rejoice. The
consequence commonly is that he makes it his
main study to raise doubts in himself, to frame objections against himself, and so to help forward his

own affliction. Whatever grounds of consolation he
reads or hears of, he disregards; and he spends his
time in darting objections against himself which he
is as unwilling as he is unable to answer. He has the
principle and habit of faith, love, joy, and every
other grace in his soul; but he perceives them not
because he will not perceive them. His views are
dark and gloomy. His feelings and exercises are
much tinctured by the disease of his natural spirits,
and his imagination and mind are more susceptible
to impressions from the powers of darkness than at
any other time. No sooner does his imagination become distempered by an alteration in the motion of
his nervous spirits than this mysterious distemper,
in addition to the corruption that remains in the
imagination, affords Satan an avenue for assaulting
him with the most terrifying of his temptations.
Immediately, that infernal enemy pours in, like a
torrent, blackness of darkness, frightful illusions,
and distracting terrors, so that the dejected Christian becomes a terror to himself. Oh! what anguish,
what horror fills his soul when Satan is permitted,
by means of that malady, thus to tyrannize over him!
How dreadful is this distemper which leaves the
imagination so exposed to that merciless enemy,
and which enfeebles the mind and impairs the
judgment to such a degree, that the Christian, while
he is feeling the deepest anguish of spirit, is at the
same time unwilling to receive that consolation
which is freely offered to him, and which only can
relieve him! If he can take pleasure in anything, it is
in solitariness and darkness, in sadness and wailing.
The mysterious distemper under which he labors

turns fancies into realities and realities into fancies;
fictions into truths and truths into fictions. It renders every sweet thing bitter, and every bitter thing
bitter in a tenfold degree.

Dejected believers may, from what has been said,
see what ground they have to hope that the Lord will
not deal with them according to what they are or
what they do under deep melancholy. God in Christ
is infinitely gracious and merciful, and He will not
consider the inevitable consequences of a dire malady, which none but Himself can remove, as sins
against Him. He will indeed treat believers according to what they are and what they do when their
understanding is sound, but not according to what
they think, speak or do when their imagination is
distempered, and their mind disabled and perplexed. A tender-hearted father will not be angry
with his beloved son for those injurious expressions
and actions which are the effects of frenzy; but he
will, on the contrary, feel and discover the more
tender sympathy with him. Now, "as a father pitieth
his children, so the Lord pitieth them that fear
Him" (Psalm 103:13). Let no good man then conclude, from his inconsistent and strange behavior
under the disease of melancholy, that he never was a
child of God.

Last, however doleful the distemper of melancholy is, it is infinitely more desirable even to be a
melancholy saint than a mad sinner. Solomon, who
could not be mistaken, informs us, when speaking
of unregenerate sinners, that "madness is in their
heart while they live" (Ecclesiastes 9:3). Now suppose (which very seldom happens) that a holy man

should be afflicted with melancholy all his days; still it is infinitely less dreadful to have that dire malady affecting the mind during the short period of human life, and then followed by endless and ineffable delight, than to have that madness in the heart while one lives which afterwards will increase into hideous and endless rage. Impenitent sinners, like Saul of Tarsus, are "mad against the saints" (Acts 26:11), and "they are mad upon their idols" (Jeremiah 50:38). The prodigal, under conviction of his sin and misery, is said to have "come to himself" (Luke 15:17), which intimates that hitherto he had been beside himself. Unregenerate men, with respect to the concerns of their souls, are madmen, and all their joys are but like the pleasant dreams of a man who has been deprived of his understanding, whereas those regenerate men who are under the deepest melancholy still have the principle and the habit of pure, solid, and everlasting joy.

6

*The Designs of God in Permitting Some of His
Children to Lose Their Spiritual Comfort*

The throne of the incomprehensible and only
wise God is established in righteousness, but it is, at
the same time, surrounded with clouds and thick
darkness. "He maketh darkness his pavilion round
about him" (2 Samuel 22:12). "His judgments are a
great deep" (Psalm 36:6). They are too deep for us to
fathom. His counsels are unsearchable, and His
ways of providence are past finding out. When,
therefore, we would try to penetrate into the mysterious designs which the infinitely wise God has in
permitting any of His redeemed so to lose their spiritual consolation as to fall under spiritual trouble,
and even sometimes under melancholy, it becomes
us to do it with the most profound reverence, and
only so far as the holy Scriptures are our guide. Now
from these we discover that the Lord suffers believers to deprive themselves of their sensible comfort,
and to continue for a season under trouble of mind,
not in order that they may thereby give the smallest
degree of satisfaction to His justice for their sins.
Their divine Surety has endured for them the whole
punishment due for all their iniquities, and so has
fully satisfied the offended justice of Jehovah (Isaiah

189

42:21; Galatians 3:13). We also find that He does not permit this from any pleasure that He takes in their perplexity of soul, considered merely in itself; for His nature is so infinitely merciful that he can take no pleasure in their sorrows, considered as disunited from the purposes intended to be served by them (Lamentations 3:33; Jeremiah 31:20; Isaiah 63:9). We likewise discern that He does not suffer any of the saints to fall under depression of spirit with a view to discourage any unregenerate sinner from coming to Christ, or from entering upon a holy life; for, said the Apostle, "God cannot be tempted with evil, neither tempteth He any man" (James 1:13). But He permits them, I humbly apprehend, to lose their spiritual comfort so as to be disquieted and distressed in spirit, especially for the following purposes:

1. That He may thereby render them the more conformable to His beloved Son, their Read and Representative in the new covenant. So delighted is Jehovah the Father with the image of His infinitely dear Son, who, as the second Adam, is the firstborn among many brethren, that He has resolved that the objects of His redeeming love shall, as much as possible, consistent with their eternal salvation, be conformed to that image not only in point of holiness, but of suffering. "Whom He did foreknow," said the Apostle Paul, "He also did predestinate to be conformed to the image of His Son, that He might be the first-born among many brethren" (Romans 8:29). Now, seeing that the Lord Jesus, in His state of humiliation in this world, suffered not only in His body, but in His soul, God the Father has determined that the spiritual seed of

Christ shall in this world resemble Him by suffering more or less in their souls as well as in their bodies. As Christ endured in His soul an awful suspension of divine consolation, together with a dreadful impression of vindictive wrath, so believers, in order to resemble Him, sometimes endure the hiding of their heavenly Father's countenance and the sense of paternal anger, which they often mistake for vindictive wrath. Hereby they drink of His cup; they are partakers of His sufferings, and so are able from experience to say, "As He was, so are we in this world" (1 John 4:17). For though they never actually experience in their trouble of soul that vindictive wrath which Christ Jesus felt in His, yet by this conformity to Him they have fellowship with Him in His sufferings, and attain some small experience of the bitterness of what He endured for them. And so they learn the more highly to esteem Him, the more ardently to love Him, and the more gratefully to remember His immense love for them.

2. *He suffers them to lose, for a season, their comfort that He may make them feel more clearly the deep depravity of their nature.* We read that Jehovah led the Israelites "through a great and terrible wilderness, wherein were fiery serpents, and scorpions, and drought, and where no water was; that He might humble them, and prove them, to do them good at their latter end," by revealing to them what was in their hearts (Deuteronomy 8:15–16). In like manner, He sometimes withholds His influences of comfort from believers, and leaves them for a season under depression of spirit in order that He may prove them and give them more clear and humbling discoveries of

the depth and strength of the corruption which remaineth in them (2 Chronicles 32:31). The hearts of
believers are like the waters of the sea, which in a
calm appear to be clear, but no sooner does a storm
arise and agitate them than they begin to cast up
mire and dirt.

When Christians are at ease, they sometimes
think that their corruptions are not so strong, and
that their graces are not so weak as they really are.
They flatter themselves that their sanctification is
much further advanced than it actually is. But when
their comfort is gone and their hearts are troubled,
what unbelief, what pride, what deadness, what enmity against a holy God, what impatience, what
murmuring, what strange unbecoming thoughts of
God arise and appear in their hearts which they
never before could either feel or believe to be there!
Mental trouble serves, in the hand of the Holy Spirit,
to show them how deeply rooted, how inveterate,
how malignant their depravity is, and what reason
they have to be greatly ashamed and blush before
the omniscient and holy Lord God. It was upon
Job's having been grievously afflicted in spirit that
he discerned more vileness in his heart than he
could formerly have suspected to be in it (Job 40:4),
and that he learned deeply to abhor himself as a
sinner (Job 42:6).

There are abominations which, like nests of
vipers, lie so quietly within that believers do not suspect them to be there till the rod of spiritual trouble
disturbs and arouses them. Some corruptions lie so
very deep in their hearts that they can hardly discern
them. But as fire under a pot causes the scum to rise

up and run over, so trouble of mind brings up from the bottom of the hearts such deep corruptions to view as the most enlightened of the saints could otherwise scarcely have conceived to be there. And discoveries especially of these are necessary for deep humiliation of spirit before the Lord.

3. *Another design which God has in inflicting trouble of spirit upon some of His children is that He may thereby chasten them for their sins, and so embitter sin to them.* Disquietude of soul is to believers a fatherly chastisement. The Lord resolves thereby to correct them. He determines that by their bitterness of soul they shall "know and see that it is an evil thing and bitter, that they have forsaken Him" (Jeremiah 2:19). By this most afflictive dispensation, He thus speaks to each of them: "Thy ways and thy doings have procured these things unto thee: this is thy wickedness, because it is bitter, because it reacheth unto thine heart" (Jeremiah 4:18). As the Lord never chastens any of His children but for their profit (Habakkuk 1:12), so He never afflicts them with spiritual trouble except when it is necessary for that purpose. Accordingly the Apostle Peter said, "Ye are now for a season (if need be) in heaviness, through manifold temptations" (1 Peter 1:6). By suspending His influences of consolation from their souls, and so embittering their sins to them, the Lord weakens the remains of corruption in them. He thereby renders them more wise and circumspect, and so He prevents much sin into which they otherwise would fall (2 Corinthians 12:7). By this painful discipline, their souls are purified, and made white and tried; and so by sad experience they are made to feel, as well as to

see, that their sin is exceedingly sinful. By withholding, for a season, consolation from them, He shows
them the evil of their not having improved their
former comfort well; of their having made for themselves a savior of their pleasant frames by relying on
them rather than on Jesus Christ.

By permitting distrust and despondency to prevail against them, and so to occasion much trouble
and perplexity of mind to them, He teaches them
the exceeding sinfulness of their unbelief and distrust. His design in hiding His face from them is to
teach them that they did wrong in setting a small
value upon His favor and the light of His countenance. If He lays them under a painful sense of His
anger, it is to make them sensible of their folly, as
well as ingratitude, in provoking His displeasure. By
piercing their hearts with deep sorrow, He teaches
them the sinfulness of their having pierced His
beloved Son and grieved His Holy Spirit. If He makes
them experience the terror of His vindictive wrath,
or the dread of suffering through eternity the pains
of hell, it is to teach them the extreme folly of their
not having been afraid of sinning against Him.

One part of His design in suffering His fiery law
to re-enter and distress their consciences is to make
them deeply sensible of the great evil of their legal
spirit. By permitting them, for a time, to lose sight
of their evidences of grace, He teaches them that
they ought never to be proud of their attainments in
religion, nor to trust in grace received. If He appears
not to stand in the relation of a Father to them, it is
to render them more sensible that they have not
acted the part of obedient children to Him. By seem-

ing to shut out their prayers, He reproves them for restraining prayer, and for their unbelieving, wandering, and vain thoughts in prayer. When He permits them to be afraid that they are yet under the dominion of spiritual death, it is to teach them the great evil of deadness and coldness of heart in their acts of worship. If He denies them His reviving and consoling presence in reading and hearing His blessed Word, it is to make them deeply sensible of the sinfulness of their having despised His glorious gospel. And if He leaves any of them to fall into some gross and open sin, His design may be to chasten them for having suffered themselves to commit secret iniquity. By thus chastening them, the Lord instructs them ("chastening" and "instructing" are, both in Hebrew and in Greek, expressed by one word) in the exceeding sinfulness of their sin in order that they may so bewail and abhor it as to turn with fuller determination of heart from it to Him as their gracious God and Father. Hereby He also teaches them that if He leaves them but for a single moment, they will instantly fall even into the most atrocious crimes. Ah! How deep, how inveterate is their disease, when a potion so bitter is requisite to accomplish their cure!

4. *The Lord withholds consolation from some of His people, and suffers them for a season to walk in darkness, in order to try and exercise their graces. Hereby the graces of the Spirit in them are tried or proved, and their truth, as well as their weakness or strength, is manifested to them.* "Now for a season," said the Apostle Peter, "ye are in heaviness, through manifold temptations; that the trial of your faith, being much more precious than of gold that

perisheth, though it be tried with fire, might be found unto praise and honor and glory at the appearing of Jesus Christ" (1 Peter 1:6–7). No affliction is so grievous and so trying as spiritual distress. The Lord therefore inflicts spiritual trouble, sometimes, upon believers in order that He may try their faith and other graces, and so reveal these to them. It appears to have been one of the designs of Job's spiritual trouble to try, and so to manifest to himself and others, the strong faith and invincible patience which God had given him.

There are some graces in the heart of a holy man which are discovered more clearly to him by means of spiritual trouble than by any external affliction. When he finds that he has been enabled to trust in the Lord Jesus at the very time in which He was frowning upon him, and seeming even to slay him; to love Him for Himself, when he had no reviving sense of His love for him; and to follow Him with longings and prayers in the midst of darkness and discouragement—this is afterwards a clear proof to him of the reality of these graces in his soul. Trouble of mind, during its continuance, renders the exercise of graces and the performance of duties peculiarly difficult. If believers, then, when they are under spiritual distress, continue still to cleave in some degree to God in Christ, and so to love Him as to prefer Him before every other object of affection, even when He seems to be casting off their souls and shutting out their prayers, this, when they afterwards reflect upon it, will be an evidence to them that they are sincere, and that their love for Him is supreme.

Moreover, when they are enabled under that most grievous trial to exercise in some degree their graces, those graces are not only manifested to their consciences, but are strengthened and increased by their exercise of them. The same affliction that serves, in the hand of the Holy Spirit, to try and discover their graces serves also to excite them to exercise; and the more they are exercised, the more the habit of them is strengthened. When the Lord thus chastens any of His dear children, it is invariably "for their profit, that they may be partakers of His holiness." For this chastening, though for the present it is not joyous, but grievous exceedingly grievous, nevertheless, afterwards it "yieldeth the peaceable fruit of righteousness, to them who are exercised thereby" (Hebrews 12:10–11). It supplies them in the meantime with special occasions for striving and wrestling against their spiritual enemies, for swimming against the stream, for pressing on as through an opposing crowd; and thus their graces have special opportunities afforded them of becoming stronger by frequent exercise. It affords occasion for many actings of faith and love, of repentance and resignation, and for many ardent longings and heavenly breathings which otherwise would not, perhaps, be experienced. Besides, the exercise of the graces of His Holy Spirit in believers, especially of that grace in which each of them excels, is so pleasing to the Lord that He will on no account suffer them to want occasion, nay, frequent occasion, for such exercise (Psalm 147:11; Song of Solomon 2:14 and 4:9).

5. His design also in withholding consolation is to teach

*them by experience their continual need of living upon Christ
by faith, and so to render Him the more precious to them.* "I
will leave in the midst of thee," said Jehovah, "an afflicted and poor people, and they shall trust in the
name of the Lord" (Zephaniah 3:12). Paul and
Timothy "had the sentence of death in themselves,
that they should not trust in themselves, but in God
who raiseth the dead" (2 Corinthians 1:9).

It is not enough that the saints merely believe
their need every moment of fresh supplies of grace
from the fullness of Christ; they must be made to see
and to feel that need. Nor is it sufficient for them
merely to believe that it is their duty at all times to
trust in Him for those supplies. They must be made
to see clearly and feel deeply their extreme need to
do so. They must by experience be made deeply sensible that without a fresh supply of grace at the time
they are as unable to perform spiritually a single
duty as they were even in their unregenerate state
(John 15:5; 2 Corinthians 3:5). So very unwilling are
they to believe this, and to regulate their spiritual
exercise according to it, that ordinarily they must be
trained for it by sad experience. Now the Lord
suspends influences of comfort from any of them,
and for a season inflicts upon them a greater or
lesser degree of mental trouble, in order to make
them see and feel how much need they have at all
times to trust in Christ for continued supplies from
His fullness, and to render them deeply sensible
that they cannot otherwise perform even the least
degree of acceptable obedience without trusting
solely and firmly in Him for new communications
of sanctifying grace to enable them to perform it.

To trust daily, and with unsuspecting confidence, in the great Trustee of the new covenant, that He will by His Holy Spirit work in them, both to will and to do, is of such necessity and importance to their growing in grace that, rather than leave them ignorant thereof, God will teach His children, even by the most painful discipline, how needful it is to do so. He will permit them to feel what anguish of soul their neglecting the daily exercise of faith in the Lord Jesus will occasion to them in order that He may reduce them to the happy necessity of placing, at all times, the confidence of their hearts in Him only, and that for comforting as well as for sanctifying influences. He will embitter a life of sense to them that He may dispose them to relish a life of faith. He will make them know by experience what their having trusted in their habits of grace has procured for them, that they may discern the exceeding sinfulness of a legal spirit, and see that, without faith, or the daily exercise of direct confidence in the incarnate Redeemer, it will be impossible for them to please Him (Hebrews 11:6).

The death of their sensible comfort will show them the necessity of a life of faith. The Lord gives to many of His saints frightful discoveries of sin and wrath in order that, by being shaken, they may learn to rely more firmly on the sure foundation which He has laid in Zion (Isaiah 28:16). He hides Himself from them, and delays to help them, till they are in extremity, so that they may learn the high and difficult art of living by faith and not by sight. Living by signs of grace is most natural and pleasing to them, but living by faith is most acceptable to Him. The

sight of their evidences of grace, indeed, cannot fail
to be delightful to them; but the sight of Jesus, by
faith, ought to be a thousand times more delightful.

But when they pore so much and so long upon
their evidences as to be thereby prevented from direct and frequent actings of trust in the Savior, they
so far dishonor and displease Him. When they build
their comfort and hope upon their evidences, instead of building all their comfort and hope upon
Him, they at once greatly dishonor Him and deeply
injure themselves. Thus they render it necessary that
He hide His face, cloud their evidences, and wither
their comforts in order that they may learn to prefer
Himself before their clearest evidences and their
liveliest frames; to set a higher value upon the husband of their souls Himself than upon the bracelets
and jewels which they receive from Him; and that
they may study the art, in the absence of evidences
and frames, of living above them upon Himself, who
is their life and consolation, their hope, and all in
all.

In this manner, He wisely and graciously trains
them up to trust as sinners in Himself; to rely on
Him not as felt by them, but as offered to them; to
depend on Him only, and to stay upon Him as theirs
in the gospel offer when feelings and comforts fail
them (Isaiah 50:10; Psalm 42:11; Song of Solomon
8:5). As nothing done by believers glorifies the great
Redeemer so much as their acting of particular trust
in Him for salvation, so, if necessary, He will rather
hide every other object of confidence from their
view than suffer them to continue resting on it instead of trusting in Him (Psalm 42:4–5). In few

words, His grand design is to render Himself and His redeeming grace more precious to them; to show them experientially that none can calm the tumults of a troubled soul but Himself only (Isaiah 57:19); and that without Him they can do nothing that is spiritually good (John 15:5).

6. *Another end which the Lord proposes to achieve in afflicting believers with trouble of mind is that they may be stirred up to search the Scriptures more earnestly and more frequently.* It is to make them capable of relishing and esteeming His glorious gospel the more. One great design of the doctrines and promises of sacred Scripture is to comfort the saints under their manifold afflictions. Accordingly, the greatest part of the precious promises is adapted and made to serve them when they are in circumstances of trouble; for although they assent to the truth of them, yet they cannot, so well and with such feeling, experience the suitableness and sweetness of them unless they are sometimes brought into the circumstances to which they refer. The Lord said, "Call upon Me in the day of trouble; I will deliver thee" (Psalm 50:15). "I will be with him in trouble; I will deliver him, and honor him" (Psalm 91:15). "I have seen his ways, and will heal him; I will lead him also, and restore comforts unto him, and to his mourners" (Isaiah 57:18). Now, till the day of trouble comes, believers do not know by experience either the use or the value of such promises as these, because they are not in the condition to which they relate. Were they to continue long without affliction, and, especially, without some degree of spiritual trouble, they would, at least many of them, be but slightly affected with the doc-

trines and promises of the gospel, because they
could not feel their need of that consolation which
many of these are designed to afford. If they had no
burdens to weigh them down, no fears to disquiet
them, no distress of conscience to exercise them,
much of the good Word of God would comparatively
be of little use to them.

Without such trouble in a greater or lesser degree, the saints could not have an opportunity of ex-
periencing the truth, suitableness, and sweetness of
many of the promises. They could not feel the need,
nor understand the true meaning, of a great part of
the Bible. Indeed, were believers always triumphing
in the unmingled light of God's countenance, they
should thereby, as one expressed it, "be cut off from
half of the promises of the gospel."

In order, then, that they may feel their need of all
the declarations and promises of the blessed gospel,
and so be trained up to set such a high value upon
the Scriptures as to search them carefully and diligently, the Lord permits them, sometimes, to fall
under distress of mind. At those times, a sense of
need urges them to look eagerly and frequently into
His blessed Word in order to see if there are any
doctrines, directions, or promises in it suited to revive their drooping spirits or console their disquieted souls. And when they find, as they sooner or
later shall do, any passages of it which through
grace afford direction or consolation to their troubled souls, each of them will from experience be
able with the holy Psalmist to say, "This is my comfort in my affliction; for Thy word hath quickened
me" (Psalm 119:50). "Thy testimonies also are my de-

light, and my counselors" (Psalm 119:24). "It is good
for me that I have been afflicted, that I might learn
Thy statutes" (Psalm 119:71).

7. *God inflicts trouble of spirit upon many of His children
to the end that, by supporting them under it and delivering
them from it, He may the more effectually recommend to them
the infinite suitableness, riches, and freeness of His redeeming
grace.* It is impossible for a man who has never experienced in any degree the distress of a wounded
conscience highly to esteem and admire the grace
of the Lord Jesus Christ. It is only when his conscience has been distressed by a galling sense of
guilt, and his soul troubled with a fear of deserved
wrath, as well as renewed by the Holy Spirit, that he
can eagerly desire and cordially embrace the
promises of redeeming mercy, or see the inestimable value of super-abounding grace. One of the
designs of God, therefore, in laying any of His people in the depths of spiritual trouble is that they may
in their deliverance see what reason they have
highly to prize, and gratefully to adore, the transcendent riches and freeness of His glorious grace;
so that when they are delivered from "the sorrows of
death which compassed them, and from the pains of
hell, which got hold upon them," each of them may
from experience be able to say with the Psalmist,
"Gracious is the Lord, and righteous; yea, our God is
merciful. The Lord preserveth the simple; I was
brought low, and He helped me. Return unto thy
rest, O my soul; for the Lord hath dealt bountifully
with thee. For Thou hast delivered my soul from
death, mine eyes from tears, and my feet from
falling" (Psalm 116:3–8). When in their deliverance

believers are made to see that from the thickest
darkness the Lord has brought them forth to the
light; that He has overruled the greatest evils in
their hearts for their good; that when they were
bleeding inwardly, and when no man nor angel
could afford them relief, He kept them from bleeding to death; that after they had been hearing the
tremendous thunders of His fiery law He has caused
them to hear for themselves the reviving sound of
His gospel; that after they had been at the very
mouth of hell, and had, as it were, been smelling
the fire and brimstone, He has exalted them to the
hope of heaven; that notwithstanding their distrustful and hard thoughts of Him, He has been gracious
to them; that after they had been very undutiful to
Him, He has been kind and compassionate to them;
that after they had, by their desponding fears, reflected much dishonor upon Him, He has caused
their souls to hope in His mercy; and that after they
had been sinking in the waters of trouble, He has
set their feet upon a rock, and filled them with joy
and peace in believing—when, I say, they are made
to experience so great a deliverance, they cannot fail
to be deeply affected with the sovereignty, the riches,
and the freeness of redeeming grace.

One design of God, then, in the infliction of
mental distress upon any of His saints, and afterwards in delivering them from it, is to afford them
special opportunities of esteeming, admiring, and
adoring His immense love and boundless grace toward them. Hereby His glorious method of salvation
by Jesus Christ is exceedingly endeared to their
souls.

8. Another end which the Lord has in permitting some of the saints so to lose their spiritual comfort as to be disquieted in spirit is that thereby He may rouse them to greater diligence in watching and praying. Disquietment of soul serves, in the hand of the Holy Spirit, to stir them up to greater watchfulness. A man who walks in the dark finds it necessary to be more careful where and how he treads. To be lifted up and cast down, to be emptied, as it were, from vessel to vessel is of great utility to excite believers to be always watchful.

By these means the Lord also rouses them to pray more earnestly and more frequently. Accordingly, Heman, when he was in his deep distress of soul, was much employed in prayer. "O Lord God of my salvation," said he, "I have cried day and night before Thee" (Psalm 88:1). So was David: "Thou didst hide Thy face, and I was troubled. I cried to Thee, O Lord; and unto the Lord I made supplication" (Psalm 30:7–8). "I poured out my complaint before Him; I showed before Him my trouble, when my spirit was overwhelmed within me" (Psalm 142:2–3). And Hezekiah likewise: "O Lord, I am oppressed; undertake for me" (Isaiah 38:14). And Jonah: "When my soul fainted within me, I remembered the Lord; and my prayer came in unto Thee, into Thine holy Temple" (Jonah 2:7). It was not until Peter was beginning to sink in the sea that he cried, "Lord, save me" (Matthew 14:30). There are, I believe, more prayers in the writings of David and Jeremiah than in any other parts of the sacred volume. Indeed, many of the saints would not be so frequently on their knees as they are if trouble of spirit did not weigh them down.

This, then, is one of the Lord's designs in going
away, that believers may pursue Him. And He will
never so hide Himself from them as to render it impossible for them to find Him; nor will He depart
any faster or farther than He will enable them so to
follow as to overtake Him (Psalm 63:8). A long continuance of ease has a tendency to render them cold
and formal in prayer, especially in secret prayer; but
spiritual troubles and painful changes tend to rouse
their spirits and impel them to seek the Lord and
His face with greater earnestness and importunity,
for it is then, especially, that they deeply feel their
want of that help which He only can afford to them.

9. *Many of the saints are afflicted with trouble of mind to
the end that they may thereby be the more prepared for spiritual
comfort, and that their consolation in time to come may be the
greater.* Sometimes the Lord inflicts spiritual distress
upon many of His children in order that He may afterwards give them the more comfort, and that their
comfort may be the more pure, sweet, and solid. He
inflicts it in order to prepare them for that strong
consolation which He has designed for them to
make them relish and value it the more, and be the
more solicitous to possess and retain it.

When the church, after Christ had withdrawn
Himself and departed, found Him again, "she held
Him, and would not let Him go" (Song of Solomon
3:4). As a tree, by being shaken with the stormy
wind, is the more deeply and strongly rooted in the
ground, so believers are sometimes "tossed as with
tempest, and not comforted" (Isaiah 54:11), that they
may by faith cleave the more closely to Christ, and
thereby derive the more strength and consolation

from His fullness, for the more they continue in the faith, grounded and settled, the greater will their peace and their comfort be (Isaiah 26:3). Moreover, when the Lord, by the witnessing of His Spirit, assures them that they have been enabled to love Him, even when He seemed to be hating them, and with lamentation and desire to follow after Him when He appeared to be going away from them, such a clear evidence of the truth of grace in them as that cannot fail to yield a pleasing satisfaction to their souls. It is the manner of the Lord Jesus to empty the souls of His children that He may fill them, to cast them down that He may lift them up, to trouble them that He may the more effectually comfort them, and to take away from them a smaller degree of mental serenity that He may prepare room in their souls for a greater measure of pure consolation (Psalm 71:20–23). He commonly suffers the bitter waters of trouble to swell in order that the sweet waters of holy consolation may afterwards rise higher than ever in their souls. Inward trouble is, in His hand, a means of enlarging the capacity of the holy soul; and the more capable that soul is of comfort, the more consolation is poured into it.

Heaviness of spirit also humbles such a soul, and true humility is, as it were, the vessel into which the wine of consolation is poured. A humble spirit is a deep spirit, and the deeper the spirit is, it is fitted to contain the more consolation. Besides, as food is doubly sweet after hunger, and light after darkness, so is consolation after anguish of spirit. By their want of spiritual comfort for a season, the Lord teaches His people to know more of the value of it;

and when they learn to prize it, and to trust constantly and solely in the great Redeemer for it as a
part of their salvation, the more of it shall they receive.

   *10. Another design of God in laying some of His children
in the depths of spiritual trouble is to render them the more
compassionate toward other saints around them when they see
them depressed in spirit.* As no outward affliction, however painful it may be, is so dreadful and overwhelming as anguish of spirit is, so, if it is the duty
of a Christian to show compassion to such fellow
Christians as are under the former, much more
ought one to show pity to such of them as are under
the latter. Surely, the most tender compassion from
fellow saints is due to those who have "the arrows of
the Almighty within them, the poison of which, is
drinking up their spirits" (Job 6:4). Such perplexing
distress calls aloud for the greatest sympathy, the
tenderest pity, as that of Job did from his friends.
"Have pity upon me," said he, "have pity upon me, O
ye my friends; for the hand of God hath touched
me" (Job 19:21). Those Christians are deeply
wounded in their spirits, and such wounds require
being touched with a tender as well as with a skillful
hand. But none of their fellow Christians are so well
qualified to treat them with gentleness and tenderness, or to speak to them with mildness and pity, as
they who were themselves in the same doleful condition, and have been mercifully delivered from it.
The Lord, then, permits some of His saints so to
lose their comfort as to become disquieted in spirit,
in order to render them the more compassionate
towards others of their brethren who are in spiritual

trouble; and also the more capable, as well as desirous, of being instrumental in binding up their wounds with a tender heart and a gentle hand. In that way, He teaches them most effectually to "put on bowels of mercies, kindness, humbleness of mind, and meekness" (Colossians 3:12) toward such as are in any trouble, especially in mental trouble. And so He qualifies them to be merciful and helpful to such.

Moreover, in inflicting upon some of the saints a painful sense of His anger, the Lord may also have it in view to teach them so to pity unregenerate sinners around them as willingly to seize every fit opportunity of instructing them in the way of salvation (Psalm 51:12–13), and of laboring from their own experience of the terror of the Lord to persuade them to flee speedily from sin to the compassionate Savior of salvation. Those saints who have been in trouble of mind can, from the anguish and terror which they themselves have experienced, feel a compassionate and a deep concern for the dreadful condition of secure sinners, and can say more than others can to assure them that "it is a fearful thing to fall into the hands of the living God" (Hebrews 10:31).

11. The Lord also permits some believers so to forfeit their comfort as to fall under depression of spirit in order to qualify them for speaking comfortably to others who are in a similar condition. As a humble, patient, and compassionate spirit is, perhaps, not attainable by any other means, so neither are readiness and skill in comforting them who are cast down. They who have been led through the depths of dejection and temptation are better acquainted than other Christians are with the various griefs, fears, perplexities, and conflicts of the heart in those depths; and therefore they know better "how to speak a word in season to them who are weary" (Isaiah 50:4). They have had experience of great and sore trouble, of being supported under it, and, afterwards, of being comforted with deliverance from it. The Lord therefore casts some, yea, many of the saints down, and, in a little, raises them up again that they may learn from experience not only to pity, but with meekness of wisdom to comfort others who are cast down.

The Apostle Paul, accordingly, was troubled on every side, cast down, and then comforted, in order that he might attain eminent skill in comforting other saints. "Blessed be God, even the Father of our Lord Jesus Christ," said he, "who comforteth us in all our tribulation, that we may be able to comfort them which are in any trouble, by the comfort wherewith we ourselves are comforted of God. Whether we be afflicted, it is for your consolation and salvation . . . or whether we be comforted, it is for your consolation and salvation" (2 Corinthians 1:3, 4, 6). The Lord has work for some of His children to do which none of them can perform so well as they who are thus qualified for it. He has sin-sick souls to be visited and healed, tempted souls to be relieved, drooping spirits to be revived, weak hands to be strengthened, and feeble knees to be confirmed. It was necessary that the Apostle Peter should have sad experience of his own weakness in order that he might be qualified for strengthening his brethren (Luke 22:31–32). Besides, as a man under a dangerous malady will choose rather to entrust himself to the care of that physician who, by having been afflicted with the same distemper, has much experience of it than to that of another who never was afflicted with it, so troubled souls will be more attentive to, and more affected by, the advice and encouragements suggested by that Christian who speaks to them from his own experience than by those of any other Christian.

12. It is likewise the intention of God, by that most painful discipline, to prepare some of His children for special and eminent service to Him. Some believers continue all their days in a low way, and have neither much trouble nor much comfort. They experience little distressing fear and as little joyful hope. These are believers of a lower class. Others, again, are raised up aloft in flashes, and even in raptures, of sensible joy; but they do not perceive distinctly the objects which are below. Various mistakes, failings, and improprieties in their mind and conduct almost entirely escape their notice. These too are Christians of an inferior rank.

But when the Lord is training up any of His redeemed for special and eminent service to Him, He commonly brings them low, and employs them in deep exercises and sharp conflicts, with motions of sin within and temptations of Satan from without. He brings them into depths of spiritual trouble, and gives them deep, humbling, and even frightful discoveries of the strength and sinfulness of the unbelief, and other abominations, which lie deep in their hearts. He hides His face from them, and permits their spiritual enemies frequently to assault

them, and sometimes to prevail so against them as
to threaten their eternal destruction. At the same
time, He secretly upholds them; and when the design of the dispensation is gained, He comforts
them with deliverance. Thus He advances them to
higher degrees of experiential knowledge, to more
enlarged views of themselves and of Christ, of sin
and of holiness, and of the suitableness, riches, and
freeness of redeeming grace than other believers attain. He thereby renders them more intelligent,
wise, and humble, more deeply sensible of their infinite obligations to Him, more disposed to trust
firmly at all times in the Lord Jesus and to be more
zealous, lively, and active for His glory than the gen-
erality of other believers. And so He prepares them
for special service and eminent usefulness to their
generation. Some think, and indeed it is probable,
that Heman was laid in the darkness and the depths
expressed in the 88th Psalm in order that he might
be qualified for that eminent station in the church
to which he was raised. Doubtless, it is in proportion
as believers attain deep experience that they have
the capacity, and especially the wisdom, required for
superior usefulness in the Church of Christ.

*13. Another purpose which the Lord intends to serve by the
spiritual trouble of many of His people is to encourage and
confirm their hope, and so render them the more lively in their
exercise of graces and performance of duties.* "We glory in
tribulations also," said Paul, "knowing that tribulation worketh patience; and patience, experience;
and experience, hope" (Romans 5:3–4). And Jeremiah: "This I recall to my mind, therefore have I
hope" (Lamentations 3:21). God suffers some of His

dear children to lose, for a season, their tranquility
of mind in order that He may take occasion from
their perplexity to favor them with such experience
of His grace and mercy, power and faithfulness, in
supporting them under it, in freeing them from it,
and in sanctifying it to them as also, with such experience of the truth of their faith, and the uprightness of their heart under it, as will encourage and
confirm their hope of eternal life.

Although it is not the experience of a holy man,
but the righteousness of Christ and the promises of
God offered to him in the gospel, that are the foundations of his hope of salvation, yet his past and present experience encourages him to hope. Such experience as is a proof to him of his personal interest
in Jesus and His great salvation works hope inasmuch as it affords him great encouragement both to
expect and to deserve complete salvation. His experience also of deadness of frame and coldness of
love, of dejection of mind and sadness of heart, of
powerful support under these and of comfortable
deliverance from them, serves exceedingly, through
the power of the Holy Spirit, to make him abound in
hope. And the more he abounds in the delightful
exercise of that living hope which is founded upon
the living Redeemer, and which has for its object
the eternal enjoyment of the living God, the more
lively and cheerful will he be in all spiritual exercise
and holy obedience. When he reflects that his great
Redeemer has, in His love and in His pity, delivered
him from the greatest of all troubles, and restored to
him the joy of his salvation, he is encouraged, yea,
and sweetly constrained to expect from such a Savior

the greatest blessedness, the highest felicity, of which his nature will, through all eternity, be capable.

14. One end which the Lord may have to accomplish by inflicting spiritual trouble upon some is the instruction of others of His children. He seems, in His adorable sovereignty and infinite wisdom, to have resolved that some of His redeemed should be afflicted with inward as well as with outward trouble for the instruction of the rest. By subjecting some to that most painful discipline, He appears to have determined that others of them shall thereby learn the exceeding sinfulness of their own unbelief and other sins, the necessity of trusting simply, cordially, and at all times in the Lord Jesus for sanctifying grace, the unspeakable importance of constant reliance upon Christ for the countenance and increase of it, and the duty of being more thankful to Him for the peace of conscience which they enjoy, as well as of being more circumspect and more solicitous not to provoke His displeasure. Spiritual trouble seems peculiarly adapted, as an instrument, to convey spiritual and holy instruction to the minds of all who believe. Accordingly, the 32nd, 42nd, and 88th Psalms, in which mental trouble is described, are each of them entitled *Maskil*, which signifies "giving instruction."

15. Another design which God may have in afflicting many of the saints for a season with trouble and terror of conscience is to assure wicked men around them of a judgment and of wrath to come. His intention thereby seems to be to give assurance to unregenerate sinners, and that by their very senses, that there shall be a future judgment in which it shall be ill with the wicked, seeing "the reward of his hands shall be given him" (Isaiah 3:11); that "if the righteous shall be recompensed in the earth; much more the wicked and the sinner" (Proverbs 11:31); and that "if judgment begins at the house of God," inexpressibly dreadful, "what shall the end be of them that obey not the gospel of God?" (1 Peter 4:17).

The saints are the objects of Jehovah's immense and unchangeable love. They are unspeakably precious in His sight, and are kept by Him as the apple of His eye. They love Him supremely, and study sincerely to please and honor Him. Jesus Christ, their divine Surety, has fully satisfied His justice for all their offenses; and yet He afflicts many of them in this world with a grievous and perplexing sense of His anger against them for their sins, and even with an overwhelming dread of His eternal wrath. Now, may it not be partly the intention of God, by thus afflicting many of His own dear children, to show unconverted sinners what a dreadful punishment must be inflicted on them if they still continue impenitent? Hereby He affords them evident warning of their danger before it is too late, and gives them repeated opportunities of making, each of them, this reflection: "If even God's own children experience such terror and anguish of soul when they are only under the mild rod of His fatherly anger, and that for their salvation, how inconceivably more horrible and intolerable will the torment be of His enemies, and of me in particular, if I continue but a little longer an enemy to Him, when we shall lie, through eternal ages, under the unrelenting strokes of His vindictive wrath, for our destruction!"

16. Last, the Lord inflicts trouble of spirit upon many of the saints on purpose to manifest His own glory. To display the glory of God in Christ is, indeed, the chief and ultimate end of that dispensation to which every other end is subordinate. His chief design in inflicting spiritual trouble is the manifestation of the infinitely glorious perfections of His nature. Next to that unparalleled display of the glory of His attributes which has been made in the sufferings of Christ, their Covenant-Head, is, perhaps, the display of it which is afforded in the sufferings, especially in the mental sufferings, of the members of His mystical body.

The glory of His manifold wisdom shines illustriously in devising those circumstances of their mental trouble which are, of all others, the most fit for subserving the designs of His grace in their sanctification; the glory also of His infinite power, both in supporting them under that greatest of all afflictions, and then in delivering them from it; the glory of His holiness in hiding His face from them, and in laying them, on account of their sins, under dreadful impressions of His anger, even though they still continue to be the objects of His redeeming love; the glory of His justice in raising them to the full enjoyment of the salvation purchased for them, even by the most painful discipline, rather than suffering them to come short of it; the glory of His love, grace, and mercy in dispensing, whenever it is needful, temporary trouble in order to prevent that eternal torment which they deserve, and in mitigating that trouble and in delivering them from it as soon as the ends of inflicting it are served; the glory of His faithfulness in performing the promise of that kind of paternal chastisement, which is the most grievous, rather than leave a single promise unperformed to them; and the glory of His sovereignty in thus afflicting, for their good, whomever, whenever, and in whatever degree He pleases.

He displays the glory of His infinite sovereignty by dispensing to His people trouble and comfort, sorrow and gladness, just as it pleases Him. Upon that ground, Elihu vindicated the Lord's afflicting of Job without questioning, as Job's other three friends had done, His integrity. "I will answer Thee," said he, "that God is greater than man. Why dost thou strive against Him? For He giveth not account of any of His matters" (Job 33:12–13). By inflicting mental trouble on some of His saints, the Most High shows them, and others around them, what He could do with them if He would. By so doing, He makes it manifest that it is He "who formeth the light, and createth darkness; who maketh peace, and createth evil" (Isaiah 45:7). He thereby makes them deeply sensible that all their comforts, whether outward or inward, depend as entirely on His sovereign pleasure as their election and regeneration did.

From what has here been said, disconsolate believers may see that the Lord never withholds sensible comfort from them but when His doing so is for their good in subservience to His own glory. Although the loss of spiritual consolation and the trouble of mind which ensues are in themselves discouragements from holy practice, and even obstruc-

tions to it, yet the Lord has appointed that many of
the saints shall sometimes be afflicted with these in
order that they may, in His hand, subserve the designs of His grace in their sanctification and salvation. Were believers always alike, were they continually in a lively frame, could they invariably exercise
ardent love and sensible joy, they would begin to
think that the power to do so was inherent, and that
it was in a great measure their own. But when, by
means of their want of consolation, they are made
deeply sensible that of themselves they can do nothing, and that they need to depend continually on
Christ for supplies from His fullness, they are hereby
prepared to glorify Him both by trusting in Him and
by advancing in conformity to Him.

Disconsolate Christian, you are laid in the furnace of spiritual trouble only when it is necessary
for your good. Love, therefore, your gracious God
and Father, who in all His dispensations consults
your welfare; who never chastens you but for your
profit, that you may be "a partaker of His holiness"
(Hebrews 12:10). "Rest in the Lord, and wait patiently for Him" (Psalm 37:7). "For a small moment He
hath forsaken thee, but with great mercies will He
gather thee" (Isaiah 54:7). Why has the glorious
gospel often appeared to you as too plain to be
practically understood, and too good to be believed
with application? It is your pride, your self-righteous
spirit. Endure, then, with faith and patience that
greatest of all afflictions, distress of mind; for by it
your heavenly Father is, in answer to your own
earnest prayers, destroying the pride of your heart.

From the foregoing particulars, exercised Christians may also see that, when outward and inward troubles, at any time, meet upon them, this is no proof either that they are unregenerate, or that God is their enemy. Believer, when you are under great and sore troubles, Satan will try to persuade you that they are proofs of your hypocrisy, and that if God loved you He would never subject you to such long, complicated, and grievous calamities. The construction which Job's three friends put upon his complicated and grievous afflictions was that they evidenced him to be a hypocrite, and God to be his enemy. When waters of a full cup are measured out to you, do not conclude that God does not love you, or that you are not one of His children. For great as your distresses are, they are not only consistent with His love for you, but they proceed from it. "Whom the Lord loveth He chasteneth, and scourgeth every son whom He receiveth" (Hebrews 12:6). Others whom God has loved have endured as great troubles as you, if not greater. Heman suffered terrors which threatened to overwhelm his amazed soul, and that not for a short season, but from his youth up. And yet, instead of concluding that God was his enemy, or that He did not love him, he addressed God as the Lord God of his salvation (Psalm 88:1).

Believers may hence see that they have no reason to be offended at the ways of godliness on account of any trouble, however grievous it may be, which they sometimes endure in those ways. They have no sufficient reason to be weary or faint in their minds. Their gracious God and Father proposes to Himself the best of all ends in afflicting them, namely, their sanctification, in subordination to His own glory.

220 A Treatise on Spiritual Comfort

And they may rest assured that they shall at no time
be afflicted with any degree either of inward or outward trouble, but what infinite wisdom sees necessary for attaining those ends. The kind, degree, and
continuance of their troubles are all fixed by the
immutable decree of their heavenly Father who
loves them; whose wisdom could not have devised
less, and whose love could not have appointed more
affliction for them than is requisite for the purposes
of His glory in their salvation. They have, therefore,
no reason to be displeased with any afflictive dispensation, or to think the worse of His ways of grace
and providence, because of any of their sufferings.

Once more, let every disconsolate Christian endeavor, in the diligent use of appointed means, to
have those ends accomplished in him for which the
Lord is afflicting him. If he does not know the particular design which the Lord may more immediately have in view in visiting him with his present
distress of soul, let him study to have at least all
those ends of it gained upon him which have been
explained previously in this chapter. His duty is to
trust firmly in the Lord Jesus, and also to pray frequently that all the designs which God usually has
in thus afflicting any of His children may be ob-
tained upon him. Perhaps the particular intention
of his spiritual trouble is for a season, concealed
from him in order that his heart may be set on having all the ends of the Lord in that most afflictive
dispensation gained upon him. "It is the glory of
God to conceal a thing" (Proverbs 25:2). "Clouds and
darkness are round about Him" (Psalm 97:2).

And, therefore, though it is the duty of a holy

man to inquire into the Lord's principal design in hiding His face from him, that he may in his exercise comply with that design, yet it becomes him to search into it with the deepest reverence and humility, and not to be so disappointed if he succeeds not as to sink lower in depression of mind, or to be deterred from any part of spiritual exercise. On the contrary, he ought, by the frequent exercise of every grace and the diligent performance of every duty, to grow up into Christ in all things. And he may warrantably hope that in proportion as he is enabled to do so, the end or ends of his mental trouble will be gained upon him.

7

*The Means Which Disconsolate Believers
Should Employ in Order to Recover
Their Spiritual Comfort*

Spiritual consolation is a commodity of heaven not to be imported but from that distant and better country. It is God only, the God of all comfort, to whom infinite mercy and power belong, who can impart holy consolation to the sorrowful heart or pour the balm of peace into the wounded spirit. It is only the adorable Spirit, the Comforter, who, like Noah's dove, can fly with the olive leaf of peace to assure the troubled soul that the winter is past and the rain is over and gone. When a holy man is walking in darkness, the day of comfort will not dawn, nor the shadow flee away, till "the Sun of righteousness arise with healing in His wings"; and he can no more command at his pleasure the rising of the spiritual sun within than he can that of the natural sun without. All that he can do is, in the strength of the grace which is in Christ Jesus, use means of recovering comfort, or, like the mariners in the ship with Paul, to cast anchor and wish for the day.

The means which he ought to employ for that purpose must be means of divine appointment, especially the following:

1. He ought, in humble reliance on the grace of Christ, to search out and confess to his heavenly Father those iniquities which have provoked Him to hide His face from him. He must without delay resolve, as did the Jewish Church in captivity, to "search and try His ways, and to turn again to the Lord, until the Lord look down, and behold from heaven" (Lamentations 3:40, 50). He ought to imitate David, who, when he was in distress of conscience, said to Jehovah, "I acknowledged my sin unto Thee, and mine iniquity have I not hid. I said, 'I will confess my transgressions unto the Lord'; and Thou forgavest the iniquity of my sin. For this shall everyone that is godly pray unto Thee, in a time when Thou mayest be found" (Psalm 32:5–6). One special design of the Lord's hiding His face, sometimes, from any of His children is so to chasten them for some latent sins in their hearts or lives as to make them deeply sensible of them, and of the horrible malignity of them, in order that they may attain deeper humiliation and self-abhorrence. The omniscient eye of God has seen all those secret evils which either have escaped their own notice altogether, or which they have carefully concealed from that of others, while they could not but know that they were open to His view. And it has also beheld how much His own glorious majesty and spotless holiness have been affronted and insulted by them. Hence comes His righteous displeasure, and that painful sense of it, under which they languish and mourn (Isaiah 59:1–2). It is their own evil tempers, and especially their unbelief and self-righteous spirit, that are the principal bars to their enjoyment of holy consolation.

When, therefore, they complain of desertion and darkness, they ought to search impartially and diligently into the hidden abominations which have procured for them that anguish of spirit which they feel they should examine strictly their consciences to see if some sinful inclination, opinion, or practice has not been indulged by them. They must listen to the softest whispers of conscience. If conscience reports that this has been neglected, or that something has been done wrong, they ought to trace that report to the grounds of it, and search even into the deepest recesses of the heart. And when their discovery of lurking depravity, or of secret iniquity, is as deep as they can make it, they should next, with holy shame, sorrow, and self-abhorrence, make ingenuous and particular confession of that to the Lord (Hosea 5:15).

2. *The disconsolate believer must likewise, if he would recover spiritual comfort, study without delay to be deeply convinced of the exceeding sinfulness and hurtfulness of his sins in general, and especially of his unbelief.* "When the Comforter is come," said Jesus Christ, "He will reprove (or, convince) the world of sin, because they believe not on Me" (John 16:8–9). He will convince the world of unbelief, as if there was no other sin in the world to be compared to that. Refusing to believe or trust in the great Redeemer is the radical evil of the human heart, the principal sin, the most malignant of all sins; and therefore, to be truly convinced of the strength, the sinfulness, and the perniciousness, especially, of that sin is necessary to the Christian's attaining holy comfort. Indeed the Spirit of Christ, ordinarily, never restores consolation to

troubled saints without previously convincing them of the exceeding sinfulness of their refusing to trust as sinners in Christ for all their salvation. When they are under distress of conscience, they commonly see and bewail their other sins; but they still continue, and cannot but continue, to be without comfort because they do not see that their not believing with application the record concerning the Son of God, and their not relying with the confidence of their hearts on Him for their salvation are the greatest of all their provocations. They cannot be favored with true consolation till they are made deeply sensible that by their unbelief and distrust they have done what they could to make the God of truth a liar (1 John 5:10). Ah, little do they think what reproach, what indignity they have reflected on the infinitely holy and faithful Jehovah by giving the lie to His immutable veracity! They do not consider that by refusing or even hesitating to trust in Jesus the Son of God for their salvation in particular, they have charged the God of truth with disingenuousness and treachery, as if He had said one thing in His Word and intended another in His heart; as if He had not been earnest in His offers of a Savior and of salvation to them; or as if He had not spoken the truth, and so did not deserved to be trusted.

Jehovah swears by His life that He has no pleasure in their death, but rather that, through the compassionate Savior, they should turn to Him and live. And, therefore, to doubt after all that He is willing to save them is to charge Him not only with insincerity, but with perjury. The high authority of the great and holy God is, in a special manner, inter-

posed in His commandment to believe on the name
of His Son Jesus Christ. He calls it "His commandment," as if it had been the only one that He ever
gave to the children of men (1 John 3:23).

Now disconsolate Christians, by their not believing on the name of His dear Son, fly in the face of
all that sovereign authority. Their presuming on any
pretense whatsoever to disobey that high command
is a crime of the deepest dye. It is more criminal
than the sin of Sodom and Gomorrah (Matthew
10:14–15). It is even worse than the sin of the Jews in
crucifying the Lord Jesus, for they crucified Him
when He was disguised under the form of a servant;
but disconsolate Christians, by refusing to trust in
Him for salvation, crucify Him afresh after He has,
by His resurrection from the dead, been declared to
be the Son of God and the true Messiah (Romans
1:4). Nay, it is even more heinous than the sin of
devils, for they never had a Savior offered to them,
nor a commandment given them to believe in Him.
Ah! How inconceivably sinful it is not to trust for
salvation in the Lord Jesus, the faithful Trustee of
that everlasting covenant, which is well-ordered in
all things, and sure! Alas, why do saints not shrink
with horror from the first risings of unbelief in
them, as they would do from a temptation to commit
murder or any other enormous crime? Unbelief is
the radical evil of the depraved heart from which every other abomination issues.

It is also requisite in order to attain comfort that
disquieted Christians be deeply convinced of the exceeding hurtfulness of their sins in general, and especially of their unbelief. They must, without delay,

study to become deeply sensible that the unbelief which prevails against them, and which passes in their minds under the disguise of humility and a dread of presumption, is a most deep, dangerous, and destructive evil. Their unbelief is the source to which every other departure of their hearts from the living God may be traced. It is the principal cause of all their spiritual trouble. What is it but their distrusting of Christ, and their apprehending of God to be their enemy, that increases the enmity against Him, the deadness of spirit, the hardness of heart, and the indisposition of soul to meditate on Him as a God of grace or to pray to Him which they feel? What is it but their fearing that He does not love them, and their apprehending that He is laying snares for them, or is watching for evil against them, that fills their souls with trouble and anguish, terror and dismay, aversion to Him, and weariness in every act of service done to Him? Is it not their disbelief of His care and their distrust of His mercy that dispose them to put a dark construction upon His dispensations to them, and to sink even under the slightest pressures? Let the disconsolate Christian, then, assure himself that he cannot attain holy comfort until he is convinced that his refusing to trust as a sinner in Jesus Christ for his salvation is not only exceedingly sinful in the sight of God, but inexpressibly hurtful to himself.

3. *He should, in order to recover spiritual consolation, take heed that he does not make rash and desperate conclusions against himself, respecting that which is either past, present, or future.* When a holy man concludes rashly, after he has had good evidence of his having been

in a state of grace, that he is still in a state of nature, he bears false witness against himself and reflects dishonor on his faithful Redeemer.

He must, therefore, strive against forming rash and sad conclusions against himself, with respect to that which is past. He ought not to conclude that he never had the grace of God, and that all his past experience has been but delusion merely because he is now walking in darkness, and is not able to discern the evidences of that grace. He should be much on his guard against thinking that he never was renewed in the spirit of his mind, or that he never passed from death to life because all his former experiences appear now to him to have been counterfeit. When, under a sense of divine anger, he rashly calls into question all that the Lord has done in and for his soul, this is a sin which is highly provoking to the holy Comforter. Asaph seems to have been guilty of it, when his remembrance of God and of his song in the night did not lessen his trouble (Psalm 77:3–9).

Neither ought the disquieted believer to conclude rashly against himself with regard to his present state. He must take heed that he does not grieve the Holy Spirit by concluding that he has at present no true work of grace in his heart, no vital union with Christ, no personal interest in Him, or that God is his enemy and has utterly cast him off. As the hypocrite is always disposed to hope upon false grounds that he is a true believer, so the true believer is frequently disposed, especially if troubled in soul, to fear upon improper grounds that he is a hypocrite. The ancient Church in her captivity said,

"My way is hid from the Lord, and my judgment is passed over from my God" (Isaiah 40:27). Jonah likewise said, "I am cast out of Thy sight" (Jonah 2:4); and David, "I am cut off from before Thine eyes" (Psalm 31:22). But these, and other instances of the same kind, are left on record not for the believer's imitation, but for his admonition. It is a great sin in a holy man to deny Christ within him, a sin of which he must be made deeply sensible in order for him to attain pure consolation.

Moreover, he must take heed that he does not form desperate conclusions against himself respecting the future. He ought to be on his guard against concluding, with respect to his spiritual condition, that it will never be better with him. He should tremble at the impious thought of making this peremptory and desperate conclusion: "The Lord will be favorable to me no more. I shall undoubtedly perish forever." He ought to be aware even of doubting whether God will be merciful to him or not, but much more of concluding rashly that He never will have mercy on him. Is he plagued all day long, and chastened every morning? He must not hence conclude that the Lord will never lay aside the rod or be favorable any more. There is nothing in the Oracles of God, nothing in the dealings of God with him, and nothing in himself which can render that conclusion warrantable.

The disconsolate Christian, indeed, is often prone, under the influence of temptation, to make such a dismal conclusion; but let him remember

that it is a very heinous sin to do so.* It tends greatly
to harden his heart, and to strengthen his remaining enmity against the God of his salvation. The
saints in Scripture who had been guilty of that sin
afterwards bitterly bewailed it. When David said that
he was cut off, he informed us that he said it in his
haste (Psalm 31:22). After Asaph had expressed the
thoughts of his desponding soul, "Will the Lord cast
off forever?" he said, "This is mine infirmity" (Psalm
77:7–10).

The dejected Christian, then, must beware of
provoking in a still higher degree the displeasure of
God by casting away his confidence in the
Redeemer, and giving himself over as undone forever. If, in the darkness of spiritual trouble, he can-

---

* It is lamentable to reflect how ready some of the saints, when
in trouble of mind, have been to form desperate conclusions
respecting their eternal state, and thereby to gratify the tempter,
as well as to reflect much dishonor on redeeming grace. And it
is no less wonderful how often infinite mercy has interposed for
their support, and even their deliverance, at the very times in
which they have been making such conclusions. I read the following account of one Mrs. Honeywood, who lived more than
a century ago, in England: When she was "under deep desertion, she refused all comfort, and seemed to despair utterly of
the mercy of God. A worthy minister was one day with her, and
reasoning against her separate conclusions. She took a venice-
glass off the table and said, 'Sir, I am as sure to be damned as
this glass is to be broken;' and therewith threw it forcibly to the
ground. But to the astonishment of both, the glass remained
whole and sound. The minister, with admiration, took it up,
rebuked her presumption, and showed her what a wonder
Providence had wrought for her satisfaction. This greatly altered the temper of her mind" (John Flavel's *Divine Conduct*).

not discern evidences of his being in a state of grace, he ought on no account rashly to conclude that he certainly is not in that state, much less that he never shall be in it. But leaving, in the meantime, that matter undecided, he should, by the direct actions of faith, entrust to the compassionate Savior the whole affair of his eternal salvation; for that is the way to recover in due time the joy of that salvation.

4. *He must, for the same purpose, call his soul to a strict account for its dejection and disquietude, and charge it again and again to trust in Jesus Christ, and in God through Him.* He ought without delay to call his troubled soul to account. This was a means of recovering comfort which David employed, and which he did not employ in vain. When his soul was cast down and disquieted in him, he called upon it to give an account of itself: "Why art thou cast down, O my soul, and why art thou disquieted in me?" (Psalm 42:5). The grief of holy David was not without a cause, and yet it must not be obstinate or exceed due bounds. It must not continue to depress and disquiet his soul, and so to discompose it as to disqualify it for the spiritual performance of present duty.

The disconsolate believer ought, in like manner, to commune with his own heart and call upon his soul to assign a sufficient reason why it suffers itself to be disquieted and cast down. He should call upon his troubled soul to answer such questions as these: "Is the cause of this dejected, this despondent frame a just one? Why, O my soul, are you this disquieted? What ground have you for these perplexing fears? You will say, 'I have good reason indeed to be trou-

bled, yea, to be so troubled as to be disqualified for
the acceptable performance of every duty!' But have
you sufficient reasons, such reasons as will endure
to be tried before the awful tribunal of the omniscient and righteous Judge of the world? Have not
other believers as much cause as you to be uneasy,
who yet do not yield themselves as you do to gloomy
dejection and obstinate grief? Why should you be
cast down, as if you had no grounds of hope or encouragement in the blessed gospel? as if you had a
God without mercy, a Savior without merit, a
Comforter without a right of access to Him, and
trouble without a promise, either of support under
it, or of deliverance from it? Will you be still miserable and not know why? Why, O my soul, do you, by
your despondency and sadness, dishonor your God
and Savior, injure yourself, and deter others from
the way of holiness? Can you give a good account of
this tumult?"

Were a holy man but to make strict inquiry into
the grounds of his uneasiness of soul, it would soon,
in some happy measure, be lessened. He can at no
time have any real ground to be afraid that the Lord
has either totally or finally forsaken him.

Moreover, he should frequently charge his disquieted soul to hope in the Savior, and in God
through Him. "Hope thou in God," said David to his
troubled soul, "for I shall yet praise Him for the help
of His countenance." After the Christian has urged
his soul to search into the grounds of its disquieting
fear, he must next charge it not to harden itself in
sorrow, but, on the contrary, to trust in God, to hope
that it "will yet praise Him for the help of His coun-

tenance," that is, for His favor and the comfort of it.

5. *If a good man, troubled in mind, would recover spiritual comfort, he must labor to understand and consider well his warrant as a sinner of mankind to trust in Christ, and in God through Him, for complete salvation.* When he cannot discern evidences within himself of his having formerly believed in Jesus, it would, through grace, relieve his mind much if he could see a full warrant in the Scripture to believe now in Him. He should, therefore, in order to attain consolation, consider well that in the gospel Christ, with His righteousness and fullness, is wholly, freely, and particularly offered to him as a sinner of mankind (Exodus 20:2; Isaiah 60:4; John 6:32 and 3:16; 1 John 5:11); that the calls or invitations of the gospel to accept all that is offered, are addressed to him (Proverbs 1:22–23, 8:4; Isaiah 55:1–3); that an authoritative commandment to comply with the invitations, and so to accept the offers of the gospel is given him (Exodus 20:3; Psalm 62:8; Proverbs 3:5; 1 John 3:23); that all the promises, being in Christ, are in and with Christ, freely offered to him for his acceptance (2 Corinthians 1:20; Proverbs 1:23; Acts 2:39; Hebrews 4:1); and that these and other such promises are in a special manner given him: "Him that cometh to Me, I will in no wise cast out" (John 6:37). "He that believeth and is baptized shall be saved" (Mark 16:16). "Believe on the Lord Jesus Christ, and thou shalt be saved" (Acts 16:31).

He ought to know and to consider that these four things—the offer, the invitation, the commandment to believe or trust in Christ, and the promise—being all addressed or directed to him as

a sinner of Adam's race, form his warrant, or afford
him a right, to come as a sinner in himself, and
without a moment's delay to trust firmly in the Lord
Jesus for eternal salvation. He should study clearly to
understand that those things, being founded on the
intrinsic sufficiency of the obedience and death of
Christ for the salvation even of all mankind, afford
him, as a sinner of mankind, a sufficient right or
warrant to come as he is; to come with all his sins,
all his wants, and all his griefs, and to rely with assured confidence on that divine Redeemer for complete salvation for himself in particular. He ought to
understand distinctly that as they are all directed as
particularly to him as if there were not another sinner in the world besides himself, so they afford to
him a particular, present, and sufficient warrant to
confide, for all salvation for himself, in Christ and
in God through Him; that they afford to him a full
right, not indeed to believe that Christ is already his
in possession (his assurance of this must be
founded on evidences), but to trust, and to trust cordially, that Christ now gives Himself, with His righteousness and salvation, to him in possession. He
must, in order to recover true comfort, learn spiritually and clearly to understand that Christ's being his
in offer gives him a right to trust in Him for possession.

The disconsolate Christian should likewise have
it firmly settled in his mind and conscience that, as
the great commandment to believe on the name of
Jesus Christ forms a main part of his revealed warrant to trust in Him, so it makes it his duty to trust
in Him; and that if it is his duty to trust in Him for

salvation, it cannot at the same time be his sin. He must labor to be fully persuaded that his endeavoring to trust cordially and confidently in the Lord Jesus for all his salvation is not presumption or sin, but that it is his present duty, yea, his first, his principal, his greatest duty, without the performance of which it will be impossible for him to please God in any other duty (Hebrews 11:6). It cannot surely be presumption in him to do that which God commands. Could the disquieted Christian be but convinced that his distrust of the great Redeemer is his chief, his greatest sin, the source of all his other sins—and that trusting in Him for his salvation is his first duty, the principal of all his duties—it should be a sure step toward his attaining holy consolation. Oh, that he but knew what an unspeakable comfort it is that the God of all consolation has made it his duty, his first duty, to trust at all times in the infinitely compassionate Savior! Oh, that he would instantly and frequently try to place the confidence of his heart in Him for salvation, and not stop a moment to look into himself for any good qualification to add to or strengthen that warrant for doing so which the Lord has graciously afforded him in His holy Word!

6. *He should also, in order to attain consolation, consider the encouragements which he still has to trust in the blessed Redeemer.* Those things mentioned above, which afford the disconsolate Christian, in common with all the other hearers of the gospel, a warrant, give him, at the same time, an encouragement to rely with confidence on the Lord Jesus. But there are various other things which, though they, strictly speaking,

form no part of his revealed warrant, yet serve greatly, when he properly considers them, to encourage him to trust in the Savior. These are:

The infinitely gracious and merciful nature of God in Christ; the consummate righteousness of the Lord Jesus (Jeremiah 23:6);

The infinite fullness of grace which is in Him, and that for the chief of sinners (Psalm 68:18);

The plenteous redemption which is with Him (Psalm 130:7);

The forgiveness of iniquity which is dispensed by Him (Psalm 130:4);

The absolute promises of His gracious covenant (Ezekiel 36:25–28);

His infinite ability and willingness to save even the chief of sinners (Jeremiah 9:24; John 6:40);

His intercession for the transgressors (Isaiah 53:12);

His experimental sympathy with all the members of His mystical body, or His being touched with the feeling of their infirmities (Hebrews 4:15);

His moderating all their afflictions, or keeping them within measure (Jeremiah 30:11);

The secret support which He has hitherto afforded them (Psalm 73:23);

And the intervals of relief from grief and fear with which, even in their greatest extremity, He has favored them.

Moreover, when a holy man is in trouble of mind, he may be conscious of several things in his own present experience which ought also to encourage him to renew his exercise of trusting in Christ, and thereby to receive comfort from Him.

Some of those would be these: He finds no righteousness or strength in himself in which he can confidently trust. He now perceives, and feels more of the depravity of his heart than ever he did before, which is an evidence that he has attained more spiritual light and life. He feels now the sin which dwells in him rising, struggling, threatening to carry all before it, and indisposing him for the practice of holiness more than he did formerly. His deadness of spirit,[*] his hardness of heart, his enmity against God, his legal temper, his worldly-mindedness, and his inability to hate and mourn for sin are a burden and a trouble to him. His inability to believe in Christ, and to pray in faith, is a ground of much uneasiness and complaint. He counts sin to be the greatest of all evils, and he is conscious of no sin in himself but what he either loathes, or is troubled because he cannot loathe it as he should; he is conscious of no sin but what he utterly disapproves, and from which he would count it a mercy to be saved. He dares not allow himself deliberately to displease the Lord, but desires above all things to please Him. He highly esteems the Lord Jesus, and concludes that the loss of Him is greater than the loss of ten thousand worlds. He is persuaded that

---

[*] Thomas Shepard of New England said that "more are drawn to Christ under the sense of a dead and blind heart than by all sorrows, humiliations, and terrors." And Thomas Brooks, who was a famous instrument of converting many to God, used to say that for his own part, he had no other evidence in himself of being in a state of grace than that he was sensible of his deadness (Brooks' *Cabinet of Jewels*).

the possession of the whole universe could not
make him content to be without Christ. He is troubled greatly because he can discern no satisfying evidence of his being personally interested in Christ,
and in God as a covenant God. He is greatly alarmed
and deeply perplexed because all his past experience
now appears to him to have been counterfeit. He
finds that he is utterly unable of himself either to
perform spiritual duties or to resist spiritual enemies. He is grieved because he cannot approve the
covenant of grace as he should, because he cannot
trust cordially in Christ for salvation, and because
he is unable to exercise godly sorrow for the evils of
his heart. He finds that he cannot rest upon Christ,
and, at the same time, that he cannot rest or be easy
without Him. He desires the presence of God and
the light of His gracious countenance, and he often
fears that he is not sincere in his desire for communion with Him. He also mourns for the absence of
God and cannot be kept from Him. He loves the
company of the saints more than that of others.
Those of his relations and acquaintances who appear unconverted, he regards with pity; and he endeavors to recommend the Savior and His great salvation to their esteem.

   These things, in the present experience of the
disconsolate Christian, of which, for the most part,
he may be conscious, though they do not, strictly
speaking, afford him a warrant to renew his sense of
confidence in Christ for salvation, nor in the least
degree strengthen his revealed warrant for doing so,
yet, if he is conscious but of any one of them in
himself, it should encourage him to trust afresh,

and not to be afraid. He ought not indeed to trust in
it, nor to make it the ground of his right to trust in
the Savior; but he should be animated and embold-
ened by it to avail himself of his warrant to renew
his acting of trust in Him.

Besides, the disquieted Christian should, for his
further encouragement to trust in Jesus Christ, and
in God through Him, consider frequently that he is
not only commanded, in common with all other
hearers of the gospel, but that he is in a special
manner commanded to trust in Him. "Who is
among you that feareth the Lord, that obeyeth the
voice of His servant, and walketh in darkness, and
hath no light? Let him trust in the name of the
Lord, and stay upon his God" (Isaiah 50:10); as if
Messiah, who is the speaker in the immediately preceding verse, had said to the professed members of
the Jewish Church, "Whoever is among you, though
it were but one, who has a sincere regard for the
commandments of the Lord, and a humble venera-
tion for His high authority; who is also willing to
listen attentively to the instructions and to obey sincerely the laws of His righteous servant; and who is
in the darkness especially of spiritual trouble, without the light of deliverance or comfort—tell him
that I have a special command to lay and urge upon
him: Let him trust, let him confide in the name of
Jehovah; yea, let him continue resolutely to rely with
firm confidence upon his God for all grace and
consolation."

Although the believer, when he is walking in the
darkness of mental trouble, cannot ordinarily perceive that God is his God in possession, yet he is at

least firmly to believe that He is his God in offer, and frequently, as well as cordially, to say that He is his in choice, and in preference to every other God; and so he is to place an unsuspecting confidence in Him. The gracious and special command, then, which Messiah here gives him to confide constantly in Him, and in God through Him, should be regarded by the disconsolate Christian as the very highest encouragement to entrust to Him all the concerns of his disquieted soul.

7. *The troubled Christian, accordingly, in order to recover consolation for his wounded spirit, ought without delay to trust in the Lord Jesus, and in God as reconciled in Him.* He should, in dependence on the grace of Christ, instantly strive to trust that God the Father loves him, and has good will toward him (1 John 4:16); that Jesus Christ saves him, and that He will save him to the uttermost (Isaiah 33:22); and that the blessed Spirit will in due time restore comfort to him. Let him not delay trusting in the Savior till he is in a better frame, or till he is so brought forth to the light as to discern some good qualifications in his own heart. But let him, even while he is in darkness, endeavor to trust, and to say, "Though He slay me, yet will I trust in Him" (Job 13:15). "If I perish, I shall perish casting myself down at the feet of the Savior for mercy. He who is the Lamb of God is too gracious, too merciful to suffer any to perish there. If He saves me not, I cannot be much worse than I am. In this way, I can but perish; and it may be that I shall be saved."

When a good man is in the darkness of spiritual trouble, let him not sit down desponding in that darkness, but let him walk on in it, and walk by faith. Let him presently and resolutely, humbly and confidently trust in the infinitely faithful and compassionate Redeemer. Elihu's exhortation to Job, when he was in darkness, is addressed also to him: "Although thou sayest thou shalt not see Him, yet judgment is before Him; therefore trust thou in Him" (Job 35:14). He ought then to adopt without delay the resolution of the holy Psalmist, and to say to the Lord, "What time I am afraid, I will trust in thee" (Psalm 56:3). It is his present duty to place the confidence of his heart in Jesus, that faithful Trustee of the everlasting covenant, and to say with the afflicted Psalmist, "Though I walk in the midst of trouble, Thou wilt revive me; Thou wilt stretch forth Thine hand against the wrath of mine enemies, and Thy right hand shall save me. The Lord will perfect that which concerneth me" (Psalm 138:7–8). "Thou wilt light my candle; the Lord my God will enlighten my darkness" (Psalm 18:28). "Thou wilt guide me with Thy counsel, and afterwards receive me to glory" (Psalm 73:24).

Let him trust not only that the Lord Jesus will, according to His promise, save him with an everlasting salvation, but that He will in due season comfort him. And let him say with holy David, "Thou, who hast shown me great and sore troubles, wilt quicken me again, and wilt bring me up again from the depths of the earth. Thou wilt increase my greatness, and comfort me on every side" (Psalm 71:20–21). It is as if he had said, "I shall in due time see nothing dark or discouraging on any side." The disconsolate Christian should confide likewise in the

Father of mercies, the God of all comfort, and, with
the church of Israel, say, "My God will hear me.
Rejoice not against me, O mine enemy; when I fall, I
shall arise; when I sit in darkness, the Lord will be a
light unto me. He will bring me forth to the light,
and I shall behold His righteousness. He will turn
again, He will have compassion upon me; He will
subdue my iniquities; and He will cast all my sins
into the depths of the sea" (Micah 7:7–9, 19). He
ought to trust even in a frowning and withdrawing
God, to trust Him though he cannot trace Him; like
the woman of Canaan, he should be resolute and
peremptory in trusting Him.

Nor should he be afraid that his endeavoring
thus to trust is presumption. Presumption is unwarrantable or groundless confidence. It cannot then
be presumption so long as he is conscious that he
trusts only in Christ and in God, and that he places
confidence in Christ and in God not upon the
ground of any good thing in his own heart or life,
but only upon the divine warrant which is afforded
him in the gospel. Nor ought he to fear that he is
acting presumptuously so long as he consciously endeavors to trust in the Savior, not for a part merely,
but for the whole of salvation; not for salvation in
any sin, but for salvation from every sin; not for salvation with sin or to sin, but for that salvation which
comprises universal holiness of heart and life; not
for salvation by his own righteousness, but for salvation by grace, reigning through the righteousness
of Jesus Christ unto eternal life (Acts 15:11; Romans
5:21); and for salvation not for his own glory, but for
the glory of Christ, and of God in Him.

Presumption also is unreasonable confidence. But nothing can be more reasonable than that a needy sinner comes at the command of God, and trusts with firm confidence in Jesus Christ for all that salvation which is laid up in Christ, laid out in the promise, and brought near in the offer of the gospel. And nothing, on the contrary, can be more unreasonable than to trust for that which it is impossible even for omnipotence itself to afford, and which the Savior has never promised to give—salvation in sin: salvation consistent with a man's retaining some darling lust, salvation merely from the punishment of sin, salvation in order to be at liberty to commit sin with impunity. In few words, the disconsolate Christian should not fear that his trusting in the Lord Jesus for his salvation in particular is presumptuous confidence, if it is accompanied with fear that he does not approve cordially the whole scheme of redemption delineated in the gospel, with desire so to approve it, and with diligence in the use of all the other means of grace within his reach.

In his endeavoring to trust cordially in the blessed Savior for salvation, he must not overlook the promises of salvation. All the promises of God, being in Christ yea and Amen, are in and with Christ offered in the gospel to him. He should, therefore, in applying Christ to himself, embrace or apply the promises not indeed separate from Christ, but in and with Him. And believing that the absolute promises especially are, in the offer, directed to him for his acceptance, he must rely on the faithfulness of God in them, which is pledged for the performance of them, and so trust in Christ for the performance of them to himself. To trust for salvation is to rely with confidence not only on Christ and His righteousness, but on the truth of the promises. It is to rely and live upon Christ not as felt in the heart, but as offered and promised in the gospel; and it must be of the same extent as the promises. The absolute promises of the eternal covenant are open. They are free. The disquieted Christian, therefore, should cast himself freely upon them when feelings and evidences fail. He has been trying to determine if he already had a personal interest in the Redeemer; and he has found no satisfying evidences of it in himself. Let him, for a little while, forbear that inquiry and, in the meantime, put the matter out of doubt by trusting that Christ now gives him a saving interest in Him. Every scriptural evidence of a personal interest in the Redeemer is either comprised *in* faith or is a consequence *of* faith. Let his actings of faith in Christ, and in the promise, then, be distinct and explicit in order that he may be conscious that he is acting it (Psalm 91:2; Lamentations 3:24). And, at the same time, let him rest not on the act, but on the glorious Object of his faith, and draw consolation not from the act, but by the act from Christ and the promises.

To trust simply in the Lord Jesus for his salvation is the principal means which the disconsolate Christian should employ for attaining spiritual comfort. Without this, no other means will be of the smallest avail. To rely with cordial and unsuspecting affiance upon the faithful Redeemer and the free promises is not only in itself an ease to the troubled soul (Hebrews 4:3), but is, according to the covenant of grace, the appointed instrument of deriving consolation, as well as holiness, from the fullness of Christ. After Job had said, "I know that my Redeemer liveth" (Job 19:25), he was so relieved from the extremity of his trouble that he no more uttered such doleful complaints as before. "The Lord is my strength and my shield," said David. "My heart trusted in Him, and I am helped; therefore my heart greatly rejoiceth, and with my song will I praise Him" (Psalm 28:7). Again, "I had fainted, unless I had believed to see the goodness of the Lord in the land of the living" (Psalm 27:13). And again, "I have trusted in Thy mercy; my heart shall rejoice in Thy salvation" (Psalm 13:5). The Lord Jesus said to His disconsolate disciples, "Let not your hearts be troubled; ye believe in God, believe also in Me" (John 14:1). If the disquieted Christian, then, would recover spiritual consolation, let him "hold the beginning of his confidence steadfast unto the end" (Hebrews 3:14). Let him come frequently to Jesus, the Consolation of Israel, and come every time as if it were the first time, or as if he were but beginning to come. Let him come as a sinner in himself, and trust that Christ will save him from his sin and from his trouble. So will the joy of God's salvation be in due time restored to him. By thus casting all his care upon his gracious Redeemer, who cares for him, his depressed spirit will become easy and cheerful.

8. *He must also, for the same purpose, hope in the Lord Jesus, and in God as the God of all comfort.* Spiritual hope comprises a cordial desire and expectation of all promised good things, both in time and in eternity.

It is a certain, and a longing, expectation of all the
good of the everlasting covenant, and is grounded
on the declarations and promises of the gospel; on
the perfections of God in Christ, and His relations
to His people; and on the office, righteousness,
fullness, and intercession of Christ. It has an ines-
timably precious object, and a heart-purifying and
enlivening influence (1 John 3:2–3; 1 Peter 1:3). It is
a consequence of saving faith, and is inseparably
connected with it. Faith is trusting that the faithful
Redeemer will perform all the promises of His eternal covenant to me. Hope is a desire and expectation of all the future blessings which are therein
promised. It is a living principle which revives and
supports, strengthens and elevates the soul of the
true believer, and which carries him beyond this finite scene into that which is infinite, where he is
transported with the joyful prospect of life eternal,
in the immediate presence of God and the Lamb; of
seeing his glorious Redeemer as He is; of being like
Him, and of the full enjoyment of Jehovah, Father,
Son, and Holy Spirit, forevermore.

Now the dejected believer should, for his comfort, endeavor frequently to exercise this living
hope, this "hope of an inheritance incorruptible,
and undefiled, and that fadeth not away, reserved in
heaven for him" (1 Peter 1:3–4). He must, in dependence on the grace of Christ, hope for all necessary
grace, and especially "for the grace that is to be
brought unto him at the revelation of Jesus Christ"
(1 Peter 1:13). He ought to hope that the Lord will in
due season comfort him; that "the God of hope will
yet fill him with all joy and peace in believing"

(Romans 15:13). He must, if he would recover holy consolation, charge his soul, as the Psalmist did, to "hope in God" (Psalm 43:5); to hope that he shall yet have comfort from God; that he "shall yet praise Him for the help of His countenance" (Psalm 42:5), for the manifestation of His favor to his soul, and for the consolation which will ensue. He ought to hope even against hope, to hope continually, and "to show diligence to the full assurance of hope, unto the end" (Hebrews 6:11). His Redeemer is the great God, and He resolves to act like Himself. The believer should therefore expect great as well as good things from Him—great consolations, great mercy and peace, and a great salvation (Jeremiah 33:3).

The Lord Jesus is the hope of Israel, and the Savior thereof in time of trouble. He will often disappoint the fears of the timorous believer, but will never disappoint his hopes insofar as they are grounded on, and regulated by, the promises. Let him therefore build his hope no longer upon any good thing wrought in or done by himself; but let him build it wholly upon the righteousness and grace of Christ, and upon the promises and faithfulness of God. The exercise of a well-grounded hope tends to settle the heart and calm the troubled spirit. "It is good, therefore, that a man should both hope, and quietly wait for the salvation of the Lord. For the Lord will not cast off forever, but though He cause grief, yet will He have compassion, according to the multitude of His mercies" (Lamentations 3:26, 31–32). That hope, when it is accompanied in its exercise with filial fear, pleases the Lord greatly; and it is a special means of attaining the light of His gracious countenance (Psalm 147:11).

The disconsolate believer should at no time suspect that his endeavoring to hope is presumption, so long as he is conscious that his expectation is founded solely upon the grace and power of God exhibited in the declarations and offers of the gospel, upon the spotless righteousness of Jesus Christ, and upon the faithfulness of God in the promises (Psalm 130:5–7). True hope is grounded not upon that which Jesus felt in his stead, not upon what he does for Christ, but upon what Christ did, and is still doing, for him. Evidences of grace in the heart and life are indeed great encouragements to exercise hope; but they are not the grounds upon which true hope is built. He who exercises a living hope is diligent in using all appointed means of grace; and yet he does not rest upon the use of those means, but upon the Lord as speaking to him in His word of grace.

9. *Another means of recovering spiritual comfort is diligence in the exercise of evangelical repentance.* If the disconsolate Christian would exercise repentance in an upright and acceptable manner, he must first of all, in the faith of pardoning mercy and sanctifying grace, repent of his unbelieving, distrustful, and desponding thoughts, and, next, of all his other sins. His unbelief and distrust of the Savior are his radical crimes; and therefore, in his exercise of repentance, he ought to begin with them. And in order to exercise repentance sincerely and acceptably, he should trust that the Lord Jesus, the exalted Prince and Savior, gives repentance to him, and forgiveness of

sins (Acts 5:31). It is faith in pardoning mercy that
breaks the heart, and that opens all the sluices of
godly sorrow for sin. Trusting, then, in the mercy of
the Lord Jesus Christ, and of God in Him (Psalm
13:5; Joel 2:13), he should endeavor to attain a true
and humbling sense of his iniquity. Without placing confidence in redeeming mercy, a man may
have a sense of sin, but not a true sense of it; he may
have a sense of sin as hurtful to himself (Genesis
4:13), but not as hateful to God (Habakkuk 1:13); a
sense of the danger and demerit, but not of the deep
malignity and pollution of sin.

The dejected Christian, therefore, should study
to attain by faith a spiritual sight and sense of the
horrible malignity, as well as of the infinite demerit,
of his unbelief and other transgressions. He must
without delay, and in the exercise of faith, look
upon Jesus whom he has pierced in order that his
grief for the loss of his comfort may be turned into
godly sorrow for those iniquities which have pierced
his dear Savior, and procured for himself that
grievous loss (Zechariah 12:10). Viewing his iniquity
as laid on Christ, and Christ as pierced for it in his
stead, he must also, with holy self-loathing and deep
abhorrence of his sin, turn not from one sin to another, but from all sin to God (Isaiah 6:5; Hosea 6:1).
Let him hate sin, and hate it as sin (Psalm 119:104).
Let his hatred be universal against all sin, and ir-
reconcilable to any sin (Psalm 101:3). He must, in
the faith of redeeming mercy, turn from all iniquity,
and especially from the sins for which the Lord is
pleading a controversy with him (Ezekiel 14:6). Let
him say with Ephraim of old, "Turn Thou me, and I

shall be turned, for Thou art the Lord my God" (Jeremiah 31:18). Trusting that the Lord his God turns him, he should "turn to the Lord with all his heart, with fasting, and with weeping, and with mourning" (Joel 2:12). He ought to turn to the love of God (Isaiah 26:13), and to the spiritual performance of every duty to Him (Psalm 119:106). This is what the Jewish Church in her captivity resolved to do: "Let us search and try our ways, and turn again to the Lord" (Lamentations 3:40).

If the disconsolate believer would recover pure consolation, let the exercise of his faith and hope be penitential. And if, after all his endeavors, he finds that he cannot shed a tear, or feel such bitter sorrow for sin as he longs to feel, let him not be discouraged, but recollect that turning with holy abhorrence from all iniquity to the Lord is the very essence of true repentance. Let him turn from his sins of omission, and especially from his sin of suffering himself to be discouraged by a sense of the corruption of his nature from the great duties of believing and rejoicing in Christ Jesus (Philippians 3:3), by which he has brought up an evil report upon the good ways of the Lord. And he ought not to fear that his repentance is legal or hypocritical, so long as he is conscious that he endeavors to exercise godly sorrow for all sin as sin, and to turn from it because it is sin. The repentance of the legalist or hypocrite is not so much sorrow for sin, as a sullen grief that he is not allowed to sin with impunity; not so much a turning from sin to the Lord as a turning from one sin to another.

As the exercise of evangelical repentance is an

appointed means, so it is a sure means of recovering
holy consolation; for thus said the Lord: "To this
man will I look, even to him that is poor, and of a
contrite spirit, and trembleth at My Word" (Isaiah
66:2). "The Lord is nigh unto them that are of a
broken heart, and He saveth such as be of a contrite
spirit" (Psalm 34:18). "He healeth the broken in
heart, and bindeth up their wounds" (Psalm 147:3).
As soon as Ephraim's heart is troubled for his iniquities, God's bowels are troubled for Ephraim; and
He will surely have mercy upon him (Jeremiah
31:20). Godly sorrow for sin is not only a means of
attaining future comfort, but is accompanied with
present consolation. There is more joy in the penitential mourning of a humble believer than in all
the vain mirth of an unregenerate man.

*10. He ought, for the same end, to meditate frequently on
the blessed Jesus, and on God as a God of grace in Him.* He
is disposed to muse often on the trouble of his own
mind, but he should rather contemplate the
sufferings of Christ's soul. Were he frequently to
meditate on the unparalleled anguish, the doleful
agony of his dear Redeemer's soul when He was en-
during for him the vindictive wrath of God, and was
not allowed to discern the least smile in the countenance of His righteous Father, it might be a happy
means of calming the tumult of his own soul. The
compassionate Savior, in love for him and for his
salvation, drank a cup of unmixed wrath. And He
puts into his hand only a cup of suffering, mixed
with many sweet and salutary ingredients. What are
his sorrows, then, to those of the Lord Jesus? There
is no comparison. There was more bitterness in one

drop of Christ's sufferings than in an ocean of his. Devout meditation on the loving, agonizing, dying Redeemer has often been a reviving, delightful exercise to holy souls. "My meditation of Him," said the Psalmist, "shall be sweet" (Psalm 104:34). It has, many times, been sweet and soothing to holy men, even under spiritual trouble.

The disquieted believer should, moreover, think frequently on God in Christ as a God of mercy and grace, and on His amiable perfections and precious promises. In Christ, God manifests Himself to be a gracious, promising, and performing God; to be just such a God as an afflicted saint would choose to have to do with. In Him, God exhibits His infinitely glorious excellencies in the most amiable, attractive and encouraging way. He manifests Himself to be "the Father of mercies, and the God of all comfort." To present Him often to the mind, therefore, from that point of view will, in the hand of the adorable Comforter, be a sovereign cordial to a drooping spirit.

Hence the afflicted Psalmist said, "O my God, my soul is cast down within me; therefore will I remember Thee from the land of Jordan, and of the Hermonites, from the hill Mizar" (Psalm 42:6). It is as if he had said, "I will, in order to cheer my drooping spirit, remember Thee as a God of mercy. I will call to remembrance Thy love and faithfulness, Thy power and presence in the sanctuary. I will remember Thee from the most distant countries to which I may be driven." To the same purpose, he says in another Psalm, "My soul shall be satisfied as with marrow and fatness, and my mouth shall praise Thee with joyful lips, when I remember Thee upon my bed, and meditate on Thee in the night watches" (Psalm 63:5–6). Asaph, likewise, when his soul was in trouble, said, "I will remember the years of the right hand of the Most High. I will remember the works of the Lord; surely I will remember Thy wonders of old. I will meditate also of all Thy work, and talk of Thy doings" (Psalm 77:10–12).

The dejected Christian must, in order to attain peace and comfort, meditate on God especially as a God in covenant; as a God offering and promising to be a God to him, and that from regard to no worthiness in him, but merely to the glory of His own free and sovereign grace. He ought frequently to contemplate the covenant of grace in the making, fulfilling, and administration of it; for the Lord has devised and established that gracious covenant as the rule according to which all His dispensations of grace and providence are adjusted. There, the timorous believer will see that all is of infinitely free grace; that every blessing is to be received as a free gift; that the great Redeemer Himself is given for a covenant of the people; that God is first in the obligation of the covenant; and that there is no tie upon the believer but what depends on, and is similar to, the tie which the believer has upon God.

11. He should also, in order to receive comfort, pray much in the name of Christ, and so pour out his heart before His gracious God and Father. This was the exercise of David when his soul was disquieted: "O my God, my soul is cast down within me." And again, "I will say unto God my Rock, 'Why hast Thou forgotten me? Why go I mourning because of the oppression of the enemy?' "(Psalm 42:6, 9). He had already charged his soul to hope in God, and no longer to yield to disquieting grief and fear, but had found no relief. And therefore he betook himself to his Covenant-God and complained of his disquietude to Him. Although he could not himself command a calm in his troubled spirit, yet he knew that his redeeming God could. He therefore complained *to* the Lord, but did not complain *of* Him. He complained not that afflictive dispensations had troubled his soul, but that his soul had troubled itself. "When my spirit was overwhelmed within me," said he, "I poured out my complaint before Him. I showed before Him my trouble" (Psalm 142:2–3). He presented this supplication to Him: "O Lord, rebuke me not in Thine anger, neither chasten me in Thy hot displeasure. Have mercy upon me, O Lord, for I am weak; heal me, for my bones are vexed. My soul is also sore vexed, but Thou, O Lord, how long? Return, O Lord, deliver my soul; oh, save me for Thy mercy's sake" (Psalm 6:1–4).

The Apostle James said, "Is any among you afflicted? Let him pray" (James 5:13). The Lord Jesus recommends this duty to disconsolate believers by His own example, for we read that when He was "in an agony, He prayed more earnestly" (Luke 22:44). The prayer of faith is a sure means of obtaining relief; for thus said Jehovah: "Call upon Me in the day of trouble; I will deliver thee, and thou shalt glorify Me" (Psalm 50:15).

Does the distressed Christian say that he feels himself sadly indisposed for the duty of prayer, or that he has been long attempting the exercise of it,

but that the Lord "shutteth out his prayer"
(Lamentations 3:8)? Let him nevertheless persist in
trying to pray, and in looking up for an answer
(Luke 18:1). Is he ready to say that he cannot pray
acceptably? Let him attempt it as he can, and commit it, notwithstanding all the imperfection attending it, to the Lord Jesus, his Advocate with the
Father. Jesus will, with infinite ease, understand it,
and will put it into such language as will be accepted in the court of heaven. He should, therefore,
come boldly to the throne of grace, and present
such requests as would show that he has honorable
sentiments of the riches and munificence of the
King of glory.

He ought to come firmly persuaded that, though
a little is too much for his reward, yet that much is
too little for his great Redeemer's bounty.[*] By so do-

---

[*] In order to illustrate the sentiment here expressed, I cannot
forbear mentioning a heathen story: Alexander had a philosopher in his court who once was greatly straitened in his circumstances. He, on that occasion, applied for money to his
sovereign, the conqueror of the world. No sooner was his request made than granted. Alexander gave him a commission to
receive from his treasurer whatever sum he wanted. He immediately went and demanded a hundred talents, which amount
to about ten thousand pounds sterling. The treasurer, surprised
at so large a demand, refused to comply, but waited upon the
King and represented to him how unreasonable he thought the
petition was, and how exorbitant the sum. Alexander heard
him with patience, but as soon as he had ended his remon-
strance replied, "Let the money be immediately given him. I
like that man. I am delighted with his way of thinking. He has
done me a singular honor and, by the largeness of his request,
he has shown what a high idea he has both of my great riches

ing, he will greatly honor the marvelous loving-kindness of the Lord. When he prays for spiritual comfort, or for any other spiritual blessing, let him pray in faith; and according to his faith it will, in due time, be unto him (Mark 11:24). He ought, as the Canaanite woman did, convert even the greatest discouragements into so many encouragements, to trust and plead the promises. He must not conclude that his prayers are lost or are hypocritical, merely because he does not experience comfort in them, and does not receive the very thing for which he asks. Mercies seldom do good to that man who is overly peremptory in asking them. It is only the prayer of faith, founded on the promises and regulated by them, that is the outlet from trouble and the inlet of consolation. Even the desire thus to pray is a forerunner of success, and an earnest of the blessing implored. "Thou drewest near," said Jeremiah, "in the day that I called upon Thee; Thou saidst, 'Fear not' " (Lamentations 3:57). The more speedily God seems to be departing from the disconsolate believer, he ought to pursue after Him with the firmer trust and the greater importunity. And in praying for spiritual consolation, he should ask only that measure of it which the Lord may see proper to give him, and should ask it not so much for his own relief as for the glory of redeeming grace. In continuing so to do he shall, in the fittest season, experience a heavenly sweetness diffusing itself over his troubled soul, and shall from his experience know that it is better to seek the Lord than to find all

---

and my royal munificence."

things else.

When the afflicted believer is praying, he must endeavor to praise and thank the Lord. This also is a special means of recovering holy consolation. We read in a passage of Scripture cited above that the Psalmist said to his dejected soul, "Hope thou in God, for I shall yet praise Him" (Psalm 42:5), as if he had said, "I hope yet to praise Him. I long to praise Him." This grateful and adoring frame was not only an evidence of David's beginning to emerge out of the depth of his trouble, but was likewise a means of his emerging. The depressed Christian, then, if he would attain spiritual comfort, should study in his prayers to occupy at least as much time in thanking the Lord for the mercies vouchsafed to him as in confessing the sins committed by him. This would tend greatly to remove his bitterness of spirit, and to bring refreshing consolation to his weary soul. The frequent mentioning of things that are sweet and cheering is a means of sweetening the temper of the mind, and of promoting cheerfulness of spirit.

Were the disquieted believer to take special notice of the manifold blessings which are still vouchsafed to him, and frequently to bless the Lord for them, he would not remain long afterwards in an uncomfortable frame (Lamentations 3:22–24). He ought therefore to esteem it his privilege, as well as his duty, in every condition to give thanks to God (1 Thessalonians 5:18). He should be thankful that his heavenly Father condescends to be angry with him, and to reprove him for sin; that He has not given him over to a reprobate mind (Job 5:17); and that the sin which dwells in him is in any measure a burden to him. If he is unworthy even of the least of all the mercies bestowed upon him, he surely ought to be thankful for the least of them (Genesis 32:10).

12. He ought, moreover, to wait patiently for the Lord. If the disquieted believer would regain holy tranquility of mind, he must "both hope and quietly wait for the salvation of the Lord" (Lamentations 3:26). He must say, as Messiah Himself did, "I will wait upon the Lord, who hideth His face from the house of Jacob, and I will look for Him" (Isaiah 8:17). The way to recover his comfort is to say to his soul, "My soul, wait thou only upon God; for my expectation is from Him." His duty at all times, and especially when his soul is disquieted, is to "rest in the Lord, and wait patiently for Him"; to "wait on the Lord, and keep His way" (Psalm 37:7, 34). "Though the vision tarry," he ought to "wait for it, because it will surely come; it will not tarry" a moment longer than the appointed time (Habakkuk 2:3). He should consider that the Lord, who has appointed that great affliction for him, is infinitely wise, righteous, and good; that He is His own God, the God of his salvation (Psalm 88:1); and that by such methods as please him least God often does him the most good.

Moreover, the time that he has to wait is but short. Yet a little while and the compassionate Savior will come and save him. The Lord Jesus waited long for him, and He waits still for a fit opportunity to comfort him more than he himself can wait for the enjoyment of comfort. "Therefore will the Lord wait," said Isaiah, "that He may be gracious unto you, and therefore will He be exalted, that He may have mercy upon you; for the Lord is a God of judgment" (Isaiah 30:18). Although he has no prospect of deliverance soon, yet let him still wait unto the time to favor him, even the set time to come; and let him wait with a patient and silent resignation to the divine will (Isaiah 28:16).

The Lord is waiting for the very same day of comfort for which the disconsolate saint is to wait; and if the Lord cannot be disappointed, so neither can he. There is, in the love of Christ toward him, an earnest longing, as it were, that the day might come. And therefore he may, in submission to the will of his gracious God, lawfully pray as the holy Psalmist did (Psalm 31:2 and 102:2), even for a speedy deliverance. But if his mental trouble still continues, he must resolve to wait patiently, and to justify the infinitely wise God in His delaying to return with comfort to him. Let him still "hope, and quietly wait," for it is the time of his extremity that is commonly the Lord's opportunity of appearing for his relief.

Holy consolation is worth his waiting for it. It is, as it were, the opening of heaven upon the soul. Let him therefore wait, and the Lord will, at the time appointed, so console his troubled spirit as to cause him from experience to say, "Lo, this is my God. I have waited for Him, and He will save me. This is the Lord. I have waited for Him, and I shall be glad and rejoice in His salvation" (Isaiah 25:9). The longer he stays in expectation for spiritual consolation, the sweeter and purer, at length, will the enjoyment of it prove. Let his patience, then, be the patience of hope. It is hope that gives life and vigor to patience. He must not suffer his exercise of patience to be interrupted either by fretting himself, or by turning for comfort to any creature. He should not fret himself in any way, but should, with humbleness and calmness, resolve to wait for God's time and to bear His frown (Micah 7:9), in humble expectation that He will at length return and visit him with the light of His countenance and the joy of His salvation.

13. It is also requisite, in order to recover true comfort, that a holy man be constantly on his guard against yielding to any motion of sin in his heart, and that he be pressing on toward more holiness of heart and of life. He must, in dependence on the promise of sanctification, always take heed that he does not yield to any secret motion of sin in his heart. If he would have his conscience pacified and peaceful, he must strive to keep it pure. Sin, like Achan in the camp or Jonah in the ship, is that which causes trouble. If the disconsolate believer allows himself, for a season, to yield to any motion of sin, or temptation of Satan or the world, he cannot be at ease or comfortable in his mind. Although a traveler was sure that he was to safely reach the place to which he was going, yet if he traveled with a thorn in his foot he could not but be sensible of pain at every step.

If the Christian suffers himself to connive, especially at that in himself which he knows to be wrong, he cannot but be disquieted. Uprightness and singleness of heart are necessary to recover lost comfort. God has made an eternal separation between continuance in the love and practice of any sin and holy tranquility of mind. Let therefore the afflicted believer, in the faith that Christ will strengthen him, maintain a resolute and continual struggle against the first risings, the secret motions of depravity in his heart. It is as natural for sin indulged to raise and increase doubt and fears in his mind as for rotten wood to breed worms. Every instance of his yielding to a motion of sin will be like a blot upon his evidences for heaven. Let him, then, in all his conflicts with the risings of sin, diligently study both to discover and mortify the corruption of his nature; both to sigh under the burden and to act against the power of the sin that dwells in him. It should always be his manner to attack and mortify sin in its first risings; for as that which usually destroys his peace of conscience is his indulging of corrupt desires, so his constant endeavor, through grace, to resist and quell them before they have time to acquire strength is a sure means of recovering spiritual comfort.

He should also endeavor daily to attain more and more holiness of heart and life. True holiness consists of loving the Lord our God supremely, of delighting in Him as manifested in Jesus Christ, and of studying habitually to serve Him with gladness (Psalm 100:2) as well as with abhorrence of all iniquity. Spiritual comfort, accordingly, is a part of holiness. The more a believer advances in universal holiness, the more of the principle and habit of pure consolation he possesses; and the more of the principle and habit of this holy comfort he attains, the more of the enjoyment of it shall he have in every time of need.

The disconsolate Christian, then, to the end that he may recover sensible comfort, should, by faith, receive out of the fullness of Christ greater measures of sanctifying grace that he may not only die daily to sin, but live to righteousness. He ought, from principles of faith and love, and for the glory of his redeeming God, to become more and more diligent in all the duties of holiness. This, though it shall not merit consolation for him, yet will, in his experience, be connected with consolation; yea, it will itself be a comfort to him. "Our rejoicing is this," said the Apostle, "the testimony of our conscience, that in simplicity and godly sincerity, not with fleshly wisdom, but by the grace of God, we have had our conversation in the world" (2 Corinthians 1:12). To be advancing sensibly in conformity to the Lord Jesus, and in holy activity for His glory, cannot fail to be very pleasing and encouraging to a holy man. Although the beginning of comfort in the soul is necessary to the practice of true holiness, yet the practice of holiness is requisite to the increase of comfort, and to the recovering of it after it has, in any measure, been lost (Isaiah 32:17; John 14:21; Galatians 6:16).

Let it, then, be the ardent desire of the believer's soul, and the settled purpose of his heart, to advance daily in the love and practice of universal holiness. Let perfection of holiness be the ruling wish of his heart and the great purpose of his life to which he uniformly directs all his efforts. Let his will be always in union with the will of Christ and the glory of God, and then Christ "will give him the desires of his heart" (Psalm 37:4). Then he shall know by experience that a supreme regard to the will and glory of God is the health and happiness of the soul.

14. As a means of attaining the spiritual comfort which he desires, the Christian, if he is capable, must perform diligently the duties of his lawful calling. Though this forms a part of the holiness mentioned in the particular immediately preceding, yet the special importance of it as a means of comfort requires that it be considered by itself. Let the disconsolate believer take care that he regard idleness as a continued omission of the duty required in the eighth commandment of the moral law, and that he abhor it as a continued crime, and as a reproach to his holy profession (1 Timothy 5:8). To be idle, even for a single day, without real and evident necessity, is dangerous to any Christian, but especially to a Christian in trouble of conscience. It is tempting Satan to come and find employment for him; and it is leaving himself at leisure to weigh one after another the temptations of that subtle and malicious enemy. A heathen philosopher termed idleness "the grace of a living man," and a holy minister of the gospel called it "the hell of a living Christian."

Let the disquieted Christian, then, be constantly upon his guard against idleness, and especially against a disposition to be idle. Let his heart as well as his hands be exercised in a voluntary and diligent performance of the various duties of some honest and useful vocation. Otherwise, his heart will work out of itself a still greater degree of trouble to him. Idleness feeds and increases the distemper of a troubled soul, whereas lawful employment occupies the mind and takes it off from poring incessantly upon the causes and aggravations of the trouble. When Elijah the prophet was in depression of mind, the Lord would not suffer him to sit still in any place. When he sat down under a juniper tree, "an

angel touched him, and commanded him to arise
and eat." When he again lay down, the angel of the
Lord, a second time, roused him to action. When he
went to a cave at Horeb to lodge there, "the word of
the Lord came to him, and said, 'What dost thou
here, Elijah? Go forth, and stand upon the mount
before the Lord.' " Soon afterwards, when he was
standing in the entrance to the cave, the Lord again
disturbed his repose and said to him, "Go, return on
the way to the wilderness of Damascus" (1 Kings
19:4–16). If it is a Christian's duty, even when he is
under the disease of melancholy, to be diligent in
business, it is no less his duty when he is troubled in
soul, merely on a spiritual account. He must not
therefore say, either that he is disinclined to work or
that his trouble is so great that he is unable to work,
until he first is well satisfied from the Oracles of
Truth that such excuses will be sustained at the tribunal of Christ, the omniscient and righteous Judge
of the world. The holy Comforter has, in wonderful
condescension, visited with the joy of His salvation
many thousands of His saints, at the very times in
which, from regard to His authority, they have been
employed in the business of their various callings.

15. *If he has reason to apprehend that he is, in any degree,
under melancholy, which, as has been observed above, is a
bodily disease, he should frequently entrust his imagination to
the blessed Redeemer, that sovereign Physician of soul and
body, in the hope that He will cure the distemper of it.* So
long as the imagination continues weak and disordered, it will present to the understanding even the
most encouraging and amiable objects in a distorted, discouraging, and unnamable form. And so

long as that is the case, trouble of mind or sadness of spirit, must, in a greater or lesser degree, continue. The melancholy Christian, therefore, should not only trust in the compassionate Savior for consolation to his troubled soul, but he should, in the use of other appointed means, trust that, so far as it can subserve the glory of God in his salvation, Jesus will deliver him from the distemper of his natural spirits. He ought to trust in the great Redeemer for the health of his body, which is the temple of the Holy Spirit (1 Corinthians 6:19), as well as for the happiness of his soul, in order that both soul and body may be prepared to serve the Lord with gladness. He is fully warranted to rely with firm confidence on the Lord Jesus for all that is necessary to enable him to glorify God in his body and in his spirit, which are God's (1 Corinthians 6:20).

16. *To disclose the condition of his soul to some experienced and judicious minister or private Christian is also a means of recovering tranquility of mind which the disconsolate believer should not fail to employ.* He ought, if possible, to select for this purpose some holy and humble minister, or private Christian, who had himself been in trouble of mind, but has mercifully been delivered from it, and who appears now to be confirmed in faith, and to be filled with joy and peace in believing. He should, without delay, reveal the condition of his soul to such a one. He ought to reveal to him, as fully and distinctly as he can, what it is that more immediately troubles and depresses his mind; what it is that makes him conclude himself to be yet unregenerate, and his former experience to have been but counterfeit; what the grounds of his present

doubts and fears are, and especially why he cannot trust in the infinitely compassionate Savior for his own salvation in particular. He should, if he can with prudence, hint to such a one the sin or sins which he apprehends have provoked the Lord to plead this controversy with him in order that he may afford him an opportunity of speaking pertinently to his condition (James 5:16). "When I kept silence," said David, "my bones waxed old, through my roaring all the day long" (Psalm 32:3). It is as if he had said, "The sin which I did not freely and ingenuously confess to the Lord, and also to persons skillful in assuaging trouble of mind, rankled inwardly, and occasioned unspeakable anguish in my soul." The affliction of the soul, as well as that of the body, should be made known to such a fellow Christian as appears qualified to suggest suitable advice and encouragements, to the end that these may be afforded seasonably as means of relief.

When the Holy Spirit comforts a dejected saint, He does it usually by the instrumentality of some other saint. If the disconsolate believer is providentially favored with an opportunity to open the case of his soul to another believer, the holy Comforter will very seldom in an immediate manner bring him his peace. Rather, he usually "creates the fruit of the lips, peace" (Isaiah 57:19). That is, he will comfort him by means of the presence and the speech of those whom He has comforted, and so qualified to be instruments of consolation to him (2 Corinthians 1:6). Faithful ministers of the gospel, especially, are helpers of the Christian's joy. But how can they be helpful to it, in the case of a disquieted Christian,

who stands most in need of their help, if he does
not afford them an opportunity? How can they
answer objections, resolve doubts, or loose, as one
expresses it, the knots of conscience, if these are not
proposed to them?

Moreover, the disconsolate believer should not
forget to request the fervent prayers not only of him
to whom he has disclosed the condition of his soul,
but of other Christians with whom he is acquainted.
Some have observed that those believers, in former
times, who were the most accustomed to request the
aid of each other's prayers were commonly the most
flourishing Christians, and that those who neglected this part of their duty were usually the most
languishing and hesitating. If "the effectual fervent
prayer" even of one "righteous man availeth much"
(James 5:16), how much more will the prayers of
many such avail (Acts 12:12)!

*17. Finally, if he would attain pure consolation, he must
not expect it from the means which it is his duty to employ.*
Let him use diligently all the means of divine appointment, and especially those explained above.
But let him take heed that he does not trust in them,
nor in his using them, for the smallest degree of
comfort. He ought to use them as diligently as if he
were to merit by his action not merely spiritual consolation, but even eternal life; and at the same time
he should trust as little in them, and in his use of
them, as if he had never known nor used so much as
one of them. His employing them is a duty which he
is bound to regard in point of performance, and to
renounce in point of dependence. He is, in his constant use of them, to rely for consolation only upon

the Lord Jesus, and upon God in Him, as the God of all comfort (Psalm 62:5). If he would recover a peaceful serenity of mind, he must renounce all confidence in his use of means, and expect consolation only from his God and Savior, saying, "Asshur shall not save me; neither will I say any more to the work of my hands, 'Ye are my gods.' What have I to do any more with idols?" (Hosea 14:3, 8).

He may expect all necessary comfort *in* his diligent use of the means, but no comfort *from* it. He must not presume to think that his utmost diligence in employing them will give him either a meritorious or contractual title to holy consolation. Spiritual comfort is a free gift, a gift of grace; and all the appointed means of attaining it are means of grace. There is, indeed, a tendency in those means to comfort the disquieted believer who diligently uses them. It is not, however, any virtue in them, nor in his use of them, but it is the power of the Holy Spirit accompanying them that imparts all the comfort. He ought not, therefore, as Christians in spiritual trouble too often do, to promise himself relief by such and such a duty at this or that time or place; for if his expectation is not answered (and it would indeed be a wonder if it should), he will be ready to conclude that the promise of God failed, and that the disappointment, especially if repeated, is a sure indication that the Lord has cast him off forever. This, instead of bringing peace of comfort to his troubled soul, will contribute greatly to plunge it into still deeper perplexity, and to enchain it the faster under perturbation and terror.

Thus, I have endeavored to point out the means

which the disconsolate believer should chiefly employ in order to regain his spiritual comfort. If he perseveres in the diligent use of them, and in complying with the advice concerning them given in this chapter, he shall, through grace, as soon as it will serve the glory of his God and Savior and the sanctification of his own soul, recover holy consolation. He perhaps may never, while he remains in this valley of tears, experience rapturous joy; but he shall, by the grace of the Lord Jesus, recover solid tranquility and sweet satisfaction of mind. "In hope of eternal life, which God, who cannot lie, promised before the world began" (Titus 1:2), his soul, by the consoling influences of the holy Comforter, shall enjoy a calm and pleasing resignation, in all things, to the holy will of his redeeming God.

Objections Answered

From the foregoing particulars, it appears clearly that disconsolate saints have no allowance from the Lord Jesus to refuse to be comforted, or to harden themselves in sorrow. The holier any of the saints are, they are, when under desertion, usually the more troubled. The more they love their God and Savior, the more it troubles them to lack the light of His gracious countenance; the more are they afraid lest they sin, and the more are they troubled because they have sinned; the more are they disquieted by a sense of His paternal displeasure, and the more are they overwhelmed by the dread of His avenging wrath. Still, however, they must not yield to despondency nor harden themselves in sorrow (Job 6:10).

On the contrary, they should exert themselves in using the means of attaining holy tranquility of mind.
To persist obstinately in refusing to be comforted
will provoke the Lord to proceed in the controversy,
and to sink their souls still deeper in the waters of
trouble.

Ought the believer, when he is troubled in mind,
diligently to search out the particular sin or sins
which have provoked his heavenly Father to hide
His face from him? Let him not hence conclude
that he will, in that condition, succeed in searching
for his graces or evidences of personal interest in
Christ. While he is walking in the darkness of spiritual trouble, it will be to little purpose for him to
spend his time in searching for evidences of his being in a state of grace; for during that time they are
wrapped up in darkness and cannot be discerned.
He may sooner expect to see his face in troubled waters than to see his evidences for heaven when his
soul is troubled and covered with darkness. The only
thing which he can, at that time, do to good purpose is to entrust the salvation of his soul to Jesus
Christ, and to trust and plead absolute promises.
Times of desertion and temptation are rather seasons for mourning, and trusting and seeking the
Lord, than for judging the state of the soul. To
search at such times for remaining corruptions in
the heart is one of the means of recovering spiritual
comfort; but to try to find evidences of grace in it
when they are veiled with darkness is the way to sink
deeper into the waters of trouble.

Is trusting in Christ the principal means of recovering spiritual consolation? Let the disconsolate

Christian, then, be exhorted and entreated to trust in Him. Oh, let him endeavor to come anew, to come without delay, to come as a sinner, to come with all his burdens, all his griefs, all his fears, and cordially to trust that the infinitely compassionate Savior will save and comfort him. Resisting every unbelieving thought, and every suggestion that would disquiet his soul, let him trust in the mercy of the Lord Jesus and not be afraid. Let him come as he is, and place the confidence of his heart in the dear Redeemer for all the salvation and all the consolation which are presented to him in the offers and promises of the gospel. Let him trust with firm confidence in the Savior for the salvation for himself in particular—not only because it is necessary for his comfort to do so, but because it is his duty, his first, his main duty. Oh, if he could but be persuaded to rely with assured confidence on the Lord Jesus, peace and joy would soon be restored to his troubled soul! He would find the exercise of trusting in Christ to be most profitable to himself, and most pleasing to God. O Christian, trust resolutely in the blessed Redeemer, and persist in trusting till comfort comes. Apply promises and take the comfort of them. Suck and be satisfied with those breasts of consolation.

OBJECTION. But some dejected Christian will say, "I see no right that I have to trust in Christ for my salvation, and therefore it would be presumption in me so much as to attempt it."

ANSWER. You conclude, it would appear, that you have no right to trust in Him because you can at present see no good qualifications in yourself to give you a right. But you were informed above that your right to trust in Christ for salvation is not founded upon any good quality in yourself, but upon the offer, the call, the commandment to believe on His name, and the promise, all directed in the gospel to you as a sinner of mankind. These afford you an ample, perfect, and sufficient warrant to believe in Him; and nothing in yourself can render that warrant more complete than it already is. It is nothing within you, but it is those things in the gospel without you that give you all the right that you need to trust anew in Jesus. To say, then, that you have no right to entrust your salvation to Him, or that it would be presumption in you to trust Him, is direct unbelief. Whether you believe it or not, you have in the gospel a full, an unchangeable right to trust as a lost sinner in the almighty Savior, for all your salvation. And nothing which is good in yourself can afford you the smallest right; for all that is good in you is either *in* faith or consequent *on* faith, but nothing of it can be previous to faith.

OBJECTION. Another, perhaps, is ready to say, "I cannot trust in Christ, for I know not if I am elected to salvation."

ANSWER. You cannot know that you have been elected till after you have trusted in Him. Your election to salvation forms no part of your revealed warrant to trust in Jesus for salvation. Your warrant is that which was mentioned above. Your ignorance, then, of your election cannot lessen that warrant, and your knowledge of your election cannot add to it. The offers and invitations of the gospel are not directed to men as elect sinners, but as sinners of mankind. Although, therefore, you do not know that you are an elect sinner, yet, since you know that you are a sinner of Adam's race, the offers and calls are addressed to you. And they afford you an authentic right to place the confidence of your heart in Christ for all the blessings of salvation. As you cannot know that you are elect before you venture to trust in Christ, so neither can you know that you are not elect. Your present duty, therefore, is to approach and, upon the ample warrant afforded you in the gospel, to trust firmly in the Lord Jesus for all salvation to yourself in particular. So shall you, by believing and walking in Him, know your election of God. You can never know that God has ordained you to eternal life otherwise than by knowing experimentally that He has ordained you to believe (John 6:37). You are bound to believe before you know your particular election, and in order to know it, and also because it is the will of God that you should believe.

OBJECTION. A third is ready to object thus: "I am afraid that I have no personal interest in Christ and His salvation."

ANSWER. If you cannot perceive that the Lord Jesus has already given you a saving interest in Himself, trust, as you were directed above, that He now saves you, or, in other words, that He now gives you a personal interest in His salvation. Trust that He gives you an interest in order to see and feel that He has given it. The more ignorant you are of your interest in the Savior, the more need you have to trust that He grants you a saving interest in Himself. You must not excuse yourself from trusting for it because you do not see and feel that you have it; but

you ought to trust for it in order to see and feel that
you possess it. Instead, then, of saying, "I dare not
confide in Jesus for salvation because I fear that I
have no interest in salvation," you should, on the
contrary, say, "Because I have a revealed warrant to
do it, I will cordially trust that He gives me salvation,
and that He will in due time favor me with a sense of
my personal interest in it." You must not seek to feel
in order to believe, but you are to believe in order to
feel (Ephesians 1:13).

OBJECTION. Another, perhaps, will be reasoning thus: "All who believe in Christ rely upon the
promises; but no promise so comes to me as to be
impressed with power on my mind. Promises are not
given me, and therefore it would be presumption in
me to apply them and rest upon them."

ANSWER. You seem to think that a powerful impression of some promise on a man's mind is the
ground of his right to take and to trust that promise,
and that, because you experience no such impression of any promise, you have no right to apply any.
But this would be to build your faith upon your feeling of the promises, or to make the sensible impression of them upon your mind your ground of right
to apply and trust them. A powerful impression of a
promise made by the Holy Spirit upon your mind
and memory in time of need is indeed an encouragement to you to apply and trust that promise; but
it forms no part of your warrant to do so. It is the offer of all the promises in and with Christ to you, and
the call and command to accept that offer, that afford you a right to trust in Him, and to apply and
trust all the promises in Him. The inward impres-

sion cannot add to, and the want of it cannot lessen, your warrant. Your duty, then, is to apply and trust the promises not as powerfully suggested to or impressed on your mind, but as offered or directed to you in the gospel. One reason, perhaps, for your not being favored with comfortable impressions of promises is your not having trusted in the holy Comforter for such impressions, and your not having honored the promises themselves by trusting them upon the divine warrant which lies in the Word outside you. Know then that, in order to receive holy consolation, you must study to trust divine promises not upon the ground of their being impressed, but upon that of their being offered to you.

OBJECTION. Some other disconsolate soul may be saying, "Alas, I have a dead, hard, and deceitful heart, which greatly discourages me from trusting that the Holy One of God will ever visit me with His salvation. How can I hope that He will save and comfort such an uncommon sinner as I am?"

ANSWER. "This is a faithful saying, and worthy of all acceptation, that Christ Jesus came into the world to save sinners; of whom," says our Apostle, "I am chief" (1 Timothy 1:15). Now you should accept or believe that faithful saying with application to yourself, and say, "It is indeed true that I am an uncommon sinner, yea, the very chief of sinners; but it is equally true that Christ Jesus came into the world to save such sinners, and why not to save me? My heart, alas, is very dead, hard, and deceitful; but the deeper the depravity of it is, the more will the power and grace of Christ be glorified in saving me from that depravity. I will therefore venture to trust that

He will glorify the exceeding riches of His grace in saving me from all the sin that dwells in me, and from all the iniquity that has been committed by me."

It is your duty to humble and loathe yourself much for the evils of your heart and your life; but it is your sin to let them discourage you in the least from attempting any one of your duties. You ought, indeed, to be humbled for them in the greatest degree; but you must not be deterred by them even in the smallest degree from your duty, especially from the first and great duty of believing in Jesus Christ. If you are, in your own sight, the chief of sinners, even this must not discourage you from the chief, the first, of all duties. The deeper your sense of the plague of your heart is, this should, instead of discouraging you, excite you the more to perform diligently the duty of trusting in Christ, especially for sanctification.

OBJECTION. One may be saying, "Why should I be exhorted to trust in Christ? I have times without number been guilty of backsliding, both in my heart and in my life. I have frequently resolved to be more circumspect and diligent in the spiritual performance of every duty, but I have, upon the very slightest temptation, acted contrary to my resolutions by relapsing once and again into the same sin."

ANSWER. You have, indeed, much reason to exercise godly sorrow and self-abhorrence, but no reason to be so dismayed as to cease trusting in the Savior, or to be so dejected as to refuse to be comforted. You have much need to exercise repentance, but as much need to exercise that reliance on Christ from which true repentance flows. And it is as great a sin to suffer your backsliding to deter you from the latter as from the former. No past sin, however aggravated, must be pled in excuse for omitting a present duty. The Lord has graciously promised to keep you from total and final backsliding, but nowhere, as far as I know, to secure you against partial backsliding or relapsing in the hour of temptation into the same sins of infirmity of which you have formerly repented. Abraham was suffered again and again to dissemble; Lot to be twice overcome with wine; John to be twice guilty of worshipping the angel; and Jehoshaphat to join affinity with Ahab, and afterwards to join himself with Ahaziah king of Israel who did very wickedly.

It is not indeed usual with God to leave His dear children to relapse often into enormous transgressions, but He suffers them, for their humiliation, to relapse into sins of infirmity. Though your backsliding, then, should humble you to the dust, yet it should not for a moment discourage you from the great duty of trusting in Jesus Christ. Hearken to these gracious, cheering invitations: " 'Return, thou backsliding Israel,' saith the Lord, 'and I will not cause Mine anger to fall upon you' "; "Return, ye backsliding children, and I will heal your backslidings" (Jeremiah 3:12, 22). Apply, trust, and plead these consoling promises: "I will heal their backsliding, I will love them freely" (Hosea 14:4). "I will seek that which was lost, and bring again that which was driven away, and will bind up that which was broken, and will strengthen that which was sick" (Ezekiel 34:16).

OBJECTION. Another may say, "How can my heart, which frequently revolts from God, be upright before Him? How can that heart be sound which is often sore? I have bewailed my sin and resolved against it, but no sooner am I tempted to it than, alas, I often fall before the temptation! Indeed, I have much reason to dread that I shall one day perish by the hands of sin and Satan."

ANSWER. Your bewailing and striving against your sin are a good evidence that, though sin sometimes prevails against you, yet it does not reign in you; that though it rebels, yet it does not rule. It is a willing obedience to the commands of the body of sin which evidences the soul to be under the dominion of sin. You shall never perish by the hands of sin and Satan until God first forsakes you totally and finally. But He has graciously promised that He "will never leave you, nor forsake you" (Hebrews 13:5). The sheep of Christ hear His voice and follow Him, as you desire and endeavor to do. Now hear what He promises concerning them: "I give unto them eternal life, and they shall never perish, neither shall any pluck them out of My hand. My Father, which gave them Me, is greater than all; and none is able to pluck them out of My Father's hand" (John 10:28–29). "The God of peace will bruise Satan under your feet shortly" (Romans 16:20). "Surely He shall deliver thee from the snare of the fowler" (Psalm 91:3). The more your spiritual enemies are threatening to destroy you, the more should you apply and trust those promises of salvation. The more frequently it is suggested to you that iniquity will be your ruin, you ought to take occasion the more frequently, and the more resolutely, to trust that your almighty Redeemer will come and save you; that "He will deliver you from every evil work, and will preserve you to His heavenly kingdom" (2 Timothy 4:18).

OBJECTION. Some discouraged soul will say, "How can I venture to trust that the holy Jesus will perform the part of Savior to me when I know that my iniquities against Him are innumerable and aggravated in an uncommon degree?"

ANSWER. For that very reason you ought to be the more disposed and determined to trust in Him for salvation from them. You must permit me to inform you that so far as your desire for salvation from the love and practice of iniquity is sincere, you resolve to rely upon Him for that salvation. Without this resolution, it will be impossible for you to evidence to your conscience the sincerity either of your complaints of sin or of your desires for salvation from it. In proportion as you do not fully resolve and endeavor to trust in the Lord Jesus for salvation from your sins, you love them; and your complaining of the number and greatness of them is hypocritical. Besides, your taking occasion from your innumerable and great transgressions to say, "I dare not trust in the holy Jesus for salvation," shows that you are wishing for some good thing, either in your heart or your life, to entitle you to trust in Him. This evidences the dreadful prevalence of a self-righteous spirit as well as of unbelief in you. You should consider that the salvation of Jesus Christ is infinitely free, and that the more numerous and the more heinous your sins are, the more need you have of Him and of His salvation, and therefore the greater need to believe in Him.

If you could suppose that the omnipotent Savior never yet performed such a great work as the saving of a sinner from sins so innumerable and so great as yours are, even this could be no just obstacle to your trusting in Him because the depth of His immense love has never yet been sounded (Ephesians 3:18–19), and the greatness of His ability to save has never yet been searched out. He has never yet done the utmost that He can do.

Suppose the mountain of your innumerable sins were so high as, with its height, to reach not only the clouds, but the throne of the Eternal Himself; suppose that another, and another, and ten thousands of them were piled up, and the whole cast into the abyss of redeeming love and redeeming blood: the waters of that bottomless, boundless ocean would still be as high above them as the heaven is high above the earth (Psalm 103:11).

OBJECTION. Another, perhaps, is saying, "I do not doubt the ability, but the willingness of Christ to save me from my great transgressions."

ANSWER. If you believe His ability, in the same degree you believe His willingness; for what is His willingness to save sinners but His moral ability? To doubt His willingness, then, is to question His ability. Why does He offer Himself to you? Why does He invite, beseech, and even command you to accept and trust in Him for your salvation? And why does He say in His promises to you, "I will," but because He is willing to save you? Would He ever have made it your duty to believe in Him for salvation, or would He ever have said to you, "He that believeth not shall be damned," if He had not been willing to give you salvation? Would He ever have said, "Him that cometh to Me, I will in no wise cast out," or have complained that sinners would not come to Him that they might have life, if He had been unwilling to receive and save them? Indeed, to disbelieve His willingness is to make Him a liar. To say that He is not willing to save you is to blaspheme the kindness of His redeeming love and the riches of His glorious grace.

If you think that He is willing to save other sinners, but not to save you, know that this is one of Satan's whispers entertained by your evil heart of unbelief, and that it is not more injurious to the infinitely gracious Redeemer to doubt His existence than to doubt His willingness to save a lost sinner who desires to trust in Him. Oh, believe with application to yourself His infinite willingness. Trust not only that He is willing to save you, but that He *will* save you. And say, with the holy Psalmist, "Though I walk in the midst of trouble, Thou wilt revive me . . . and Thy right hand shall save me" (Psalm 138:7).

OBJECTION. Some other desponding Christian may say, "Alas, it is in vain to urge me to believe in Jesus, for I fear that I have committed the sin against the Holy Spirit which will never be forgiven!"

ANSWER. That horrible sin appears, from various passages of Scripture compared, to include: first, a willful, malicious, and avowed rejecting of the Savior, and of salvation by Him, and that after a manifest conviction of the truth of the gospel; next, an avowed and obstinate opposing of the doctrines of the gospel; and, last, an obstinate and spiteful

scoffing at the religion of Jesus Christ and the pro-
fessors of it, attended sometimes with a rancorous
persecution of them. And all these are consequences of a total and final apostasy from the profession of Christianity.

The man who is guilty of that dreadful sin is not
merely an apostate, but a blaspheming apostate. And
so horrible is his enmity against Christ, and the way
of salvation by Him, that he chooses rather to risk
eternal damnation than to be indebted to Him for
mercy. Now you may be assured that you have not
been guilty of this most atrocious sin, if none but
you complains of it; if you are desirous of complete
salvation by Jesus Christ; if you are content to be an
eternal debtor to His redeeming grace; if you are
afraid that you have been guilty of it; if you are in the
smallest degree grieved and troubled for the unbelief of your heart, if you are grieved and ashamed
that so much sin is in your heart and your life; and if
you wish that the glory of sovereign and redeeming
grace may be illustriously displayed in your salvation.

OBJECTION. One, perhaps, is disposed to say, "I
am not humbled, or at least not humbled enough,
for my sins, and therefore I dare not place confidence in Christ for His salvation."

ANSWER. You ought to know that true humiliation is either a concomitant or a consequent of saving faith, but is not a ground of it. It gives a man no
right to trust in Christ, no title to the divine acceptance, either of his person or his performances. It is,
indeed, in the hand of the Spirit, a means of rendering a man willing to trust in the Lord Jesus; and the

more of it he attains, he is the more willing. But it affords him no degree of warrant to trust in Him, nor is it requisite that it should. For by the offers and calls of the gospel he already is fully warranted, so well warranted that nothing in him can either diminish or increase his warrant.

When you then say that you dare not trust in the Redeemer because you are not sufficiently humbled, you thereby show that you are under the prevalence both of unbelief and a legal spirit: of unbelief, for you do not seem to believe that by the offers, calls and commands of God you are sufficiently warranted to rely on Christ, but that something more is requisite to afford you a sufficient warrant; of a legal spirit, for you regard humiliation as that which must confer upon you a right to trust in Him, since, for want of it in a sufficient degree, you dare not entrust your salvation to Him. But be assured that you cannot recover holy consolation till you come as you are, and place direct confidence in Jesus Christ for all your salvation; and that you cannot have more evangelical humiliation till you first trust in Christ for it, and so receive it by faith out of His fullness. The more of this humiliation you attain, the more willing will you be to come as a sinner to the Savior; but you cannot attain an increase of it before you trust in Him for it as a part of your salvation.

OBJECTION. Another may reason thus: "I am not sufficiently troubled for the heinous transgressions of which I have been guilty; and therefore I dare not trust in the Holy One of God for salvation from them."

ANSWER. But are you not already so troubled in

mind as to long for comfort? Are you not disquieted because you apprehend that you are not troubled enough for your sins? Are not your transgressions a real source of trouble to you? But what think you of that trouble for sin which keeps you from trusting in the only Savior, which weakens your heart and injures your health, which renders all your outward comforts unsavory to you, and which disqualifies you for the acceptable performance of your religious and moral duties? Is such trouble as that desirable to you? Is it not sinful? And do not you, by wishing for more of it, increase the number of your sins and provoke the Lord to proceed in His controversy with you? Indeed, that distress of mind, even for sin itself, which keeps you from coming to Christ is more sinful than it is possible for you to conceive. And it must be repented of before you can experience pure consolation. That uneasiness of soul for sin which indisposes a man to place confidence in Christ for salvation from sin is undoubtedly hypocritical and sinful. When a man is troubled for his other offenses, but not for his greatest sin, the sin of refusing to trust in the blessed Savior for salvation, he may assure himself that such trouble is not of the right kind. Genuine trouble of mind for sin presses a man forward to Jesus Christ; and it is accompanied with frequent attempts to trust in Him for pardon and sanctification (Hosea 6:1–3 and 14:1–3; Jeremiah 31:18–20).

OBJECTION. Someone will say, "But I am so very unworthy of Christ and His great salvation that I fear He will not receive me or admit me to share in that salvation."

ANSWER. Indeed, you are very unworthy, infinitely more unworthy than any man or angel will ever be able to conceive. You are not only far, but infinitely far from being able to deserve Christ and His great salvation. But it seems as if you wish that you could deserve salvation, or, at least, that you could merit the Savior Himself; or, if not salvation or the Savior, that you could but merit the good will of the Savior, and could so recommend yourself to His favor as freely to claim and trust in Him. But do you not hereby, in effect, declare that you are under the prevalence of strong unbelief; that you do not believe that salvation is altogether free, or that eternal life is the gift of God, through Jesus Christ our Lord. You seem at present not to believe that salvation is an infinitely free gift; that it is so free as not to admit the sinner's offering the smallest price for it (Isaiah 55:1–2); and that it is so great as to be infinitely above the highest price that he can ever afford to offer. And do not you likewise show that you are under the prevalence of a legal spirit when you are averse to trusting in Christ, because you are not worthy of Him, or because you cannot recommend yourself to His favor? Are not you thereby leaning to the covenant of works? Do you think it possible that Christ, the inestimable gift of God, can be purchased with the money of your merits, or that you can procure a title to that salvation which is wholly of sovereign grace?

Suppose you offered but a single good thought for it. Would not even that mar the freeness of it, and obscure the glory of immensely rich grace in the gift of it? Ah! Why do you try to find a cause in yourself why the Lord Jesus should save you? Why do you seek to make merit the object of redeeming grace and mercy? You are invited to take the water of life freely. Why, then, are you discouraged because you have nothing to pay for it? Why do you think it hard that you are not allowed to put something of your own into the scale with the consummate righteousness of Jesus Christ to make it full weight?

OBJECTION. Another disconsolate soul is saying, "I cannot trust in Jesus for my salvation. I have no ability to believe in Him."

ANSWER. That is a common objection, but it amounts just to this: a complaint that, however much Christ has done for you, He has not yet advanced you to a state of independence from Himself, nor set you free from your incapacity of doing anything without Him. But why should this be a ground of complaint? He knows that you cannot, by any power of your own, believe or so much as think one good thought; and yet He commands you to believe on Him. But He nowhere commands you to do it in your own strength. He enjoins you to "take hold of His strength" (Isaiah 27:5), and to "be strong in the grace that is in Him" (2 Timothy 2:1). Instead, then, of excusing yourself from trusting in the great Redeemer because you cannot do it by any strength of your own, you ought on the contrary to say, "I can do that, and all things else, through Christ which strengtheneth me" (Philippians 4:13).

Although you are not able to trust cordially in Him by your own power, yet it is your duty so to trust in Him, and your sin not to do it. You should therefore attempt it frequently, looking to Him for grace to enable you. Indeed, to say "I *cannot* trust in Him" is almost the same as to say, "I *will* not! I will trust in man who can lie, but not in God the Savior who cannot lie." Ah, what a heinous sin is this! You thereby presume to lay the blame of your unbelief upon the holy Lord God. But your impotence is voluntary, and so is wholly your own sin. Your inability consists not so much in a mere want of executive power as in the want of a willing mind. Oh, do not imagine that such inability will in the least excuse you. Inability to discharge a just debt does not excuse a debtor. Though you do not feel that Christ strengthens you for believing or other spiritual exercises, yet your duty is to trust that He strengthens you for them. Your not feeling the habit of faith in you will never excuse you from attempting the exercise of faith. Although you cannot cordially believe in Christ until the Holy Spirit works faith in you, yet you should try so to believe in Him before you feel the Spirit working it in you.

OBJECTION. To conclude, a Christian, under extreme dejection of spirit, will be ready even to say, "In my present doleful condition, I find myself neither able nor willing to trust in Jesus for salvation."

ANSWER. What? Are you not willing to trust in Him? Not willing to be saved and comforted by Him? Not willing to afford Him an opportunity of showing in your salvation the exceeding riches of His grace? He, with all His salvation, and with all the joy of that salvation, is freely and particularly offered to you (John 3:16 and 6:32; Revelation 22:17); and you are still unwilling to trust in Him? The truth is, you are in some degree either willing to trust Him and His promises of salvation, or willing to quit, henceforth, all right to Him, all interest in Him, and to forego all expectation from Him. Are you then willing to bid an eternal adieu to the only Savior, and, in testimony of your doing so, to transcribe and sign this declaration: "I do hereby, in the presence of God, the Judge of all, declare that I henceforth renounce, and that forever, all my part in the Savior and in His salvation, and that, for the future, I will never allow myself to hope in Him either for salvation or consolation"?

Are you indeed willing to subscribe this renunciation? If you are not, you bear false witness against yourself when you say that you are not willing to trust in Christ Jesus for salvation; for you are either willing in some degree to trust Him, or willing to renounce Him.* Is your heart indeed willing to be

---

* I am aware that even an unregenerate man will refuse, in a deliberate and formal manner, to renounce forever his claim to the Savior, and yet continue far from being willing truly to believe in Him for all his salvation. But there is a great difference between the refusal of the careless sinner so to renounce Christ and that of the disconsolate saint. The reason why the secure sinner will refuse to abandon forever his claim to the only Savior is merely his fear of eternal torment, whereas the reason why the disquieted saint will tremble at the thought of renouncing his part in Him is not so much his dread of eternal torment as of being forever separated from the blessed God, and forever deprived of holy conformity to Him. The unwillingness of the disconsolate Christian to renounce forever his part in the great Redeemer arises from a principle of grace in his heart; and it implies a proportional degree of willingness to trust in Him for all the parts of his salvation, though the Christian is not able under trouble of mind to discern this will-

forever separated from the Lord Jesus? Or is it matter of indifference to you whether He saves you with an everlasting salvation or punishes you with everlasting destruction? No, it cannot be!

---

ingness of himself. The unregenerate sinner may, indeed, be willing to trust in the Lord Jesus for preservation from hell; but he cannot, so long as he continues unregenerate, be cordially willing to rely upon Him for salvation from all sin. And therefore let him not flatter himself that he is, in the smallest degree, willing to exercise true faith.

8

The Means which Believers Ought to Employ in Order to Attain Increasing Comfort

It frequently happens not only in the experience of young converts, but also in that of advanced believers, newly delivered from mental trouble (especially if their preceding distress and sorrow were very deep), that the joy which succeeds these is lively and almost rapturous. We are not, however, to imagine that they are all equally joyful, or that the joy which any of them feels will always continue. It will rather subside and settle into a peaceful serenity or a pleasing tranquility of mind. They, indeed, go out usually with joy; but afterwards they will be led forth with peace. And though their joy is no longer ecstatic as before, yet it becomes more pure and spiritual, or rather subsides into a peaceful and refreshing tranquility of soul. This peace or serenity of mind, as was observed above, is indeed the lowest degree of spiritual consolation, yet still it is real and solid comfort. And although it is the office of the Holy Spirit, the Comforter, to maintain and increase it in the souls of believers, and in every time of need to elevate it to joy, or even to triumph, yet it is ordinarily in their diligent use of appointed means that He affords them the influences of consolation requisite for these purposes. If, therefore, the man who believes and experiences holy consolation would retain this comfort, and rise to higher degrees of it, he must, in dependence on the grace of Christ, diligently employ especially the following means:

1. *He must study to increase in the habit and exercise of faith, and to be more resolute and express in acting out his faith.* It will be necessary that he give all diligence to grow in the habit and exercise of true faith. "We which have believed," said the Apostle, "do enter into rest" (Hebrews 4:3). He whose heart trusts in Christ, and relies on the promise of eternal life as offered to him in the gospel, thereby enters already into spiritual rest or holy tranquility of soul. And the more he trusts with firm confidence in the Lord Jesus for eternal life for himself, the more spiritual rest he experiences. Hereby he enters further and further into rest, and, notwithstanding all temptations and troubles from sin, Satan, and the world, he attains increasing ease and comfort of soul. He comes laboring and heavy laden to Jesus Christ, and He gives him rest (Matthew 11:28). Jesus gives rest to his conscience in His own blood and righteousness, and rest to his heart in God as his God and portion. Accordingly, Isaiah says, "Thou wilt keep him in perfect peace whose mind is stayed on Thee, because he trusteth in Thee" (Isaiah 26:3).

When the Holy Spirit enables him to trust with unsuspecting confidence in the faithful Redeemer for all salvation for himself in particular, and to rely on the promises as offered to him, the very acting of this faith sets his mind at rest. He is, through the power of the Holy Spirit, "filled with joy and peace in

believing" (Romans 15:13). Committing himself,
with all his spiritual and temporal concerns to
Christ Jesus, and trusting that Jesus will save him,
uphold him, and manage for him, his soul is, in
proportion to the strength of his faith, set at ease.
He "rests in the Lord, and waits patiently for Him"
(Psalm 37:7), not only because it is his duty, but because it is the instituted means of his attaining an
increase of consolation. Knowing that the joy of the
Lord is his strength for the spiritual performance of
every duty, he studies to increase in the lively exercise of faith in order that "believing, he may rejoice
with joy unspeakable, and full of glory" (1 Peter 1:8).
Indeed, faith is the principal means not only of recovering, but of increasing holy consolation. The
way to console is to settle the heart. The increase of
comfort, therefore, will be according to the increase
of faith. If the believer would advance in pure consolation, let him endeavor diligently and constantly to
exercise faith. Let him "labor to enter into that rest"
(Hebrews 4:11). To bring his heart to the habitual
exercise of trusting simply in the Savior will indeed
cost him many hard struggles and hot conflicts with
his remaining unbelief, but still he must labor not
only to exercise, but to increase his faith; and that by
acting out his faith more frequently, and by trusting
in Christ at all times for an increase of it. He must
endeavor so to advance in the daily exercise of cordial and direct confidence in Jesus for salvation as
thereby to receive from Him a daily increase of holiness; for the more holiness he receives, the more
holy comfort he will experience.

Let him also renew frequently his application of

the blood of Jesus to his conscience, for purging away the guilt which he is daily contracting. The Apostle Paul informs us that "the kingdom of God is righteousness, and peace, and joy in the Holy Ghost" (Romans 14:17). From the spotless righteousness of Jesus Christ, applied by faith, comes peace, peace of conscience as well as peace with God, and from peace issues joy. Hence it is evident that the way to advance in spiritual peace and joy is to increase in that faith which relies on Christ and His righteousness for justification and complete salvation. Moreover, the principal, if not the only, way in which the holy Comforter administers consolation to believers is by testifying of Christ to them. It is by showing them His loveliness and love, His ability and willingness to save, His suitableness and faithfulness; and it is by enabling them so to confide in Him for their salvation as to rejoice in the hope of that salvation. It is, likewise, by enabling them to appropriate God in Christ and to place increasing confidence in Him. This was David's exercise in order to attain more comfort: "I trusted in Thee, O Lord; I said, 'Thou art my God.' " And the happy consequence of it he expresses thus: "Blessed be the Lord; for He hath shewed me His marvelous kindness in a strong city" (Psalm 31:14, 21).

If the believer would attain increasing consolation, he must likewise be more resolute and express in acting out his faith. It will be necessary for him to be resolute in looking away from every other object of dependence to Jesus. He must habitually and peremptorily resolve to trust simply in Him, and, in full assurance of faith, to entrust all his salvation,

and all his concerns, to His care. By thus casting his
burden upon the Lord Jesus, and trusting that He
will make all things work together for good to him,
his heart will become light and cheerful. He shall
be freed from a thousand anxieties which otherwise
would disquiet and distract his soul. The more distinct and explicit the actings of his faith are, the
more peace will they bring into his conscience, and
the more joy into his heart.

When his actings of faith are so lively and express that he becomes habitually conscious of them,
he thereby sits down to a rich feast of inward tranquility, and even of spiritual delight. When his faith,
under the influences of the Holy Spirit, is so direct
and so particular in its exercise as to meet Christ in
the promise, heart to heart and eye to eye, it is like a
rod of myrtle in the hand of the traveler, which, as
some say, revives his spirits and enables him to proceed without feeling himself weary. He thereby
dwells in Him who is the Consolation of Israel, the
Fountain from which all the streams of ineffable delight flow.

Let every believer, then, study diligently to be
more distinct, particular, and express in his exercise
of faith. Let him endeavor daily to be more and
more express, especially, in his trusting in Christ for
salvation from the love, power, and practice of every
sin. This appropriating and express exercise of faith
in the Lord Jesus is graciously and absolutely
promised. "Surely, shall one say, 'In the Lord have I
righteousness and strength' " (Isaiah 45:24). "I will
say, 'It is my people'; and they shall say, 'The Lord is
my God' " (Zechariah 13:9).

2. It will be necessary that he trust frequently in Christ not only for salvation in general, but for an increase of comfort in particular. Let him continue humbly and firmly to trust that the Lord Jesus will not only save him, but comfort him on every side, and that He will not merely preserve and increase in his soul the habit of spiritual joy, but that He will favor him in every time of need with an increase even of sensible comfort. He must endeavor in every condition, and in the diligent use of all other instituted means, to trust that God in Christ, the God of consolation, will "fill him with all joy and peace in believing"; that Jesus, the Consolation of Israel, will "speak comfortably to him" (Hosea 2:14), and "will never leave him comfortless" (John 14:18); and that the Holy Spirit, the Comforter, will, by His inhabiting and influence, fill his soul with an increase of holy consolation. Then, in every season of need, it will be unto him according to his faith.

Instead of refusing to be comforted by raising captious and frivolous objections against the consolation which in the gospel is offered and promised him, he should, upon the warrant of the gospel offer, habitually desire and constantly rely upon Christ for a higher degree of it, according to the promise. He ought never to forget that the comfort of the Holy Spirit is one of the fruits of trusting in the Lord (Proverbs 16:20). It is a part of the office of faith to accept and to hand spiritual comfort to the holy soul. If faith therefore is strong and frequently in exercise, such a soul will have strong consolation. If faith increases in its habit, and in the frequency of its exercise, holy comfort will increase in propor-

tion. Let the believer therefore trust at all times in
the Lord Jesus for increasing consolation. Let him
see that he takes comfort from Christ revealed
rather than from his own discoveries of Him, and
that he lives comfortably upon Christ Himself rather
than upon his own experience of Christ. He should
encourage himself continually in his God and
Savior. Amidst all his inward and outward troubles,
he must, by the frequent actings of particular trust,
derive strong consolation from the life, the death,
the resurrection, the intercession, the covenant, the
words, the offices, the victories, and the relations of
Jesus Christ. He must also trust that the blessed
Spirit loves him, and that, as His gracious Comforter, "He will abide with him forever, and will
bring all things to his remembrance" that are necessary to comfort him (John 14:16, 26).

Believer, if you would advance in true consolation, you must always trust that whenever the Lord
Jesus shall take from you any of your present comforts, it will be only to make room for better and
sweeter comforts. Entrust all your temporal comforts, without the least anxiety, to your faithful
Redeemer, and He will render them doubly sweet to
you. Or if He shall take any of them from you, He
will restore them again with much advantage, either
in kind or in value. Beware of relying partly on
Christ and partly on the creature for your comfort.
Derive all your comforts of every kind from the direct actings of faith, from Christ in the promise, and
derive them only from Him. It is the character of the
true circumcision that "they rejoice in Christ Jesus,
and have no confidence in the flesh" (Philippians

3:3). If the sufferings of Christ, or sufferings in conformity to Him, shall at any time abound in you, your "consolation also will abound by Christ" (2 Corinthians 1:5). Look therefore to Jesus, the glorious Sun of righteousness, for the light of consolation, and not to yourself; and charge it often upon your soul to rejoice in Him. When you use diligently the appointed means of advancing in spiritual comfort, do not forget to trust that He will abundantly bless them for that purpose. So shall they prove to be means to your soul of increasing in holy consolation.

3. If the believer would retain his comfort, and rise to higher degrees of it, he must exercise constantly the hope of eternal life. As hope is a means of recovering, so it is a means of increasing spiritual comfort. The more, therefore, that a good man "abounds in hope through the power of the Holy Spirit," the more shall he "rejoice in the hope of the glory of God" (Romans 5:2). Having "fled for refuge to lay hold upon the hope set before him," let him "show the same diligence, to the full assurance of hope" that many of the first Christians showed; and then he shall, like them, "have strong consolation" (Hebrews 6:11, 18). If he hopes continually for the full and endless fruition of God and of the Lamb in the heavenly world, he shall thereby be weaned from undue attachment to the present world, and so shall be preserved from being much affected either by the smiles or the frowns of worldly men. If he exercises daily "the lively hope of that inheritance which is incorruptible, undefiled, and which fadeth not away, reserved in heaven" for him, and builds his hope

upon the sure, immovable foundation laid in Zion,
remote from all the changes experienced in himself, he shall thereby "hold fast the confidence and
the rejoicing of the hope, firm unto the end"
(Hebrews 3:6).

Were the believer to exercise constantly a lively
and firm expectation of sufficient grace in time, and
of consummate blessedness through eternity, it
would be a special means of exciting and promoting
ineffable delight in his soul. It would fill his heart
with overflowings of holy gratitude, and his lips with
expressions of joy and triumph. In proportion as his
hope is grounded and frequently exercised on the
love of God, on the promise of eternal life, and on
the righteousness, grace, and faithfulness of the
glorious Redeemer, it brings more and more of
eternal life, and of that heavenly delight which
forms a part of it, into his soul. That living hope is
from above, and, in proportion as it is strengthened
and frequently exercised, it elevates the holy soul to
the things which are above. The believer, when he is
exercising it, lives in a joyful expectation and a sweet
anticipation of the ineffable and endless pleasures
which are at God's right hand. Hope settles and
cheers the heart. It disposes the Christian patiently
and quietly to wait upon the Lord for every promised
blessing (Romans 8:25). It leaves the season and the
manner of bestowing any promised blessing to that
divine Redeemer, who is infinitely wise, gracious,
and faithful. True hope is the assured expectation
that, although Christ may seem to delay long, yet He
will certainly come with every promised and necessary blessing, and that He will not defer a single

moment longer than the time appointed in the everlasting covenant.

Moreover, the exercise of hope promotes holy
consolation, inasmuch as it is a means of purifying
the soul from sin, that greatest enemy of spiritual
comfort (1 John 3:3). When a holy man is enabled to
hope that he shall abide in Christ and endure to the
end; that he shall continue to receive from the fullness of Christ rich supplies of sanctifying grace to
enable him faithfully to keep His commandments;
that he shall consequently grow in grace, and in the
saving knowledge of Jesus Christ; that he shall be
graciously upheld under, and delivered from, all the
afflictions which may still await him; that he shall at
the appointed time be prepared to die in peace, and
to pass over with joy into the embraces of his dear
Redeemer; and that he shall be with Him to behold
His glory forevermore—this hope fills his heart with
inexpressible joy. It diffuses a delightful perfume of
comfort over his soul.

*4. It will be requisite for the same purpose that he daily ad-
vance in love to the Lord Jesus, and to God in Him.* The
Christian's love to Christ is the immediate principle
of his delighting or joying in Him. To advance
therefore in supreme love to Christ is the way to increase in holy joy. The Apostle Paul, in describing
the fruit of the Spirit, mentions joy and peace in
immediate connection with love (Galatians 5:22).
And the Lord Jesus Himself, when He was comforting His disciples, said, "If a man loves Me, he will
keep My words; and My Father will love him, and we
will come unto him, and make our abode with him"
(John 14:23). Love is a pleasant, cheering affection.

Those believers, therefore, who exceed others in
love for Christ Jesus commonly surpass others also
in spiritual comfort. The exercise of supreme love to
Him, and to God in Him, diffuses a sacred sweetness
over the soul. Whether it is a love of desire to Him
when He is absent, or of delight in Him when He is
present, still, in proportion to the strength and exercise of it, it sweetly refreshes and invigorates the
soul. "There is no fear in love," said the Apostle
John, "but perfect love casteth out fear" (1 John
4:18). Although it is always attended with a holy and
filial fear of displeasing God, yet, in proportion to
the degree and exercise of it in the soul, it banishes
all slavish, diffident, and disquieting fear of Him.
Indeed, when the ardor of love decays, and the exercise of it fails, distressing fear usually arises; but
when love is revived, and is vigorous in its exercise
upon its transcendently glorious and amiable
Object, such fear usually vanishes and gives place to
holy consolation in the soul.

The vigorous exercise of ardent love toward his
dear Redeemer, excited by believing views of His infinite loveliness in Himself and of His immense love
to him, tends, through grace, to fill the mind for the
believer with a pleasing tranquility. If loving any object has in its nature a tendency to make the person
who loves take pleasure in the company of the object
beloved, notwithstanding all the infirmities which
cleave to that object, what inexpressible pleasure
must a saint experience in loving Him who is altogether lovely! All the delights of worldly men are but
like the toys of children in comparison to the pleasure of supreme love to the Lord Jesus, and to a God

of love in Him. The Apostle Paul informs us that "love thinketh no evil" (1 Corinthians 13:5). Love of God, in proportion to the degree of it, thinks no evil of Him; it fears no evil from Him. It indulges not evil surmises or groundless jealousies of Him. "He who dwelleth in love dwelleth in God, and God in him" (1 John 4:16). He counts it his highest pleasure to please Him, and his greatest joy to have intimate communion with Him. He delights in Him, as his Friend, his Father, and his God, as his only portion and his exceeding joy. And the more he delights in the Lord, the more holy consolation he experiences.

Believer, see that you advance daily in supreme and ardent affection to God in Christ, to all of God and all of Christ. Love especially the holiness, the will, and the glory of Christ. Let your soul cleave continually to Him, and it will comfort you greatly to think of Him, and of His immense and amazing love to you. To advance in supreme love to your dear Redeemer will, notwithstanding all the afflictions which may henceforth befall you in your lot, render you capable of increasing in heavenly consolation. Difficult things will, for His sake, seem easy, and bitter things will seem sweet.

5. *If the believer would advance in holy consolation, let him, in the faith of redeeming love to him, learn to delight more and more in the law of the Lord.* The more he is enabled to delight in the will of God, expressed in that holy law, the more comfortable and happy is he in doing that will (Psalm 112:1). The more pleasure he takes in performing every part of his duty, and seeing he is commanded to employ himself always in present duty, the more his present duty is his delight; the

more will he always be delighted. "Great peace," said the Psalmist, "have they who love Thy law, and nothing shall offend them" (Psalm 119:165). For the more they delight in the holiness, spirituality, and perfection of the law as the rule of their duty, and in holy obedience to it, the clearer evidence they have that they are so justified by faith as to have peace with God; the more they enjoy peace of conscience, which is a sense of peace with God; and the more are they at peace with the creatures of God. No external troubles or offenses can deprive them of this "great peace," or divert them from the path of duty in which they delight. Indeed, the more a holy man delights in the commandments of the law as expressions of the will of God the Father who loves him, of the mind of Christ who redeems him, and of the desire of the Holy Spirit who dwells in him, the more will he regard sincere obedience to them as his privilege, his pleasure, and his comfort.

Those precepts which are all "holy, and just, and good" prescribe good and pleasant work to him— such work as is not only good for him, but agreeable to the bent of his renewed nature. The more, therefore, he advances in sanctification, the more pleasure he takes in doing, and even in suffering, the will of his heavenly Father.

So much was this the attainment of the holy Apostle Paul that he gloried in tribulations; he took pleasure in infirmities, in reproaches, in necessities, in persecutions, in distresses for Christ's sake, because it was the will of God that he should endure them, and because they afforded the power of Christ an opportunity so to rest upon Him as to be gloriously displayed, and evidenced to be perfect, in his weakness (2 Corinthians 12:9–10). Doubtless, his taking pleasure even in manifold sufferings for the sake of Christ could not but be attended with such a measure of holy consolation as would make him "exceeding joyful in all his tribulation" (2 Corinthians 7:4).

Thus it is evident that the more a believer delights in the providential and, especially, the preceptive will of God, and the more spiritual and exact his obedience is, the more experience he has of spiritual comfort. Besides, his delighting in or savoring those things of the Spirit is a comfortable evidence to him not only that he has the Spirit of Christ, and that the prevailing inclination of his heart is toward spiritual and holy objects, but that the delight which he has in the Lord, and in the Word and law of the Lord, is his chief delight (Psalm 43:4 and 119:127). Oh, how cheering must it be to a holy man to be conscious that not only the grace of the promises, but the holiness of the precepts, instead of displeasing him, renders them inexpressibly pleasant to his soul (Psalm 119:143)! He cannot perish in his affliction because the law of God is his delight (Psalm 119:92). Delight in the will of the Lord is heaven upon earth, the very essence of real satisfaction, true felicity. The Lord Himself is inconceivably happy in His own will, and He has revealed it to His people that they might be happy in it.

6. *Another means of retaining and increasing spiritual comfort is frequently to exercise godly sorrow or contrition of heart for sin.* To be contrite in heart is—from a principle of faith in Christ, of love to God, and of desire

to please and honor Him—to be sorrowful for having sinned against Him. The Apostle Paul called sorrow for sin "godly sorrow" (2 Corinthians 7:10), that is, sorrow which has God in Christ for its author and its Object; or sorrow for God for having, by sin, offended a God of infinite holiness, justice, faithfulness, and goodness; or sorrow according to God, according to His holy will; or sorrow which is acceptable to God through Jesus Christ. The same apostle informs us that "it worketh repentance unto salvation," that evangelical repentance which is a man's turning from all sin to God in Christ, a God of infinite mercy and grace.

Now in order to advance in holy consolation, the Christian must, in the faith of pardoning mercy and of sanctifying grace, exercise frequently that godly sorrow for sin, especially for the sin that dwells in him. The exercise of godly sorrow is not only consistent with holy joy, but it always tends to it, and frequently issues in it; yea, it even includes it. Such refreshing of soul, such joy of heart is often experienced in the depth of godly sorrow so that the true penitent would not exchange even the lowest degree of that joy for all the carnal mirth in the world. The most sorrowful Christian would not for a thousand worlds exchange states or pleasures with the most prosperous of ungodly men. In comparison to that pure and solid joy with which the penitential sorrow of a true believer is often attended, carnal mirth is folly, and even madness (Ecclesiastes 2:2). His mourning for sin is because it has offended his gracious God and wounded his compassionate Savior; because it has pierced that heart which loves him, and shed that blood which saves him. It is a joyful mourning, a real comfort to his soul.

To mourn for sin on such accounts as these is, as one expresses it, to weep for joy. As godly sorrow cannot be exercised by the Christian without some comfortable apprehension of the mercy of God to him, or of Christ's having been pierced for his iniquities, so it is seldom exercised by him without some degree of comfort experienced either in or after his exercise of it. "Wisdom's ways are ways of pleasantness, and all her paths are peace" (Proverbs 3:17). The believing penitent takes delight in mourning for his crucified Redeemer, in sitting down at His pierced feet and bathing them with his tears. His godly sorrow is a means both of preparing him for consolation, and of introducing it into his soul. Accordingly, Jehovah promises that He will "dwell with him who is of a contrite and humble spirit, to revive the spirit of the humble, and to revive the heart of the contrite ones" (Isaiah 57:15). The Lord Jesus also said, "Blessed are they that mourn, for they shall be comforted" (Matthew 5:4); and again, "The Lord hath anointed Me to bind up the brokenhearted, to comfort all that mourn" (Isaiah 61: 1–2). Hence holy fasting is represented in Scripture as spiritual feasting (Zechariah 8:19).

The penitential grief of a holy man is also matter of joy to him. He rejoices more to feel his heart melting for sin than he would do in enjoying all the carnal delights of the sons of men. He finds a secret sweetness in the tears of evangelical repentance, a balm which refreshes and cheers his soul. Besides, godly sorrow renders him capable of receiving in a

higher degree influences of holy consolation. The
more he grieves in a godly manner of sin, the more
capable is he of rejoicing in God his Savior; yea, the
more he grieves that he cannot grieve as he ought
for his iniquity, and mourns that he cannot mourn;
the more capacity he has for receiving and enjoying
spiritual comfort. The joy of God's salvation is not to
be found but in the deep recesses of a contrite heart.
Although, then, true repentance consists more in
turning from all sin to God than merely in sorrow
for sin, yet, in order to retain and increase his comfort for the service and the glory of God, the believer
should diligently exercise that sorrow.

7. *It will be necessary, for the same purpose, that he be
more and more diligent in mortifying the sin that dwells in
him.* When the Christian finds himself yielding to
motions of sin in his heart, it cannot but occasion
to him trouble of soul; but when he feels himself, by
the sanctifying influences of the Holy Spirit, enabled to resist or act against them, it is a special
comfort to him. And the more he is enabled to
maintain a holy opposition to them, the more pure
and solid is his consolation. To mortify the deeds of
the body of sin, and the members of it which are
upon the earth (Romans 8:13; Colossians 3:5), is
constantly to apply the blood and the Spirit of Christ
for subduing, weakening, and destroying it with all
its corrupt affections, principles, and practices. It is,
by the gracious influences of the Spirit of Christ, so
to resist and subdue the vital qualities and active
powers of the body of sin in the heart as gradually to
destroy them.

Now one of the means which the believer must

employ in order to retain and increase his comfort is to maintain constantly a holy opposition to all the affections, principles, and motions of the body of sin in him until, in conformity to Christ in His crucifixion, and by grace derived from His fullness, they are destroyed. The more resolute he is, and the more pleasure he takes, in thus mortifying them, the more of spiritual and pure consolation will he attain. The more of sanctifying influences he receives by faith for the mortification of sin, the more of consoling influences will he commonly receive. Accordingly, David prayed thus: "Create in me a clean heart, O God; renew in me a right spirit"; and then, "Restore to me the joy of Thy salvation" (Psalm 51:10, 12). As the Christian advances in mortifying his unbelief and pride, his self-righteous and worldly spirit, he will increase his enjoyment of the cheering light of his heavenly Father's countenance. The more diligent and successful he is in mortifying his propensity to cavil or dispute against the freeness of the offers, promises, and grace of the gospel, the more disposed he will be to admit and to relish the comforts of the gospel.

It is in proportion as remaining sin dies in the believer that he lives a life of holiness and comfort. The weaker the body of sin in him is, the less power over him will his other spiritual enemies have; the temptations of Satan and the world will proportionally lose their influence with him. The only care of the hypocrite is to reform his life, whereas the main, though not the only, concern of the sincere believer is to cleanse his heart (Jeremiah 4:14). Luther used to say, "I fear what is within me more than what comes from without. The storms and winds without never move the earth; it is only vapors within that cause earthquakes." And the sweetness which one experiences in obtaining victory over sin in his heart is a thousand times greater than the seeming pleasure which is felt in gratifying sin. Indeed, were the least real pleasure to be enjoyed in sinning, the torments of the damned in hell would thereby be greatly lessened; for there they will forever sin in the utmost degree possible, but instead of being the less, they shall be the more tormented *by* as well as *for* their sinning.

Believer, take heed that you are diligent in mortifying the depravity of your heart. The further you advance in mortifying the sin that remains in you, and especially the sin that more easily besets you, the more pleasure will you take in mortifying it, and the more comfort will you experience in your conflicts with it. Learn to hate all sin in an increasing degree, for the more you abhor it, the greater delight you will take in opposing and subduing it. Holy joy can exsist with remaining sin, but not with retained and indulged sin. Mortify then, through the Spirit, the corruption of your nature, and Christ will not be constrained to mortify it for you by the extremity of outward or inward trouble. Study to attain more eminence in that grace, which is the direct opposite of the sin which easily besets you.

8. *The Christian must, for the same end, endeavor daily to become more and more circumspect and conscientious in the practice of universal holiness.* It is only in proportion as he "walketh in the fear of the Lord" that he can walk "in the comfort of the Holy Spirit" (Acts 9:31). To

walk circumspectly is to be habitually cautious and watchful on every side against all manner of sin, and to be always attentive to every duty, and to every circumstance of duty. Or it is to walk in all the duties of holiness with wisdom, diligence, and exactness. So far as a good man walks circumspectly, he is in all things upright, exact, and conscientious. He is "in the fear of the Lord all the day long" (Proverbs 23:17). From a principle of faith in Christ and of love to God, he dreads sin as the worst evil in the world; and, consequently, he abstains even from all appearance of that evil (1 Thessalonians 5:22). He abstains from the very appearance of it not merely because he sees that it is reasonable and prudent to do so, but because it is the will of his God and Father. And though this does not afford him the smallest title to divine consolation, yet he knows that it is a necessary means of it, and that it is inseparably connected with as much of it as the Lord sees good to afford him.

The more spiritually and closely he walks with God, the more he walks in the light of His countenance. The more he makes the practice of universal holiness his main business, a business in which he principally engages, and which he pursues with the greatest earnestness and diligence, the clearer evidence has he that the Holy Spirit, the Comforter, dwells in him. Accordingly, the Lord Jesus said to His disciples, "If ye love Me, keep My commandments: and I will pray the Father, and He shall give you another Comforter, that He may abide with you forever" (John 14:15–16).

Let the believer, then, beware of sinning, especially of sinning willfully, for that would provoke the Lord to cover His evidences with a cloud in His anger, and to suspend influences of consolation from his soul. Let it be his constant purpose and unwearied endeavor, through grace, to please God in everything, and to displease Him in nothing. To walk circumspectly is indeed the sure way to walk comfortably and advance in comfort. He who is enabled, from the principles of faith and love, and for the glory of God, so to walk, "shall sing in the righteous ways of the Lord" (Psalm 138:5), for he shall find that they "are ways of pleasantness, and paths of peace" (Proverbs 3:17).

As holy comfort is necessary to the practice of holiness, so increasing holiness of heart and of life is requisite to the maintenance and increase of comfort. As heat accompanies fire, so a greater or lesser measure of comfort usually attends the spiritual performance of holy actions (Psalm 19:11). It cannot be otherwise; for to walk circumspectly in a course of holy obedience is to walk with God, the God of all comfort, to walk in Christ, the Consolation of Israel, and to walk after the Spirit, the holy Comforter.

If the believer would walk so circumspectly as to glorify Christ and promote his own comfort, he must, first, take heed that he does not, on any occasion, walk in the dark; he should not go forward where he cannot, by the light of holy Scripture, discern his way; and he should be as much afraid of taking comfort merely from his duties themselves as from his sins.

9. *To grow in spiritual-mindedness is also the way to*

maintain and increase spiritual comfort. To be "spiritually minded" is, from the spiritual principles of grace, and under the sanctifying influences of the Holy Spirit, to have the mind and heart frequently, intently, and delightfully employed about spiritual objects. It is to have all the powers of the soul habitually concurring in spiritual thoughts and desires, and in taking a holy complacence in the things of the Spirit, especially in the things concerning Christ and the wonderful scheme of redemption by Him.

Now one special means of advancing in spiritual consolation is to increase in spiritual-mindedness. The Apostle Paul informs us that "to be spiritually minded is life and peace" (Romans 8:6). It is, in its very nature, spiritual life, and is the earnest and the beginning of life eternal, consisting in the full and immediate fruition of God and the Lamb in the mansions of glory. And in proportion as the believer increases in it, his soul is endued not only with spiritual activity, but with pleasing serenity and pure consolation. The more spiritually minded he becomes, the more of spiritual peace and comfort he attains. The more he spiritually understands, meditates, relishes, and delights in the doctrine of redeeming grace, and the glory of God displayed in the wonderful person and work of the great Redeemer, the more pleasing tranquility and refreshing delight he experiences. By how much he grows in spiritual understanding, or in the knowledge of the transcendent loveliness and love of God in Christ, and of the excellence, suitableness, and freeness of salvation by Christ, by so much does he experience holy serenity and solid consolation in committing to such a God and Savior all his spiritual and temporal concerns. In proportion as his heart becomes more deeply sensible of the unparalleled holiness and beauty of spiritual objects, and of his own personal interest in them, it is delighted, enlarged, and elevated.

Whether he contemplates the cheering truths and precious promises of the gospel, or practices the spiritual duties of the law toward his God or his neighbor, the more spiritual he is in them, the more pure, solid, and heavenly is the pleasure which he enjoys. These are the banquet of his mind. They are sweeter than honey to his taste in proportion as his spiritual understanding and his disposition to count all earthly things empty and mean in comparison to union with Christ and to conformity to Him, increase. He sets his affection on things above; he places his happiness in them, and rejoices in hope of them. When he advances in habitual desires and in holy endeavors to aim in all his exercise of graces and performance of duties at the glory of his God and Redeemer, he, in the same proportion, glories and delights in the Lord. To become more and more spiritually minded, then, is a sure way of attaining higher degrees of spiritual comfort. As the higher a bird flies, the more out of danger he is from the snares of the fowler, so the higher a believer soars in spirituality of mind above the world, the higher and safer is his consolation.

Moreover, the Christian, in order to attain increasing comfort, must be always on his guard against formality and remissness in his exercise of

graces and performance of duties. To be remiss or
formal in performing any of his duties is the very
opposite of being spiritually minded. Now he may
assure himself that he is declining into formality if
he is more studious of approving himself to men
than to God; if, instead of performing his duties
with holy delight, he performs them as a task; if, instead of habitually exercising faith, love, godly sorrow, and spiritual desire in performing them, he sat-
isfies himself with the external performance; and if
the remaining carnality of his mind is not so
grievous or burdensome to him as formerly.
Nothing will more effectually hinder his advancing
in the comfort of the Holy Spirit than remissness or
negligence of spirit in the duties of religion (Song
of Solomon 5:2, 6; Proverbs 10:4). For when the
Christian does not serve God with his spirit, he
grieves the Holy Spirit of God, and provokes Him to
suspend influences of consolation from his soul.
And when he does not ardently pursue increasing
communion with Christ in holy exercises, he cannot expect to enjoy the comfort of communion with
Him.

   *10. Another means of a believer's advancing in spiritual
comfort is to become more and more content with God in
Christ as his inheritance.* He cannot be comfortable but
in proportion as he is content. God in Christ, as
their Covenant-God, is the sure, boundless, unchanging, and everlasting portion of all the saints.
Nothing can be added to Him; nothing can be
taken from Him or diminished in Him. A holy man
may lose all his earthly possessions, but he cannot
lose his God, or anything in God. And therefore he

continues still as rich as he was before. His outward comforts are only lent him in order to be used for a season, and then to be willingly and thankfully restored. But his God is given him to be eternally enjoyed by him as his immense, unchangeable, and sure portion. And therefore he has as much reason to be satisfied with, and to rejoice in, his all-sufficient inheritance afterwards as before his outward losses.

The ancient Church, accordingly, after she had been deprived of her best external comforts, placed her happiness and her hope in Jehovah as her sure portion: " 'The Lord is my portion,' saith my soul; therefore will I hope in Him" (Lamentations 3:24). And when Asaph was emerging from his depths of spiritual trouble, he said to Jehovah, "Whom have I in heaven but Thee? And there is none upon earth that I desire besides Thee. My flesh and my heart faileth; but God is the strength of my heart, and my portion forever" (Psalm 73:25–26). The sincere believer, trusting that a gracious God bestows Himself, and all that He is and has, upon him as his infinite inheritance, should be much more content than he is with his portion. The more satisfied he is with God in Christ as his inheritance, the more pleasure will he take in Him; and the more pleasure he takes in Him, the more consolation will he receive from Him, and the more will he rejoice in Him. "Although the fig tree shall not blossom," said Habakkuk, "neither shall fruit be in the vines . . . yet will I rejoice in the Lord, I will joy in the God of my salvation" (Habukkuk 3:17–18).

In proportion as the believer is content with

God, or satisfied that his Covenant-God is enough for him, without anything else except what infinite wisdom and love see meet for a time to afford him, he attains true, lasting, and increasing enjoyment. If he has outward comforts, he enjoys God in them; or if he has been deprived of them, he still enjoys them in God, so that his spiritual enjoyment or comfort is not, strictly speaking, dependent on them. Being satisfied with God Himself as his portion, he learns to be content with all the providential dispensations of God. "I have learned," said Paul, "in whatsoever state I am, therewith to be content" (Philippians 4:11). The Lord Jesus has given to His Church exceedingly great and precious promises in order that every saint may, by faith, "suck, and be satisfied with the breasts of her consolations" (Isaiah 66:11); and God, having reconciled them to Himself in Him, has graciously promised that He will be their God. Oh, what cause, then, has the believer to be always content! He is "an heir of God, and a joint heir with Christ," and therefore all things are his (Romans 8:17; 1 Corinthians 3:21).

There is more ground of comfort in this than the heart of man can conceive. God in Christ is your inheritance, believer; and therefore whatever He is, or has, or does, or can do, all shall promote your consolation in time, and your felicity through eternity. Be contented, then, as well you may, with your glorious, boundless, incorruptible, unfading inheritance. Menedemus, being told one day that it was a great felicity to have whatever we desire, replied, "Yes, but it is much greater to desire nothing but what we have."

Live continually and comfortably upon your God.
Make up all your happiness in Him. Blame yourself
if you lack strong consolation, when the God of all
comfort is your God and your portion; for you are
never without comfort but when you are not satisfied
with something in your God and Redeemer. See that
you rejoice more in Him than in all the delights of
the sons of men. Do you know anything desirable or
delightful in the creature? You may find it in your
Redeemer, and enjoy it in your God. What if you
have lost not merely one, but all your earthly comforts? In possessing God, the fountain of living waters, you still possess all things. You have one comfort still which is worth infinitely more than all others: "This God is thy God forever and ever; He will be
thy guide even unto death" (Psalm 48:14). See the
hand of your God in that which is, and be not disquieted by it; see that which is to come in His hand,
and be not discouraged in the prospect of it. What
can you wish for in an inheritance that is not in
your Covenant-God? If you would have a large estate,
He is infinite; if you would have sure possession, He
is unchangeable; if you would desire durable riches,
He is eternal. If God were to give you all that is in
the universe without Himself, you would be completely miserable and could never be satisfied. None
can afford satisfaction to your soul but that dear
Savior who gave, and that gracious God who received, satisfaction for the sin of the soul.

*11. If the believer would advance in spiritual consolation,
he must also increase daily in holy resignation to the will of the
Lord.* He must endeavor by grace not only to be content with God in Christ as his infinite portion, but

to increase in holy resignation of heart to the will of God, with respect to all his earthly comforts. The way to advance in peaceful tranquility of soul is to become so resigned to the providential will of the Lord as always to submit without murmuring to that holy will. God's will of providence, as well as His will of precept, is not only wise and sovereign, but holy and just and good. It is infinitely wise, and therefore it cannot be liable to the smallest mistake in its determination of anything respecting the external condition of the believer. It is absolutely sovereign, and therefore it is in vain for him to attempt resistance to it. It is also infinitely holy and righteous; and for these reasons it is infinitely incapable of doing a Christian the smallest injury, or of dispensing to him anything, whether pleasant or painful, but what is right and even necessary for him. It is infinitely good, likewise, and therefore it can appoint nothing to happen in the outward condition of a believer but what is good, yea, best, for serving at the time the sanctification and consolation of his soul.

So good is the will of the Lord that it has determined never to give or to take away a single outward comfort from a saint but when this is good for him, or even necessary to promote the great designs of redeeming grace in His salvation. So wise and good is that adorable will that all things, under the direction and control of it, "work together for good to them who love God, to them who are the called according to His purpose" (Romans 8:28). If therefore a holy man would advance in pure consolation, he must study, in dependence on the grace of Christ, cordially to resign himself and all his concerns to the holy will of his heavenly Father. The more he studies to delight in the holy will of God, the more will he be disposed to acquiesce in it; and the more he acquiesces in it, the more comfort, amidst all the vicissitudes of life, shall he experience. Let him endeavor to love it in an increasing degree, for in proportion as he loves it he will be pleased with it, and will rejoice to think that everything in his lot has been, from eternity, unalterably fixed according to it. He will delight in the cheering thought that, under the direction and control of it, all objects and all events, either directly or indirectly, promote his eternal welfare, and that all hands in the universe are continually at work for good to him. If affliction comes, the storm which then arises in his natural passions is hushed into a calm; and not only does submission ensue, but sweet resignation.

So far as the believer attains holy resignation, he is secure from disappointment; for his leading desire that the will of the Lord may be done concerning him cannot fail to be accomplished. He believes that the Lord chooses better for him than he can do for himself. He is persuaded not only that he has no right to complain of any providential dispensation, but that he has no reason, because "all the paths of the Lord are mercy and truth to him" (Psalm 25:10). "I was dumb," said holy David, "and opened not my mouth, because Thou didst it" (Psalm 39:9). In proportion as he is resigned to the holy will of God, he is always pleased, always comfortable, because whatever pleases God pleases him. As far as his will is in union with the will of the Lord, he shall always have what he chooses. He shall constantly be in a state of enjoyment as having the very thing which he desires. If he is under affliction, he comforts himself with thinking that it is the appointment of his heavenly Father's will.

Believer, the more you welcome the whole will of your gracious God and Father, the more happiness and comfort shall you enjoy. Consider how unbecoming, how sinful it is to murmur against the will of the only-wise God, your Savior. Know that the moment you repine at the providence of the Lord, you secretly accuse Him. You presume to charge Him with having done you an injury, to blame Him for something wrong in His management of your affairs. But is not this the same as secretly to blaspheme Him? Oh, if you would maintain spiritual consolation, take heed that you murmur not against the holy will of your gracious God. You are not qualified to be the chooser of your own outward condition; and therefore it belongs not to your wisdom and will, but to His, to dispose of all your affairs.

12. Another means of advancing in holy consolation is to become more and more thankful for blessings, either received or promised. "To give thanks always for all things, unto God and the Father, in the name of our Lord Jesus Christ" (Ephesians 5:20) is both the duty and the privilege of a holy man. It is his duty, in every condition of life, to maintain a thankful frame of heart, and to express daily to the Lord a lively and grateful sense of the unmerited and unnumbered benefits which He has bestowed upon him. The Apostle Paul, accordingly, gave this charge to the Thessalonians: "In everything give thanks, for this is the will of God in Christ Jesus concerning you" (1 Thessalonians

5:18). And in his epistle to the Hebrews he says, "By him, therefore, let us offer the sacrifice of praise to God continually, that is, the fruit of our lips, giving thanks to His name" (Hebrews 13:15). It is also a privilege to the believer when he is enabled in every circumstance of life, to be thankful for the mercies which God bestows either upon himself or others.

A disposition to be, in every condition, thankful to the Lord for benefits received from Him is always attended with some degree of comfort in a holy soul. A saint's frequent recollection and acknowledgment of the sweet mercies which he has in hand, and of the sure mercies which he has in hope, tend to sweeten and cheer his spirit. Praise and thanksgiving, according to the following passages of Scripture, are the genuine expressions of a comfortable frame of soul: "My heart greatly rejoiceth, and with my song will I praise Him" (Psalm 28:7). "Because Thy loving-kindness is better than life, my lips shall praise Thee. My mouth shall praise Thee with joyful lips" (Psalm 63:3, 5). "My lips shall greatly rejoice when I sing unto Thee, and my soul, which Thou hast redeemed" (Psalm 71:23).

While these passages evince praise and thanksgiving to be the native expressions of holy joy, at the same time they intimate that a saint's being disposed gratefully to praise and thank the Lord for blessings, either received or promised, is commonly attended with an increase of comfort or joy. A habitual cheerfulness of spirit is thereby maintained and increased. A heart truly thankful is, in the same proportion, cheerful. The most humble and thankful of the saints are commonly the most eminent in holiness and comfort. Indeed, thankfulness and comfort imply each other. A holy man must be, in some degree, comfortable in order to be thankful, and thankful in order to be, in an increasing degree, comfortable.

If, then, he would retain and increase his holy consolation, let him frequently give thanks to God not only for the unspeakable gift of His dear Son, but for all His benefits conferred upon him. Let him, as often and as much as possible, gratefully remember them, and thank the Lord for each of them, whether it be a great or a small, a spiritual or a temporal blessing. He must be thankful, particularly, for the degree of comfort with which the Lord has already favored him; and then, if his trials or sufferings at any time abound, "his consolation by Christ will also abound" (2 Corinthians 1:5). Let him extract arguments even from the darkest dispensations of providence, for exciting him to be always thankful to his God and Redeemer. For when he is continually thankful, he will, in the same proportion, be comfortable. He should, moreover, express his gratitude daily for the inestimable and innumerable blessings vouchsafed to him by giving to God in Christ all the glory of them, and by employing them all for the purposes of His glory. So shall he enjoy them, and experience increasing comfort in using them.

13. *Further, let the believer pray with increasing importunity for the continuance and increase of his comfort.* The fervent and incessant prayer of faith is a means not only of recovering, but of retaining and increasing spiritual consolation. Let him therefore pray impor-

tunately not only for sanctifying, but for consoling influences. The Spirit is the Comforter of the saints, and God "giveth the Holy Spirit to them who ask Him" (Luke 11:13). The Christian, then, should with increasing earnestness pray to his heavenly Father in the name of Christ, and in the faith of the promise, for the refreshing and comforting grace of the blessed Spirit. The more earnestly and frequently he offers up the prayer of faith for grace and consolation, the more will his heart be strengthened with the consolation of the holy Comforter. "In the day when I cried," said David, "Thou answeredst me, and strengthenedst me with strength in my soul" (Psalm 138:3).

When the God of consolation seems, at any time, to be forgetting or passing by the exercised believer, the prayer of faith will call Him in. When the Lord Jesus, having come to Emmaus, made as though He would have gone further, the two disciples constrained Him, saying, "'Abide with us; for it is towards evening, and the day is far spent.' And He went in to tarry with them" (Luke 24:28–29). The less true Christians desire from Christ, the less do they glorify the immense riches of His grace; but, on the contrary, the more they expect, and the more they ask from Him, the more will He give, and the more will He manifest His delight in giving to them. The believer, therefore, should pray, as the Apostle Paul did for the saints at Rome, that "the God of hope would fill him with all joy and peace in believing" (Romans 15:13); and, as the same apostle prayed for the Thessalonians, "that the Lord Jesus Christ Himself, and God even His Father, would comfort his heart, and establish him in every good word and work" (2 Thessalonians 2:16–17). And he should pray, as the disciples did, that the Lord would increase his faith; for as faith is increased, so is the joy of faith. Let him pray that he may be enabled always to thirst for spiritual consolation, "as the hart thirsteth for the water brook," and, at the same time, let his desire of sensible comfort be regulated by a due submission to the sovereign will of God. Paul had not been long praying before it was revealed to him that he was a chosen vessel. It was when Jesus Christ Himself was praying that He was transfigured, and that "a voice out of the cloud said, 'This is My beloved Son, in whom I am well pleased' " (Matthew 17:5). Those of the saints who pray most have the most comfort. Prayer crowns God with the glory of His redeeming grace, and God crowns prayer with the comfort of that grace.

If a holy man would so pray as thereby to advance in spiritual comfort, he must not only pray in faith, and with importunity, but he must pray with his spirit, with understanding, with sincere desire for that which he asks, with watchfulness, attention, and ardor. He should make supplication to God as his God and Father, in the name of Christ, by the help of the Spirit, and only for things which are promised. He "ought always to pray, and not to faint" (Luke 18:1), or to continue constant in prayer; he should plead the promises, and fill his mouth with such arguments as will tend to excite and increase his faith, hope, and love. He must, moreover, be habitually disposed to pray, to intermingle ejaculatory prayer with all his other duties, and to pray

much in secret. It was when Jacob retired for secret
prayer that the Angel of the covenant came to him,
and enabled him so to wrestle with him by supplication as to receive the blessing. She who was alone
with Jesus at the sepulcher was the first who partici-
pated in the joy of His resurrection. The holy Psalmist seems to have considered the comfort which he
enjoyed with God in secret as his sweetest comfort
(Psalm 63:5–6).

*14. It is necessary, for the same purpose, that the believer
increase daily in his knowledge of the grounds of spiritual
consolation.* He must, in order to advance in true comfort, study, through grace, to attain clearer and
fuller views of God the Father as a God of love, grace,
and mercy to him; of Christ, in His person, righteousness, fullness, offices, and relations; of the
Holy Spirit as his quickener, sanctifier, comforter,
and guide; of the covenant of grace in the admirable
suitableness, fullness, and stability of it; and of the
doctrines, offers, and promises of the glorious
gospel. The more spiritual and enlarged, clear and
distinct his knowledge, especially of these grounds
of pure consolation, is, the more will he see reason
to be of good comfort; the more will the principle
and habit of spiritual joy increase in his soul; and
the more will he rejoice in Christ Jesus and glory in
His cross.

A spiritual and clear understanding of those glorious and reviving objects will make his way clear in
taking comfort. Remaining ignorance in the mind
of a good man is, for the most part, the parent of all
his doubts and perplexities of spirit, because he does
not know how far he may or may not take encour-

agement and comfort. Were he but to study the covenant of grace more, and to understand better wherein it differs from the covenant of works, his doubts and fears would proportionaly vanish as clouds before the sun shining in its strength, and he would attain more of the holiness and consolation which are herein promised him. The better he understands that well-ordered and sure covenant, and the more he meditates on it and admires it, the more cordials he will find in it to cheer him under all his pressures and faintings of soul. If he understood better that eternal and wonderful contract, he would look for less from the creature and more from the Redeemer, for less here and more hereafter. He would discern more clearly that a humbling sense of the sinfulness and strength of sin in his heart is a good evidence of spiritual life in it, and that he has, notwithstanding the sin that remains in him, much in the promises daily to afford him pure consolation. It is through the knowledge of God as his Covenant-God, and of Jesus our Lord as his Covenant-Head, that grace and peace are multiplied to the believer (2 Peter 1:2).

Let him, then, "grow in grace, and in the knowledge of our Lord and Savior Jesus Christ" (2 Peter 3:18), that sure foundation of holy comfort, "and the peace of God, which surpasseth all understanding, shall keep his heart and mind through Christ Jesus" (Philippians 4:7). If the pleasure even of natural knowledge is great, how inexpressibly great must the pleasure of advancing in spiritual knowledge be!

15. If the believer would attain an increase of spiritual and solid consolation, let him not give ear to the reports of sense. By sense here is meant the present frame, feeling, or perception of an exercised Christian, which is either pleasant or unpleasant, and is continually subject to change. To hearken to and trust the reports of sense, or, in other words, to make his feelings or frames the ground of his faith, or the rule according to which he regulates his exercise, renders the faith of the Christian unsteady, and hinders the growth of it. And if the growth of faith is obstructed, the increase of spiritual comfort will be obstructed likewise.

Sense judges and reports that he is in a state of grace, and that Christ saves him merely because his feelings are pleasant and comfortable. It concludes that his state is either good or bad only from what he feels or from his present frame of spirit. If this is lively and pleasant, sense reports that he is in a state of grace, and that Christ is acting the part of a Savior to him. If, on the contrary, his frame is dull and unpleasant, sense reports that he is not in a state of grace, and that it would be rash and presumptuous in him to trust that Jesus will save him. Thus the report which it makes to the believer's conscience of the state of his soul before God and his salvation by Jesus Christ is not founded on unchangeable grounds, which would set his mind and conscience at rest, but on things which are changeable, and which frequently expose him to perplexing doubts and fears. If, instead of the record of God, he makes his lively feelings the foundation of his faith, his acting of faith will be either lively or languid, either more or less, just as these are. If, instead of trusting in Christ, upon the warrant of the offers and calls of the gospel (which is an unchanging as well as an authentic warrant), he trusts in Christ upon the ground of his own pleasant feelings, which are perpetually changing, his exercise of faith must cease as often as his lively or comfortable frame ceases. Now how can his faith increase if it is not daily exercised? And how can he exercise it daily if he thinks that he ought not to exercise it but upon the ground of a pleasant frame, which he may have today and want tomorrow; yea, which he may not for a long season enjoy?

If, then, he would, by daily actings of faith, derive solid and increasing consolation from the fullness of Christ, he must no longer ground his actings of faith upon his feelings, but upon the immutable offers and promises of God who cannot lie. By building his confidence in Christ upon the reports of sense, he builds it upon a wrong, as well as a changeable foundation; and thereby he forfeits his comfort instead of deriving an increase of it. Faith cannot derive any increase, either of holiness or comfort, from Christ unless the exercise of it proceeds upon its proper ground. It is not the report of sense, but the record of God that is the true and warrantable ground of saving faith. If the believer, then, would attain solid and increasing consolation, he must allow his faith to stand always upon the record of God concerning His Son; for that is the only right ground of confidence in the Son of God for salvation, and is therefore called "the word of faith." Then will he see that he has ground still to hold fast his confidence in his faithful Redeemer when his pleasant frames are gone. Then will he learn to retain the confidence of his heart in his divine Savior, even when the reports of sense contradict the report of the gospel, and, like Abraham, "against hope, to believe in hope." And in proportion as he ceases to ground his confidence in the Lord Jesus for salvation upon his comfortable feelings, he will receive that pure and everlasting consolation from Christ, which will be the pleasant fruit, though not the ground, of his faith.

In order to illustrate as well as confirm what has been advanced in this particular, I cannot forbear transcribing these paragraphs from Romaine's *Life of Faith*:

> Sense judges from what it sees, and draws its inferences from what it feels, so that its report to the conscience, either of a believer's state or of his growth in it, is not from unchangeable things which would settle the conscience in peace, but from changeable things which leave room for continual doubting. Sense also looks at the fruits of faith more than at the object of it; and if the believer has been misled and taught to confound these two together, he will be at great uncertainty in judging his state. For instead of the Word of God, he will make his comforts the ground of his faith; and as these are more or less, so will his faith be. When he has comfortable feelings, then he will think himself a believer; and when he has none, then he will think himself an unbeliever, changing his judgment of himself like the wind, and varying like the weather. This is a common case.
>
> I have seen the sad effects of it in the lives of many of my acquaintances who, from being

taught thus to judge of themselves, were tossed about for several years up and down, now comforted, then doubting, and could not get any solid establishment till the Word and Spirit of God convinced them that sense was not to be the ground of their believing, nor the object to which they were to look.

Sense judges by feeling and reports what it sees. Sense says, "Now I am not in the favor of God; for I do not feel it. Now He is not my God; for I do not find Him so. I am not comforted." What can be the issue of this but continual wavering and changing? For our feelings are sometimes more, sometimes less, as every believer experiences. What a state, then, must he be in who has no way to judge of himself but by those changeable things! What room does he leave for continual doubting, and what trouble and misery does he thereby bring upon himself, as well as dishonor to the unchangeableness of God in His nature and promises!

16. It will be necessary also, for the same purpose, that the believer be always upon his guard against affected sadness. Has he already some happy measure of true consolation? Let him show that he has it by a habitual cheerfulness of temper and manner. Let him not, by assuming an air of gloominess or peevishness, show to any around him that he finds no comfort in a life of communion with the blessed Redeemer. When a believer is not afflicted with trouble of soul, and yet appears habitually dejected and gloomy, he thereby, in the view of others, gives the lie to the truth of his holy profession, as well as to the truth of God in His promises of consolation. He thereby practically declares it to be false that God is the God of all comfort, that the Holy Spirit is the Comforter, and that wisdom's ways are ways of pleasantness. By assuming an air of gloominess or peevishness, instead of recommending the way of holiness he brings reproach upon that good way. Like the unbelieving spies who, by bringing up an evil report of the promised land, discouraged the Israelites, he represents the life of faith and holiness as an uncomfortable, unamiable life, and so discourages, more effectually than one can express, sinners around him from trying to enter upon that life.

Were he, on the contrary, by a habitual cheerfulness of temper and manner, to exhibit the comforts of religion so far as he possesses them, he would resemble the faithful spies who brought with them clusters of the grapes of Canaan that they might thereby invite their brethren to enter that good land. It is his duty, as he is infinitely obliged to the Lord Jesus, to promote always the honor of His glorious name and the interests of His spiritual kingdom among men. His whole behavior, therefore, should be such as would be the means of winning souls to the blessed Redeemer.

The Apostle Peter exhorted wives to be in subjection to their own husbands, "that if any obey not the word, they also may be won by the conversation of the wives" (1 Peter 3:1). A holy man should not only be, but appear to be, habitually cheerful so that all who know him might have an opportunity of perceiving that his blessed Savior has made him happy as well as holy, and that his holy religion instead of having rendered him gloomy, has disposed him to be cheerful. Conscious that he is under the greatest obligations to invite others around him to "taste and see that the Lord is good" (Psalm 34:8), let him henceforth adopt this resolution of the holy Psalmist: "My soul shall make her boast in the Lord; the humble shall hear thereof, and be glad" (Psalm 34:2). He has cause, indeed, to be always humble and penitent, but no cause to appear gloomy. A smiling aspect is comely, and, doubtless, none have so good reason to be of a cheerful countenance as the upright in heart.

If the believer, then, would have lasting and increasing comfort, let him be continually upon his guard against affected or pretended sadness, else he will provoke the Lord to deprive him of his present degree of comfort, and to afflict him with real sadness. Although he does not always enjoy sensible consolation, yet he has the root and the habit of it, and has always good cause to rejoice. Let him therefore be always cheerful, and on every occasion show that he can distinguish between gravity and sullenness, seriousness and gloominess; and let him never appear so ignorant as once to insinuate it to be right or becoming in any true Christian to appear habitually sad and sullen.

17. If the believer would attain increasing tranquility of mind, he must frequently examine his heart and conduct in order that he may the more clearly discern his evidences of personal interest in spiritual consolation. The more clearly he perceives his personal interest in Christ and in the covenant of grace, the higher will the degree of his holy comfort usually be. The more diligently he scrutinizes his heart and life, comparing them with the Word of God, and the more frequently and clearly he perceives, in consequence of the witnessing of the Holy Spirit, his evidences of union and communion with Christ, the more will his heart be comforted and encouraged; the more will he know that he is of the truth, and with greater confidence will he assure his heart before God (1 John 3:19, 21).

Now, when he has it in view at any time to examine himself, let him begin by renewing his act of trusting in Christ for all his salvation as well as for the joy of that salvation. For if he begins this inquiry by doubting whether the Lord Jesus will save him, or by yielding to distrust and despondency, he will be afraid to search deeply into his heart or to know the worst of himself. But if he begins it by an act of humble and direct confidence in Christ Jesus for his salvation in particular, he will be disposed, as well as encouraged, to deal impartially with himself. He will be willing to find out the worst as well as the best of himself. He will not be afraid to find that his heart, so far as it is unrenewed, is deceitful above all things and desperately wicked. Besides, by means of that acting of faith, his other graces will be invigorated and excited to lively exercise; and the more he exercises them, the more easily and the more clearly will he perceive them.

Further, let him begin it also by praying that the Holy Spirit may shine upon the graces which, he trusts, are implanted in his heart, and so "bear witness with his own spirit that he is a child of God" (Romans 8:16). He may then proceed to try his graces, and he should try them by their nature rather than by the degree of their strength or liveliness. Let him more especially examine himself whether he is in the faith, and so prove himself (2 Corinthians 13:5). If he does not discern true faith in his heart, yet, if he is conscious of an earnest desire to believe cordially in Jesus Christ, accompanied by frequent endeavors to do so, he ought to conclude that he has some measure of that precious faith.

An earnest and habitual desire of grace is itself grace, in the account of God (Matthew 5:6), and a man's desire for faith, love, hope, and of all the other graces of the Spirit is sincere and earnest when he desires them for their own intrinsic excellence and amiableness, and chiefly for the glory of God in Christ. And when, though he does not perceive them, he yet feels his need of them, and is conscious that he desires them, and desires even the perfection of them, let the believer, then, trusting that the Lord Jesus gives him grace, and that the holy Comforter will, in every time of need, shine upon that grace in his soul and render it apparent to him, enter frequently upon the trial of his state and conduct. And if he finds but one scriptural evidence of his being in a state of grace, he ought for his comfort to conclude that he has all the other evidences of being in it, though he cannot at present clearly perceive them. Nevertheless, he should frequently pursue the important inquiry till he has the comfort of discerning clearly all his evidences; for the more knowledge he has of his personal interest in the blessings of salvation, the more consolation he will enjoy.

Moreover, let the believer search daily into his

heart and life, in order to find out more of his sins and wants, that by a deep and affecting sense of them he may be urged to apply and plead frequently the promises of pardon and of sanctification. This is a necessary means of "walking in the comfort of the Holy Spirit" (Acts 9:31).

18. Finally, in order to advance in spiritual consolation, the believer must endeavor diligently to mortify his fear of death. Although death is, by the almighty Redeemer, so disarmed of its sting and strength that it can do no hurt to any of His redeemed, yet it is still a dreadful enemy to nature. When the exercised Christian thinks of temporal death as armed with the tremendous curse of the violated law and as a punishment of sin, it assumes even to him the grim and ghastly visage of the king of terrors. But when he contemplates it as removed from the curse of the covenant of works to the promise of the covenant of grace; as no longer a curse, but a blessing; and as no more an enemy, but a friend to all the spiritual seed of Christ, its terror should not make him afraid.

The Apostle Paul said to the believers at Corinth, "Death is yours" (1 Corinthians 3:22). And concerning himself, he said, "To me to live is Christ, and to die is gain" (Philippians 1:21). John, the beloved disciple, "heard a voice from heaven, saying unto him, 'Write, Blessed are the dead who die in the Lord' " (Revelation 14:13).

If temporal death, then, is an article in the inventory of the believer's treasure, and if as such it is his in promise, if it is gain to him and a blessing in disguise, why should he any longer fear it with a slavish dread? Why should he suffer himself so to fear it as, for a single moment, to lose the smallest degree of his holy consolation? If a good man, therefore, would subdue and rise superior to his fear of death, let him, under the sanctifying influences of the Holy Spirit, study to fear sin more and more. As one wedge drives out another, so the godly fear of sinning expels the slavish fear of dying.

Let him also, in the prospect of dying, commit frequently his soul, with all the concerns of it, to his infinitely merciful and faithful Redeemer; and let him commit it with unsuspecting confidence to Him, trusting firmly that, as He is able, so He is willing to keep that which he has committed to Him against the great day. Let him constantly entrust to the Lord Jesus the safety, comfort, and complete salvation of his precious soul; and as often as disquieting fear arises, let him say with the holy Psalmist, "What time I am afraid, I will trust in Thee" (Psalm 56:3). "None who trust in Him shall be desolate" (Psalm 34:22). Seeing the great Redeemer, "who liveth forevermore, and who hath the keys of hell and of death," invites and even commands the saints to trust Him with their souls, their bodies, and all their concerns, they may rest assured that He will not deceive their expectation. No, He will not deceive it, for He has promised that He will never leave them nor forsake them (Hebrews 13:5).

The believer should, for the same purpose, familiarize to his mind the thoughts of dying, and of his Redeemer's glorious victory over death and the grave. He ought to meditate frequently on Christ's having, as His federal representative, disarmed death to the dying Christian. The almighty Redeemer has disarmed it of its sting and strength, and so of all its terror. "The sting of death is sin; and the strength of sin is the law" (1 Corinthians 15: 56). Now the Lord Jesus "hath put away sin by the sacrifice of Himself," and He has perfectly fulfilled the law by His obedience unto death. Thus He has, for the true believer, disarmed death of its venomous sting, and, at the same time, of its strength or dreadful dominion. And what hurt can the most poisonous and frightful monster do to him when it has entirely lost both its sting and its strength?

The Redeemer promises that, by taking away the sting and the strength of it, He will remove the plague of death to His dying saints. Nay, He promises that by raising them up in glory at the last day He will be the destruction of death to His dead saints. "I will ransom them," said He, "from the power of the grave. I will redeem them from death. O death, I will be thy plague. O grave, I will be thy destruction; repentance shall be hid from Mine eyes" (Hosea 13:14). Accordingly, we read that He "hath abolished death" (2 Timothy 1:10); that is, He has annulled or reduced it to nothing, or so destroyed it to all who believe in Him as to have turned it from a curse to a blessing.

How consoling, then, how cheering is the thought that death disarmed can do no more harm to the dying believer than if it had been completely annulled! It can, indeed, separate his soul from his body; but it cannot separate either the one or the other from Him who is the living Redeemer, the resurrection and the life. The dying of a saint is but a sleeping; it is a sleeping in Jesus (1 Thessalonians

4:14). Death to him is but the shadow of death, not the substance. It is not the Omega, but the Alpha of his consummate felicity: he then begins to live when he begins to die. It is not the end either of his soul or of his body, but only a separation between them for an appointed time.

Let him also study, by an increasing diligence in the exercise of every grace, and in the practice of every duty, to be always actually, as well as habitually, prepared for death and judgment; for when he, in this manner, gives "all diligence to make his calling and election sure," he will, through grace, overcome gradually the disquieting fear of death and judgment, and will rejoice in hope of eternal life. James Hervey wrote, "Write down the reasons which, at any time, make you afraid to die, and then endeavor, by faith, prayer, and conversation with experienced Christians, to remove the causes."

Thus I have endeavored to point out to the exercised Christian those principal means of retaining and increasing spiritual consolation which he ought diligently to employ. The illustration of such of them as the disquieted believer was directed to use for the recovery of his forfeited comfort, I have studied, as far as I could, to diversify. I have only to add that, if the sincere believer uses them diligently, and if, instead of resting in them or depending on his use of them, he relies only upon his great Redeemer for all grace and consolation, he will increase in the principle and habit of spiritual joy, and will, in every time of need, be favored with sensible comfort.

From what has now been discoursed, the pious reader may easily see that no other pleasures under the sun are to be compared to those of faith and holiness. The pleasure of true religion, or of communion with God, far surpasses all the other delights of the sons of men. In comparison to other pleasures, it is pleasantness itself, pleasantness in the abstract. The pains of sense have frequently conquered and destroyed the delights of sense; but those pains, instead of having been able to conquer the delights of faith and holiness, have, in ten thousand instances, been counterbalanced and conquered by them. And while the pleasures of sense diminish, the delights of religion increase with the using. The longer a holy man continues, and the higher he advances, in the exercise of faith and practice of holiness, the greater and the sweeter is his delight. Besides, in order to enjoy and advance in the pleasures of religion, he is not called to relinquish any of the pleasures of sense, but such as are sinful, despicable, and produce misery.

Believer, as none has so much reason to rejoice as you, see that you exercise and increase your joy in the Lord. Study to attain an increasing cheerfulness of disposition and pleasantness of manner. These, so far as they are spiritual, will greatly promote holiness in yourself, and will so adorn it as to recommend it much to others.

Are spiritual knowledge and faith principal means of advancing in holy consolation? We may hence infer that those are usually the sweetest hours in the life of a believer in which he has the deepest sense of his need of Christ, the clearest discoveries of the fullness and suitableness of the willingness and glory of Christ, and the firmest confidence in Christ for the supply of all his wants. He commonly experiences the most solid comfort when he is most enabled and excited to entrust all his spiritual and temporal concerns to his divine Redeemer, whose power and grace, whose thoughts and ways infinitely surpass the highest conceptions of men and angels.

Those of the saints who have attained much sensible joy may, from the foregoing particulars, see how necessary it is for them to take heed that the height of their joy does not elate them with the pride of self-sufficiency. The sensible joy of God's salvation should never lift them up with self-conceit; and the want of such joy should never cast them down under disquieting and discouraging fear. The want of sensible joy should not for a moment deprive believers of their peaceful tranquility of mind. Their serenity of mind should be as great when they are with Jesus on Calvary sorrowing as when they are with Him on the Mount of Transfiguration rejoicing. The proper tendency of sensible joy is to humble; but, through the depravity remaining in the heart, it does not always have that effect. Let such believers, therefore, as are favored with sensible and lively emotions of joy take heed that they never delight in them so much as in Jesus, the Consolation of Israel; that they never yield to any temptation to rest in them or trust in them; and that they never think themselves more holy or more acceptable to God because of them. The more sensible joy they experience, the more humble, as well as self-diffident, they should be, and the more fervent in spirit, serving the Lord.

Let such believers as, by grace, have attained increasing consolation learn, from what has been said, always to take heed that they do not suffer their fear of sinning and of losing their comfort to degenerate into a perplexing scrupulousness of conscience. The Apostle Peter exhorted believers to "pass the time of their sojourning here in fear" (1 Peter 1:17); that is, in filial fear, which is a fear of sinning against God their heavenly Father. The Christian, indeed, ought daily to attain more and more of this filial fear; but he ought also for his comfort to keep it within its due bounds, and not to suffer it to run out into a vain and endless scrupulosity of conscience. He should be studying the law of God concerning sin and duty, and in every particular case have his conscience well informed. If his persuasion that this or that which presents itself to be done is lawful and right is grounded upon his knowledge of the spirituality and great extent of that holy law, his persuasion, in that case, may be full and firm. And being firmly persuaded that it is according "to the law and to the testimony," he should, without scruple, resolve to do it.

But if his persuasion of the lawfulness of that which he is requested or disposed to do is grounded on opinion only—if he is of the opinion merely that it is agreeable to the law, and so he is not fully persuaded—there will always remain a secret doubt in his mind that the contrary is his duty, and not this. In such a case, if the arguments for the lawfulness of it appear to his judgment more probable than those against the lawfulness of it, he should resolve to do it without allowing his resolution to be shaken by the latter.

But if the arguments against the lawfulness of it appear to his mind more probable than those for it, or even equally probable, in that case, doubting the lawfulness of it, he ought not to do it. For Paul says, "He that doubteth is damned," or condemned in his own conscience and by the Word of God, "if he eat, because he eateth not of faith; for whatsoever is not of faith is sin" (Romans 14:23). He who does what he himself does not determine to be lawful and right, but still doubts whether it is so or not, sins; for though he does that which may, in itself, and in the sight of God, be materially right, yet he does it not rightly because he, at the time, doubts whether it is lawful or not. In order to prevent his sinning in such cases, he should be fully persuaded in his own mind of the lawfulness of an action before he resolves to perform it; and then he will not condemn himself in that which he allows himself to do. And when he is fully persuaded that he may do this or that lawfully, and yet some objections to the contrary occur to his mind, he ought not to delay doing it till these difficulties are solved; for if he does, others may arise. Scruples will multiply the more they are attended to, and will dampen the resolution, and so mar the comfort of the exercised Christian.

Has any believer, after having been in the depths of spiritual trouble, not only recovered spiritual consolation, but attained an increase of it? His duty is constantly to admire and praise those wonders of the wisdom, power, faithfulness, and grace of Christ which he has seen in those depths (Psalm 107:24).

The floods of trouble, and the waves of terror, beat vehemently upon his soul; but the Lord Jesus, who sits upon the flood, has mercifully upheld him and has drawn him out of many waters. He has seen the wonders of the Redeemer's wisdom in dispensing to him trouble and comfort, terror and hope, sorrow and joy, and in teaching him by these means the malignity and bitterness of sin and the preciousness and freeness of grace; the wonders of His power and love in sustaining his fainting soul under the pressure of his overwhelming distress; and the wonders of His mercy and faithfulness in delivering him from the darkness of desertion and in bringing him forth to the light of communion with Himself.

Let him, then, with adoring gratitude, admire and praise these wonders, and say with the holy Psalmist, "Thou art the God that doeth wonders" (Psalm 77:14). He ought likewise, with holy reverence and ardent love, to say to his redeeming God, "O Lord, I will praise Thee; though Thou wast angry with me, Thine anger is turned away, and Thou comfortedst me" (Isaiah 12:1). "Thou hast turned for me my mourning into dancing. Thou hast put off my sackcloth, and girded me with gladness, to the end that my glory may sing praise to Thee, and not be silent. O Lord my God, I will give thanks unto Thee forever" (Psalm 30:11–12). Be assured, O Christian, that "it is good to sing praises unto our God, for it is pleasant, as well as comely" (Psalm 147:1). It will infuse a double sweetness into all your enjoyments. Though the Lord does not need your praises, yet He is glorified by them; and a growing disposition to praise Him is necessary to your own advancement in holy consolation.

To conclude, the Christian who is favored with the cheering light of God's gracious countenance may, from what has been discoursed, see that he is under the highest obligations to be more and more assiduous in using all the means of obtaining a daily increase of spiritual consolation. The sweetness, and especially the usefulness, of holy comfort for the purposes of his Redeemer's glory should excite him to unwearied diligence in employing every appointed means of attaining a daily increase of it. Let him live by faith, grow in grace, and take heed that he does not rest in comfort received as an evidence of grace. Let him also guard against taking his comfort from the act instead of the object of his faith, offered to him in the gospel.

9

Directions for Attaining Establishment in Holy Consolation

To be established is to be settled firmly or fixed unalterably in the enjoyment of some privilege, either of a spiritual or a temporal kind. By a believer's being established in spiritual comfort, I do not mean his being so established in a state of grace as to persevere therein to the end (for this is the common privilege of all who cordially believe—John 10:28), but his being settled firmly in the habit of peaceful tranquility and holy joy. This is the privilege of those only who are holy in an eminent degree.

An eminently holy man is established in solid consolation when, though he is not often favored with joyful frames or lively emotions of delight, yet he is blessed with a settled tranquility of mind, and with a constant inclination of heart to rejoice in Christ Jesus and delight in God as his God in Him. After he has attained settled comfort, his frames, notwithstanding, may often change, and his afflictions may be frequent and painful; but inasmuch as he trusts in Christ, and delights in the will of God, his inward consolation, in times even of great affliction, instead of being lessened, is commonly increased. The more sharp and painful his trials are,

344

his consolation is usually the more strong, sensible, and sweet; and so his times of outward affliction are ordinarily the seasons of his greatest inward comfort. The consoling influences which then are graciously afforded him serve to render the habit of holy joy in his soul the more stable, and the exercise of it the more lively and sensible. Now this is established and even everlasting consolation. It is heaven upon earth; it is the earnest, the foretaste, and the beginning of that celestial, ecstatic, endless delight which the happy believer is soon to enjoy in the immediate presence of God and of the Lamb.

If the exercised Christian would arrive at establishment in spiritual comfort, let him, in dependence on the grace of Christ, observe diligently the following directions, which I humbly offer to him as those which appear to me to be of all others the most adapted to his purpose:

1. Let him endeavor with all diligence to attain establishment in the assurance of faith. By the assurance of faith is meant a firm assent of the heart to the truth of the gospel, and a firm or assured confidence of the heart in Jesus Christ for that salvation which is offered and promised in the gospel. Or it is meant of a cordial belief of the divine testimony, and a cordial trust in the divine Savior for the whole of his salvation. In other words, it is a man's cordial belief of the record of God, with application to himself and his trusting firmly in Christ, and in God through Him, for all that salvation for himself which Jesus has purchased for him, and which God, in the gospel, offers to him.

His assurance of faith is not an assurance that

Christ has already saved him; but it is a trusting that Christ now saves him, and that He will save him with an everlasting salvation (Acts 15:11). It is the simple, direct confidence of his heart in the adorable Savior for his own salvation in particular. It is always the duty, though seldom the attainment, of the believer to receive the Word not only in assurance, but "in much assurance" (1 Thessalonians 1:5), and in every act of worship to draw near to his gracious God and Father not only in assurance, but "in full assurance of faith" (Hebrews 10:22).

Now the way to attain establishment in solid consolation is, through grace, to become established in this assurance of faith. The Christian must, for that end, not merely trust in the Lord Jesus for complete salvation for himself, but he must endeavor to place a firm trust, a steady affiance, a settled and an assured confidence in that infinitely faithful Redeemer. It must be his habitual endeavor to honor the exalted Savior not only with the confidence of his heart, but with strong, unsuspecting, and unshaken confidence. It will be necessary that, under the almighty operation of the Holy Spirit, he study diligently to become established in the faith, to "continue in the faith grounded and settled" (Colossians 1:23), and to "hold fast the confidence and the rejoicing of the hope, firm unto the end" (Hebrews 3:6).

By being established in the assurance or confidence of faith, the exercised Christian attains establishment in spiritual comfort. His establishment in faith does not indeed merit for him establishment in consolation; but the latter is in proportion to the

former, and is inseparably connected with it. Hence
are these declarations of Scripture: "If ye will not believe, surely ye shall not be established" (Isaiah 7:9).
"Believe in the Lord your God; so shall ye be established" (2 Chronicles 20:20). "Thou wilt keep him in
perfect peace (Hebrew is "in peace, peace") whose
mind is stayed on Thee, because he trusteth in
Thee" (Isaiah 26:3). To stay the mind on the Lord
Jesus is to repose a firm or settled confidence in
Him. Now the compassionate Savior will not suffer
such a resolute believer to continue oppressed and
tossed with disquietude of soul, but He will, on the
contrary, "keep him in peace, peace," that is, in all
manner of peace, or in great, settled, and durable
peace. This is the happy attainment of the man
"who feareth the Lord, who delighteth greatly in His
commandments. He shall not be afraid of evil tidings; his heart is fixed, trusting in the Lord. His
heart is established, he shall not be afraid" (Psalm
112:1, 7–8).

Such joy is in believing, or at least such peace
and such undisturbed quietness, as is in no other
thing in the world. It is by means of his inward and
assured confidence in the love, and care, and faithfulness of his great Redeemer that the advanced believer is carried wonderfully and sweetly through all
the outward vicissitudes of life. By trusting firmly in
his exalted Lord, his heart is fixed amidst all the
tumults and changes of this world. The hearts of
other men are unsteady; and therefore they are agi-
tated by every rumor, as the leaves of a tree are
shaken by the wind, or even "as the chaff which the
wind driveth away" (Psalm 1:4). But, as no tidings of

calamity can shake the confidence of that man whose faith is established on the Rock of his salvation, so none can disturb the tranquility of his heart. He shall be enabled to say, if afflictions come, "God is the strength of my heart, and my portion forever" (Psalm 73:26). He can say, "I know in whom I have believed. I trust that He will keep that which I have committed to Him" (2 Timothy 1:12), and know also that He will perform these great promises to him: "As thy days, so shall thy strength be" (Deuteronomy 33:25). "I will be with him in trouble; I will deliver him, and honor him" (Psalm 91:15).

Thus the advanced believer attains established comfort, for the confidence of his heart is firmly fixed on Christ and on the promises. He believes that the Lord Jesus can and will sweeten every bitter thing, make up every loss, and make all things work together for good to him. And so he trusts simply in the promise and power of the Redeemer beyond, and even against, appearances. Having but one Object to rely and live upon for all things in time and in eternity, his heart is fixed; his comfort is established. Come what will, he is upon the mountain of the Lord's house, where he looks down with calmness of spirit upon all the commotions beneath. And if the storm threatens him, he entrusts all to Him, who in one moment can say, "Peace, be still." Indeed, were his trust in the Rock of his salvation as firm as his spiritual state is secure, his holy joy would almost be equal to that of one of the ransomed above.

2. Believers, in order to arrive at established comfort, must also study to be rooted and grounded in love. The Apostle

Paul, in his epistle to the saints at Ephesus, informed them that he offered up this prayer for them: "That ye, being rooted and grounded in love, may be able to comprehend with all saints what is the breadth, and length, and depth, and height, and to know the love of Christ, which surpasseth knowledge, that ye may be filled with all the fullness of God" (Ephesians 3:17–19). To be rooted and grounded in love is to be deeply fixed and firmly established in love. Saints are rooted and grounded in love when they are deeply and firmly fixed in an experimental knowledge and an assured faith in Christ's infinite love for them, and in the exercise of grateful and ardent love toward Him; or when, in the faith and sense of His redeeming love to them, they are confirmed, or firmly settled and strengthened, in the habit and exercise of their supreme love toward Him, and toward God in Him. They may be said to be rooted and grounded in love when their faith in Christ's love, and the habit of their love toward Him, are firmly rooted and strengthened in their souls.

Now in order to be established in holy consolation, the believer must be established by the Holy Spirit in his love for Christ, and for God as his God in Him. Supreme love for God is the principal grace, the spring of all the other graces in a holy soul. It is, in particular, the principle of spiritual joy. In proportion as a holy man loves the Lord and enjoys communion with Him, he delights and rejoices in Him. He delights and rejoices in all His perfections, and in all the manifested glory of them. He rejoices in the works and the Word of the Lord. He delights in His preceptive and providential will, and in His holy image, whether he discerns it in himself or in others. The infinite loveliness and love of God in Christ are objects of his supreme delight. If, therefore, he is always loving and enjoying God, he is always, in the same proportion, delighted; and in proportion as he is delighted, he, of course, must be comfortable. If he is established in the faith in God's love for him, and in the exercise as well as in the habit of his love toward God, he shall, in the same degree, be established in divine consolation. It will be an inexpressible comfort to him to reflect that He, upon whom he has set the supreme love of his heart, is infinitely worthy of it. Besides, when he is established in his unfeigned love of God, he is proportionally confirmed in his hatred of all sin; and in proportion as he is firm in his holy abhorrence of all iniquity is established in holy comfort.

To be established, therefore, in supreme love of God and Christ is the way to become established in the comfort of the Holy Spirit. Hence are these words of the Apostle Paul to the believers at Colossae, "I would that ye knew what great conflict I have for you, and for them at Laodicea, and for as many as have not seen my face in the flesh, that their hearts might be comforted, being knit together in love" (Colossians 2:1–2). It is as if he had said, "I wrestle with God in prayer for all the saints that, as they already are firmly cemented together in cordial affection for Christ and for one another, so their hearts may be filled abundantly with holy consolation." He prayed for the latter as a consequence of the former.

Love is the most delightful affection of the soul. When therefore it is set upon the Lord Jesus, who is altogether lovely, and who is, for that reason, the most deserving of it, the more fixed and strengthened it is in the heart, and the greater must the delight and the stronger the consolation be which it will produce. Accordingly, when our Apostle said, "Who shall separate us from the love of Christ?" (Romans 8:35), it was with holy joy, and even with triumph, that he expressed those words. Oh, how inexpressibly delightful and cheering is it constantly to love and always to be loved by Him who is "the chiefest among ten thousand, and altogether lovely" (Song of Solomon 5:10, 16), yea, love itself!

3. It will be necessary, for the same purpose, that the exercised Christian be established in humility and meekness. He must be established in true humility, or evangelical humiliation of mind. True humility is the deep and abasing sense which a good man has of his odiousness as a sinner in the sight of God, of his vileness as a sinful creature, and of his utter insufficiency for his own salvation, and that accompanied by poverty of spirit. It is a true sight and sense of the hatefulness of all sin, and of his own odiousness because of sin, attended with a disposition to abase himself and exalt his God and Savior alone (Isaiah 2:11).

In evangelical humiliation, he is made not only to despair of ever being able to help himself, but to renounce himself in every point of view, and freely to prostrate himself at the feet of Jesus Christ. He has self-abasing views of himself as an unworthy sinner, and admiring views of the Lord Jesus as an all-sufficient Savior. He has also a quick perception of his own defects and defilements, and especially of the pride of his heart. He is therefore like a little child, afraid of taking a single step alone; and he is so conscious of weakness and depravity within, and of snares and dangers without, as to cry continually to the Lord to hold him up that he may be safe.

He is disposed to think that his attainments in holiness are comparatively small, and to count himself little among saints, yea, even one of the very least of saints. And the more he increases in humility, the more he sees and feels the strength of his corruptions and the weakness of his graces; the greatness of his natural deformity and the smallness of his spiritual attainments in comparison to what they ought to be; the deep and dreadful malignity of the least of his sins and the inexpressible meanness and deficiency of the greatest of his performances. The saints increase in humility the nearer they get to heaven. Paul, some years after his conversion, said of himself that he was unworthy to be called an Apostle. As he advanced in holiness, he cried out, "less than the least of all saints" (Ephesians 3:8). A little before his death his cry was, "the chief of sinners" (1 Timothy 1:15).

Hence, the exercised Christian becomes proportionably poor in spirit, and disposed, in lowliness of mind, to esteem other saints better than himself (Philippians 2:3).

Now, to advance to eminence and establishment in true humility is a special means of attaining establishment in pure consolation. "Should anyone," said Augustine, "ask me concerning the Christians' religion, and the people of it, I would answer that the first, the second, and the third thing in it, and all, is—humility." "Though the Lord be high, yet hath He respect unto the lowly" (Psalm 138:6). "Thus saith the high and lofty One, who inhabiteth eternity, whose name is holy: 'I dwell in the high and holy place, with him also who is of a contrite and humble spirit, to revive the spirit of the humble' " (Isaiah 57:15). "He that humbleth himself shall be exalted" (Luke 14:11). "Whosoever therefore shall humble himself as this little child, the same is greatest in the kingdom of heaven" (Matthew 18:4). Deep humility is, as it were, the guard of spiritual consolation, as well as the soil in which it grows.

It is no less necessary for the same end that the believer grow and be established in meekness. To be meek is to be of a mild, soft, and gentle spirit. The Christian, by putting on the new man, which is created in righteousness and true holiness, puts on "the ornament of a meek and quiet spirit" (1 Peter 3:4). He is meek in proportion as he is holy. Meekness is so much the character of every saint that the Scripture says that the meek and the wicked are opposed one to another. "The Lord lifteth up the meek; He casteth the wicked down to the ground" (Psalm 147:6). In proportion as a good man is meek, he is of a loving, merciful, and forgiving disposition. At the feet of Jesus, he has learned to be meek and lowly in heart; and therefore he is not captious, nor easily provoked, nor hard to be reconciled. If he meets with unkind and unjust usage, he recollects that, though he has not deserved such treatment from men, yet they are often the instruments

employed by his heavenly Father to chasten and to
humble him.

Now it is in proportion as the Christian advances
in holy meekness that he increases in pure consolation; and it is as far as he is established in the former that he is established in the latter. "The meek
shall inherit the earth, and shall delight themselves
in the abundance of peace" (Psalm 37:11). They
shall inherit the earth. The earth, empty and transitory as it is, will be worthy to be called an inheritance to them, for they shall enjoy much of heaven
upon earth. The more of a meek and quiet spirit
they attain, the more shall they enjoy themselves
and their earthly comforts, and the more quietly and
comfortably shall they pass through the world,
whatever their lot in it may be. "Learn of Me," said
the Lord Jesus, "for I am meek and lowly in heart,
and ye shall find rest unto your souls" (Matthew
11:29). He also promised that "the meek shall eat
and be satisfied" (Psalm 22:26), and that "the meek
shall increase their joy in the Lord" (Isaiah 29:19).

*4. If the believer would reach establishment in holy com-
fort, he must study daily to grow in grace.* It must be his
earnest and continual endeavor, in the faith in
God's free favor to him, to grow stronger and
stronger in the habit, and to abound more and
more in the exercise, of every grace implanted by the
Holy Spirit in his soul. By so doing, spiritual declension and the loss of comfort will, under sanctifying
and consoling influences, be happily prevented.
The Apostle Peter, in order to prevent the believers
to whom he wrote from being so led away with the
error of the wicked as to fall from their own stead-

fastness, directed them to "grow in grace" (2 Peter 3:18). Believers, "holding the Head, and having nourishment ministered," ought in point of duty, as well as of privilege, to "increase with the increase of God" (Colossians 2:19). It is their duty to "grow up into Christ who is the Head," not only in all things, but at all times (Ephesians 4:15). Their path should always be "as the morning light, that shineth more and more unto the perfect day" (Proverbs 4:18). They ought at all times to grow inwardly by faith and love, cleaving more firmly to Christ the Head of gracious influences; to grow outwardly by being more and more fruitful in good works (Titus 3:8); to grow upward in heavenly-mindedness and joy in God (Philippians 3:20); and to grow downward in humility and self-denial. To grow thus in grace, and to grow continually in it, is the sure way to attain establishment in spiritual comfort. For the more a holy man advances in grace, the firmer his habits of grace become; and the firmer they are, the more "his heart is established with grace" (Hebrews 13:9). The more it is established with grace, the more is he established in the truth, so as to "continue in the faith grounded and settled" (Colossians 1:23); and the more this is the case with him, the more is "his heart established unblamable in holiness" (1 Thessalonians 3:13). But in proportion as his heart is established in holiness, which comprises joy, and which is the only true felicity of an immortal soul, it is established in holy consolation.

5. *It will be necessary, for the same purpose, that he be continually upon his guard against sinning in his use and enjoyment of lawful things.* The believer may assure him-

self that he pursues and uses lawful things in an unlawful manner:

• If he desires or enjoys them immoderately, if he
loves any of them so passionately as to have his heart
enflamed with it (Isaiah 57:5), and to be hindered by
it from the vigorous exercise of grace or the spiritual
performance of duty;

• If his desire and endeavor to obtain the enjoyment of some outward comforts becomes ardent and
renders him impatient (Genesis 30:1) so that he begins to say, "I must have such and such a thing,
whatever it may cost me";

• If his heart becomes so fond and tender of any
of his earthly comforts as not to be able to endure
the thought that either the Word or the rod of God
should come so near as to touch it (2 Samuel 18:5);

• If he entertains hopes of high satisfaction from
any outward enjoyment, or promises himself more
profit or pleasure from it than it is fitted to afford
(Jeremiah 2:13);

• If when the Lord is, by His providence, calling
for some one of his earthly comforts, he is so very
unable and unwilling to resign it as to become impatient and fretful, and to render it necessary that it
be forced from him;

• If he becomes so anxious about the good
things of this life as to be often ready to say, "What
shall I eat? Or what shall I drink? Or wherewithal
shall I be clothed?" (Matthew 6:31).

And if, when the Lord has been visiting him with
some special dispensation in order to wean him
from earthly enjoyments, his heart is still cleaving to
them—if, I say, he pursues or uses earthly comforts

in any of those ways—he so uses them as to abuse them. He uses lawful things in an unlawful manner, and so transgresses the law of God. He sets them up as idols in his heart and, by his inordinate and undue affection for them, he impairs his inward consolation, and provokes his heavenly Father even to leave him for a season without the comfort of communion with Him.

Now, the love of earthly things, and the deceitfulness of sin, which remain in the heart of the believer are such that they will continually expose him to the danger of sinning in one or another of those ways in his pursuit or use of lawful things. If, then, he would advance to establishment in spiritual comfort, he must continually take heed that he does not, in a sinful manner, pursue and enjoy lawful comforts. It will be necessary that he be, at all times, sober and vigilant lest he, at any time, so love the world as to use lawful things in a sinful manner. And it must be his constant endeavor, through grace, so to use his outward comforts as to enjoy the inward comfort of communion with Christ in his use of them. He must always live above them, and never place his happiness in them. He ought to keep them constantly in their own place, and to value them not so much for themselves as for the opportunities and facilities which they afford him of glorifying his God and Savior.

6. In order to be established in pure consolation, it will be no less necessary that the Christian be firmly fixed in his resolution and endeavor to avoid those places and that company which appear to have even a remote tendency to draw him into sin. He must, for that purpose, be always firm in his

resolution never, without evident necessity or a clear
providential call, to be present in the company of
worldly and wicked men. And when at any time he
has such a call, he should never stay longer in their
company than till his business with them is trans-
acted. He ought, on all occasions, to show them that
he loves their persons, but not their company, and
that he is ready to do them all the good that he can,
but not to countenance them in any evil. It must
also be his firm resolution never to venture into
their company, however clear his call is, till after he
has entrusted his temper, his manner, and his object to that Savior who "preserveth the souls of His
saints" (Psalm 97:10), and who has said to each of
them, "I will teach thee in the way which thou shalt
go; I will guide thee with Mine eye" (Psalm 32:8).

It is his duty to maintain constantly a holy jealousy over himself, and, having tasted the sweetness
of heavenly consolation, to live as distant as possible
from the ensnaring society of worldly men. As he
cannot approach too near to God, so he cannot
stand at too great a distance from sin. It will not
therefore be enough for him to keep himself merely
from acts of sin; he must endeavor constantly to ab-
stain even from all appearances of evil, and from
that company and those amusements which have
even a remote tendency to lead him into sin. Such
conduct will, indeed, expose him to the contempt
and ridicule of ungodly men. Some will account
him a designing hypocrite; others, a precise formalist; and others, a weak and gloomy enthusiast. Be it
so: "his witness is in heaven, and his record is on
high" (Job 16:19). He can say that never, till he be-

lieved in Jesus Christ, did he know what it was to enjoy real pleasure or true satisfaction. He can from
experience attest that communion with Christ in
His redeeming love and grace is so delightful, so
cheering, that one who has tasted the sweetness of it
cannot but desire more and more of it, in preference to all the mean gratifications and polluted delights of carnal men.

The men of the world, therefore, should cease to
wonder, if the experienced Christian so conducts
himself as to evince on all occasions his firm resolution to prefer the marrow and fatness of pure consolation before the husks of vanity and sin. Indeed,
such a resolution, manifested by a suitable conduct,
is indispensably necessary to established comfort;
for, though the former does not merit the latter, yet
the one is inseparably connected with the other.
The more firmly fixed a saint is in his holy resolution and endeavor always to avoid whatever has a
known tendency to draw him into sin, the more established shall he be in his enjoyment of everlasting
consolation. "I have not sat with vain persons," said
the holy Psalmist, "neither will I go in with dissem-
blers. I have hated the congregation of evildoers,
and I will not sit with the wicked" (Psalm 26:4–5).
And again, "Blessed is the man that walketh not in
the counsel of the ungodly, nor standeth in the way
of sinners, nor sitteth in the seat of the scornful. He
shall be like a tree planted by the rivers of water, that
bringeth forth his fruit in his season; his leaf also
shall not wither, and whatsoever he doeth shall
prosper. The ungodly are not so" (Psalm 1:1, 3–4).

7. If the advanced Christian would arrive at establishment in spiritual comfort, he must attain some degree of establishment in the assurance of sense. The assurance of sense is an assurance of vital union with Christ, or of personal interest in Him, founded on scriptural evidences thereof. It is the believer's certain knowledge of his being united to Christ, and is built on the sense or experience which he has of his possessing those evidences of union and communion with Christ which are stated in the Scriptures.

In this place, I shall take notice only of three of those evidences:

EVIDENCE 1. Saving faith is a sure evidence of union with Jesus Christ. While, according to the covenant of grace, faith is the instrument of vital union with the second Adam, it is, at the same time, an evidence of that union. "He that eateth My flesh," said the Lord Jesus, "and drinketh My blood, dwelleth in Me, and I in him" (John 6:56). "Verily, verily, I say unto you, He that believeth on Me hath everlasting life" (John 6:47). "He that believeth and is baptized shall be saved" (Mark 16:16).

If an exercised Christian has just and distinct views of the nature of true faith as declared in the Scriptures, if he clearly understands what it is to believe Christ and what it is to believe in Him, and if, at the same time, his actings of faith are direct and lively, he will, under the witnessing of the Holy Spirit, be less or more conscious of them. He will be enabled to reason thus: "He who believeth on Jesus Christ dwelleth in Him and hath everlasting life (John 6:46–47). But I am conscious that I believe on Him; therefore I dwell in Him and shall be saved

(Acts 16:31). I believe on Him; therefore I am united to Him, and I shall be saved."

And in order to be satisfied that His actings of faith are unfeigned and not hypocritical (1 Timothy 1:5), let him, in dependence on the enlightening influences of the Spirit of truth, attend carefully to the distinctions marked in the Sacred Volume between a true and a counterfeit faith. There he shall find that if a man, convinced of his sin and misery, believes the record of God with application to himself, and with cordial approbation of the whole plan of redemption by Jesus Christ; if he trusts in Jesus for salvation, not upon the ground of previous qualification in himself, but solely upon the warrant afforded by the gospel offer, the gospel call, a commandment to believe on the name of Jesus Christ (John 3:27 and 4:10); if he relies (unlike the hypocrite, who rests partly on his own performances and partly on the righteousness of Christ) on the righteousness of Christ only for all his title to eternal life (Romans 9:31–32); that if he trusts in the Savior for salvation from all iniquity, and especially from the sin that easily besets him, or, in other words, for the whole of salvation (2 Samuel 23:5; Lamentations 3:26; 2 Timothy 4:18); if he trusts for that salvation only which is wholly of sovereign grace, and in which the glory of redeeming grace is most illustriously displayed (Acts 15:11); and if his faith works by love and purifies the heart—there he shall find, I say, that he exercises it, and he may consider it as a good evidence that he is united to Christ, and interested in His righteousness and salvation.

That is the faith of God's elect. It is "a believing with the heart unto righteousness" (Romans 10:10), "a trusting in the Lord with all the heart" (Proverbs 3:5); and, therefore, when the holy Comforter shines upon it as His own work in the soul, it cannot fail to be comfortably evident to the Christian that he is in a state of grace.

EVIDENCE 2. Unfeigned love for God and the saints is also a sure evidence of union and communion with Christ. "He that loveth Me," said the Lord Jesus, "shall be loved by My Father, and I will love him, and will manifest Myself to him" (John 14:21). "If any man love God, the same is known of him" (1 Corinthians 8:3). "He that dwelleth in love dwelleth in God, and God in him" (1 John 4:16). "Everyone that loveth is born of God, and knoweth God" (1 John 4:7). If, then, a man loves Christ, and God in Him, for His infinite loveliness in Himself, as well as for His redeeming love toward him; if he loves all of God, all His perfections, and especially His holiness, all His purposes and providential dispensations, all His precepts, promises, and ordinances, and that chiefly because they are holy; if he loves God supremely, setting Him upon the throne in his affections; and if he laments sincerely that he does not love Him more—such love is a good evidence to him that he is "an heir of God, and a joint heir with Christ" (Romans 8:17).

A pious mother dearly loves her sucking child, but she never complains that she loves it too little: whereas she often laments that she loves the Lord Jesus too little, and often fears that she loves her infant more, or at least as much, as she loves Him. But

these complaints and fears are proofs that her affection for her Savior is greater than it is for her child.
They show that she sees much more reason to love
and admire Him than to love the most amiable of
creatures, and that she wishes to esteem Him, and to
delight in Him, more than in any creature. The
more a saint feels, and bitterly bewails, the coldness
of his affection, or the sinful deficiency of his love
for his God and Savior, the more evidence has he of
the sincerity of his love for Him. The hypocrite pre-
tends to love the Lord, but he never loathes himself
in his own sight for loving Him too little; for he
thinks that he loves Him a great deal, and is even
proud of the greatness of his love for Him. On the
other hand, the sincere believer, knowing that it is a
sinful and abominable defect *not* to love Him, even
in a perfect degree, loathes himself often in secret
for the criminal imperfection of his love for Him.

Unfeigned love of the brethren, flowing from
supreme love for God, is likewise a sure evidence of
union and communion with Christ. "By this shall
all men know that ye are My disciples, if ye have love
one for another" (John 13:35). "We know that we
have passed from death unto life, because we love
the brethren" (1 John 3:14). "My little children, let
us not love in word, neither in tongue, but in deed
and in truth. And hereby we know that we are of the
truth, and shall assure our hearts before Him"
(1 John 3:18–19). "If we love one another, God
dwelleth in us, and His love is perfected in us"
(1 John 4:12).

If, then, a man is conscious that, while he loves
all others as creatures of God with a love of benevo-

lence, he loves all the saints with a love of complacence; that he regards all with cordial esteem and
affection, to whatever denomination they belong,
who appear to be saints of the Most High; that he is
pleased with them, and delighted in their company,
not so much because they are generous or kind or
serviceable to Him as because they are holy and devout; that he loves them not so much for their upright, peaceable, and courteous demeanor, or for
their charity, fidelity, and usefulness in society, as
for the truth's sake which dwells in them, and for
the holy image of the Son of God which shines forth
in their conversation; and that he regards them in
proportion to the degrees of holiness which appear
in them, with such affectionate kindness and tenderness as to be always careful not to hurt, neglect,
or offend them—if, I say, he is conscious that he
thus loves the saints, he may consider such love of
them as a comfortable evidence that he himself is
one of their number. He may, for his comfort, conclude that his love of the image of Christ in others is
a valid proof of the grace and image of Christ in
himself. For as no saint can love a sinner as a sinner
(Psalm 139:21–22), so no hypocrite or sinner can
love a saint as a saint, however much he may regard
him with affection on other accounts.

EVIDENCE 3. The practice of universal holiness,
or obedience of heart and life, to all the commandments of the moral law as a rule of life is, likewise, a
sure evidence of a man's union and communion
with Christ. "He that hath My commandments, and
keepeth them," said the Lord Jesus, "he it is that
loveth Me" (1 John 3:14). "Therefore, whosoever

heareth these sayings of Mine, and doeth them, I will liken him unto a wise man who built his house upon a rock" (Matthew 7:24). And the Apostle John: "Hereby we do know that we know Him, if we keep His commandments. Whoso keepeth His word, in him, verily, is the love of God perfected; hereby know we that we are in Him" (1 John 2:3, 5). "He that keepeth His commandments dwelleth in Him, and He in him" (1 John 3:24).

The behavior or practice of every man who is vitally united to the holy Jesus is universally conformed to the law as a rule of duty. Such a holy practice is the grand business of his life—the business in which he is chiefly engaged, and which he pursues with more earnestness and diligence than he does any other. His understanding is divinely enlightened to see the transcendent beauty of holiness; his will is renewed to choose holiness, and his affections are sanctified to love, desire, and delight in it. He is also constrained by the love commanded by the law, and enabled by the Spirit of Christ, to be "holy in all manner of conversation" (1 Peter 1:15). He, therefore, makes the constant practice of universal holiness his choice, his delight, and, in an eminent degree, his employment. Relying on the righteousness of Jesus Christ for all his title to eternal life, trusting in Christ for continual supplies of grace, and aiming in all his performances at the glory of God, he perseveres, through all changes and under all trials, in the love and practice of universal holiness to the end of life. He may indeed be left to be guilty in some degree of spiritual declension, and may be suffered to yield so far to some temptations as even to fall occasionally into great sins; but he shall never be permitted so to fall that it will cease to be his manner, even in the most difficult situations, to perform sincerely all duties required of him, even the most difficult.

Now, when a man is conscious that he is relying on the suretyship and righteousness of Jesus Christ for all his title to life eternal, that he is trusting in Christ for all promised supplies of sanctifying grace, and that he is believing the love which God has for him, he is enabled cordially to perform obedience to all the commandments of Christ. When he finds that he is enabled to yield universal obedience, not that it may secure him from hell or entitle him to heaven, not merely because he is bound to perform it, but because he is constrained by the love for Christ and because he wishes and delights and resolves to do it; when he is conscious that he purposes and practices universal holiness, according to the law as a rule, from principles of supreme love to God and unfeigned gratitude to Jesus Christ, who fulfilled all righteousness for him, according to the same law and covenant; and when he knows by experience that he has been enabled under manifold trials resolutely to cleave to Christ and His Word, and habitually to make the glory of Christ, and of God in Him, the chief end of all his performances—he ought to consider this holy obedience as a sure, distinguishing evidence that he is united to the Lord Jesus.

Indeed, universal holiness of heart and of life is the most sure, the most unquestionable evidence of a personal interest in Christ. It is the sign of signs, the chief of all the signs of grace. No faith is an evidence of union with Christ but that which is made perfect by works (James 2:22). No love is a sign of it but that which is perfected in keeping His Word (1 John 2:5). Holy practice is the highest evidence of connection with the holy Jesus, the great mark of distinction between the children of God and the children of the devil (1 John 3:10).

It is very remarkable that this evidence is much more insisted on in the Scriptures than any other. "Blessed are the undefiled in the way, who walk in the law of the Lord" (Psalm 119:1). "Then shall I not be ashamed, when I have respect unto all Thy commandments" (Psalm 119:6). "If ye love Me," said our Lord, "keep My commandments. If a man love Me, he will keep My words. He that loveth Me not keepeth not My sayings" (John 14:15, 23–24). "Herein is My Father glorified, that ye bear much fruit; so shall ye be My disciples. Ye are My friends, if ye do whatsoever I command you" (John 15:8, 14). "Little children," said the Apostle John, "let no man deceive you: he that doeth righteousness is righteous, even as He is righteous. Whosoever doeth not righteousness is not of God" (1 John 3:7, 10). "This is the love of God, that we keep His commandments" (1 John 5:3).

The man, therefore, who is truly conscious that, from principles of faith and love, and for the glory of God, he forsakes with abhorrence every known sin, and studies to know and perform cordially every commanded duty, may warrantably assure himself that he is united to Christ, and is in a state of grace. Let the believer, then, endeavor diligently to attain

more and more of this high evidence of grace. So
shall he arrive not only at sensible assurance of his
union with Christ, but at establishment in that assurance. Indeed, when a man trusts, with cordial
and strong confidence, in Christ Jesus for salvation,
he trusts that Christ will afford him evidences of salvation; and the consequence will be that his mind
will never be entirely at ease till he sees that he has,
at least, the evidences mentioned above. Whatever
degree of the assurance of faith he attains, he will,
in the same degree, be diligent to attain, as soon as
possible, the assurance of sense and establishment
in this assurance.

And here I must remind the exercised Christian
that however diligent he may be in the practice of
holiness, he cannot attain this holy assurance,
much less establishment in it, but by the testimony
of the blessed Spirit, the Comforter. It is the same
Holy Spirit who has implanted in his heart all saving graces who can, by shining upon them, make
him "know the things which are freely given to him
of God" (1 Corinthians 2:12). As the sun cannot be
seen but by its own light, so the graces and fruits of
the Spirit cannot be certainly known but by the light
of the Spirit. The believer cannot be assured that the
Spirit dwells in him as a Sanctifier otherwise than by
the same blessed Spirit as a Comforter. "The Spirit itself," or, "the same Spirit," said the Apostle Paul,
"beareth witness with our spirits, that we are the
children of God" (Romans 8:16). The same Spirit
that works habits of grace and holy dispositions in
the hearts of believers, by shining upon these, by exciting their attention to them, and by enabling

them to compare them with the signs of adoption mentioned in Scripture, concurs with their consciences in witnessing that they are the children of God. In order, then, to attain such establishment in sensible assurance as will introduce establishment in spiritual comfort, the Christian must frequently trust, as well as pray, for the witnessing of the Holy Spirit; and he should continually take heed that he does not grieve the Spirit (Ephesians 4:30).

8. Moreover, in order to be established in pure consolation, the believer must endeavor, with all diligence, to make a right and profitable use of the holy Sacraments. These are the seals of the covenant of grace, for they were instituted in order to confirm that holy covenant with true believers (Daniel 9:27). They, accordingly, in the hand of the holy Comforter, are special means of confirming that everlasting covenant with them; and they confirm it with them not by making it firmer in itself than it is already, but by confirming their faith in it, and by clearing up or confirming to them their personal interest in it, and in all the blessings promised in it.

The believer, then, in order to be established in spiritual comfort, must improve his baptism both to confirm his assurance of faith and his assurance of personal interest in the everlasting covenant. He ought, for these purposes, to improve it at all times, but especially when he is called either to present a child for baptism or to witness the dispensation of baptism to the child of another. Seeing baptism, in the place of circumcision, is a seal especially "of the righteousness of faith" (Romans 4:11), he should, in witnessing the dispensation of it, renew his cordial

application of the spotless righteousness of Jesus
Christ which, in the gospel, is revealed from faith to
faith. Since the water in baptism represents the
cleansing virtue of the blood and the Spirit of Christ
(Revelation 1:5; Titus 3:5), he ought, when he sees
the baptismal water applied to the body, to seize the
precious opportunity afforded him of applying the
justifying blood of Christ to his conscience for
cleansing it from its guilt and pollution, and the
sanctifying Spirit of Christ to his heart for cleansing
it from the power of sin. And, relying on the righteousness and blood of Jesus for a complete title to
deliverance from the guilt, power, and pollution of
sin, and trusting in the Lord Jesus Himself for all
his salvation, he should then within himself say, "As
certainly as I have now seen the baptismal water
sprinkled upon the body of that infant, the blood
and the Spirit of Christ are mine not only in offer,
but in possession; and while they are mine to justify,
sanctify, and comfort me, Christ Himself is mine as
my Covenant-Head, and God is mine as my
Covenant-God, from henceforth and forever." And
seeing that the child is, in its baptism, solemnly
dedicated to the Lord, he ought further to say, "O
Lord, I devote myself and all that I am to Thee, to be
Thine wholly, only, and forever, to be saved by Thy
grace, and to be employed for Thy glory."

That the exercised Christian may attain establishment in true consolation, he must likewise improve the holy Sacrament of the Supper. He must,
with increasing diligence, improve it for the con-
firmation of both his assurance of faith and his assurance of union and communion with his great

Redeemer. When, after due preparation, he has sat down at the communion table, he ought, with suitable affections, not only to remember and meditate on the amazing love of Christ in serving and suffering for him, but upon seeing the sacramental bread given him he should say, "As certainly as the sacred bread is now given me, with a command to take and eat of it, Jesus, my gracious, my crucified Redeemer, is now given me in offer; and the offer, together with the commandment to believe on His name, affords me a warrant to accept and to trust in Him."

When he is taking and eating of the bread, he should from his heart say, "O Lord Jesus, upon the warrant of Thy offer and command, I now accept Thee as my only Savior, and trust with firm confidence in Thee for all my salvation." Upon seeing the cup of blessing presented to him, he should not forget to say, "As certainly as this cup is now given me, with my Redeemer's express command to drink of it, His righteousness, and all the promises and blessings of the new testament in His blood, are given me in offer; and the offer, together with the commandment to believe on His name, affords me a full right to receive and rely on them."

When he is taking and drinking of the cup, he ought to say, "O my adorable Redeemer, I now, upon the warrant of Thy free offer and authoritative command, accept Thy consummate righteousness, and rely upon it only for all my title to the inestimable blessings promised and bequeathed in the new testament, and ratified by Thy death; and believing that Thy righteousness, and all the benefits merited by it, are given me in offer upon the warrant of Thy authentic offer and command, I trust cordially that Thou givest them to me also in possession."

Appropriating and feeding thus upon the body and blood of the incarnate Redeemer, the believer's faith is confirmed, and all his other graces are proportionally strengthened; for it is unto him according to his faith.

Moreover, conscious that his heart is accepting and trusting in the Lord Jesus for all the blessings bequeathed in His testament, the believer ought, upon hearing these cheering words from Luke 22:19–20 ("This is My body broken for you," and, "This cup is the new testament in My blood, which is shed for you"), assure himself that Christ, with His righteousness and salvation, is his not only in offer, but in possession. And he should regard the bread and the cup now given him as visible tokens and pledges of his union and communion with his dear Redeemer, and of his personal interest in all the promises and blessings of the new covenant.

In other words, having, in the exercise of trusting in Jesus Christ for his salvation in particular, received the bread and the cup, he ought to consider them as visible signs and pledges that the body of Christ was broken for him, and that the blood of Christ was shed for him. And if, through infirmity, he, when sitting at the Table of the Lord, forgets this, or any other part of the exercise of taking communion, let him not be discouraged; but let him attend to it after he rises from the Table and when he sees others communing. Thus, by the blessing of Christ, he shall find this holy ordinance to be not only an instrument of conveying more grace to him, but a seal and a pledge to confirm both his assurance of faith and his assurance of interest in Christ and the covenant of grace. And in proportion as these are confirmed, his holy tranquility of mind is established, and his cordial resolution of heart to devote himself wholly to the service and glory of Christ is strengthened.

9. Last, if the believer would attain established consolation, he should endeavor diligently, according to the opportunities afforded him, to promote the extension and establishment of the Redeemer's spiritual kingdom. This is a sure means of his arriving at solid and durable comfort. "Pray for the peace of Jerusalem; they shall prosper that love thee" (Psalm 122:6). "Let them shout for joy and be glad, that favor my righteous cause; yea, let them say continually, 'Let the Lord be magnified, who hath pleasure in the prosperity of His servant' " (Psalm 35:27). "I will make thee an eternal excellency, a joy of many generations" (Isaiah 60:15). "Rejoice ye with Jerusalem, and be glad with her, all ye that love he. Rejoice for joy with her, all ye that mourn for herr that ye may suck, and be satisfied with the breasts of her consolations; that ye may milk out, and be delighted with the abundance of her glory" (Isaiah 66:10–11).

When the Apostle Paul had reviewed the success of his ministry among the Corinthians, he addressed them thus: "Great is my glorying in you; I am filled with comfort, I am exceedingly joyful in all our tribulation" (2 Corinthians 7:4). The constant and earnest endeavors of the saints to promote and extend, according to the law of Christ's kingdom, the interests of His Church militant do not indeed entitle them to stable comfort; but they are usually connected with it. The glorious King of Zion has decreed that they who, by His grace, are habitually disposed to contribute, by their prayers, their labors, and their substance, to promote so great and so glorious a design shall, even in this valley of tears, participate with Him in that ineffable joy wherewith He always rejoices over His church (Zephaniah 3:17).

If a Christian, instead of being of a liberal and public spirit, is contracted in his views, and concerned mainly for his own welfare, and that of a particular party, he is not qualified for strong and durable consolation. Established comfort, like fame, will elude the grasp of him who pursues it merely or chiefly for himself and for its own sake. One reason, perhaps, why some believers at this day have little spiritual and lasting comfort is that, in comparison to it, they care little for more weighty things. If they were more employed in seeking the glory of Christ, the success of His blessed gospel, and the extension of His spiritual kingdom, both at home and abroad, than in seeking ease and comfort for themselves, they would find that holy and lasting consolation would come, as it were, of its own accord, and flow freely into their souls. Were they to seek first the kingdom of God and His righteousness, they would experience more frequently, and in a higher degree, that righteousness, peace, and joy in the Holy Ghost of which His kingdom consists (Romans 14:17).

From what has been here advanced, the following reflections are obvious:

If any of my readers is destitute of true religion and spiritual consolation, he may hence see that he is yet an entire stranger to true happiness. It is impossible for a man to be happy if his soul is miserable; but the soul of a sinner cannot *but* be miserable so long as he continues destitute of evangelical holiness and pure consolation. The greatest variety and highest degree of sinful pleasures leave the soul as miserable as they found it; but the lowest degree of holy comfort renders it happy. Be persuaded, then, O unregenerate man, that so long as you continue under the guilt and dominion of sin, "thou art wretched, and miserable, and poor, and blind, and naked" (Revelation 3:17).

You are a sinner against the infinitely holy and righteous Jehovah, a sinner in Adam, a sinner by nature and by practice. Your transgressions are innumerable, for you have been a transgressor from the womb. And as the smallest sin that ever you have committed deserves the infinite wrath of the great and terrible God, you are at this moment under the tremendous curse of His violated law. You are condemned already, and the wrath of God abides on you. Death is already on its way to you, and perhaps is so near that you have not a day or even an hour to live. If it should surprise you in your present state, the condemning sentence of the broken law must be executed upon you without intermission and without end. The faithfulness, as well as the holiness and justice, of that God whose eternal indignation you have deserved renders it necessary, if you die under the guilt but of a single sin, that the dreadful curse be eternally executed upon you. Ah, if you die impenitent, and without union with the great Redeemer, you must go away into everlasting punishment. You must be punished with endless torment, with everlasting destruction, with the vengeance of eternal fire. You must be punished in "the lake which burneth with fire and brimstone," till that divine justice which you have insulted is fully satisfied, and till that terrible wrath which you have incensed is to the uttermost endured.

Oh, how inexpressibly miserable must you at length be if you shall be condemned to sink through all eternity in the bottomless abyss of infinite wrath! How can your heart endure, or your hands be strong, in the days when God almighty will thus deal with you? How shall you be able to dwell with the devouring fire, to dwell with everlasting burnings? The day is coming when, if you die in your sins, the omniscient Judge of the quick and the dead will say to you, "Depart from Me, thou cursed, into everlasting fire, prepared for the devil and his angels." You now take pleasure in committing some secret, darling sin; and this is a sure evidence that you are an entire stranger to Christ and to holy consolation from Him. Now you love and enjoy the pleasures of sin; but hereafter, if sovereign mercy prevents it not, you shall feel the pains of it. It will bite like a serpent, and sting like an adder. The gnawing worm will never die; the consuming fire will never be quenched.

You are now surrounded by a multiplicity of objects with which you gratify your depraved desires, but in the place of torment, while these desires will continue and even increase, you shall have no opportunities of gratifying them. Now you are so desirous of the delights of sense and of sin that you continue to reject the compassionate Savior, and that everlasting consolation which is enjoyed in Him, for fear that you may lose those base and sordid delights. But yet a very little while and these pleasures shall not only be irretrievably lost, but shall be followed by the dismal sorrows of eternal death and be expiated with everlasting pain. For thus it is written: "Upon the wicked He shall rain snares, fire and brimstone, and a horrible tempest; this shall be the portion of their cup" (Psalm 11:6). God "will render to every man according to his deeds . . . To them that are contentious, and do not obey the truth, but obey unrighteousness, indignation and wrath, tribulation and anguish, upon every soul of man that doeth evil" (Romans 2:6; 8–9). Ah, secure sinner, eternal destruction is ready at your side. God is angry with you every day, and to Him vengeance belongs. His sword is drawn; His bow is bent; and His arrows are set to destroy you. But why, oh, why will you die? Why will you continue a moment longer to prefer sin, which is infinitely detestable, before holiness, which is infinitely amiable, and the base pleasures of sin before the exalted, ennobling, everlasting joys of God's salvation?

The God of all grace and consolation now offers Jesus Christ, with His righteousness and salvation, to you, a lost sinner of mankind. He offers Him wholly and freely, presently and particularly. Jesus, the faithful and true witness, said, "God so loved the world that He gave His only begotten Son, that whosoever believeth in Him should not perish, but have everlasting life." And, "My Father giveth you the true bread from heaven." And, "Him that cometh to Me, I will in no wise cast out." And the Apostle John said, "This is the record, that God hath given to us eternal life; and this life is in His Son."

The compassionate Savior, with infinite earnestness and tenderness, invites and entreats all, even the chief of sinners, to accept the gracious offer. He now says to you, "Come, eat of My bread, and drink of the wine, the wine of spiritual consolation, which I have mingled. Forsake the foolish and live. Come, yea, come, buy wine and milk without money, and without price. Whosoever will, let him take the water of life freely."

Sinner, *now* is the accepted time; *now* is the day of salvation. Oh, comply now with the gracious, endearing invitation, and look to Jesus for the Spirit of faith. Comply because it is your first, your principal duty, without which no other duty can be so performed as to please God. I beseech you to accept the authentic offer of a gracious Savior, and of a free salvation. I earnestly entreat you, by all the transcendent glory and incomparable excellence of the only begotten of the Father, by all His saving offices and endearing relations, by all His service and suffering for your redemption, by all His love and tears and blood, by all the exquisite torments of His body and all the doleful anguish of His soul, by His glorious triumphs and unbounded fullness, by His mercies and judgments, by all the ordinances of His grace and all the necessities of your soul, by all the consolations of the blessed gospel and all the terrors of the fiery law, by all the ineffable joys of heaven and all the dire torments of hell; to believe, with application to yourself, the record of God concerning His Son. Whether you have hitherto been a profligate sinner or a formal hypocrite, come now to Christ. Come, because you are warranted by the unlimited offers and calls of the gospel, and because you are peremptorily commanded in the law, and trust in Him for all His salvation.

The moment that you begin to trust cordially in Him for salvation not only from the guilt but from the love, dominion, and practice of all sin, you will pass from death to life, from sin to holiness, and from a slavish fear of endless punishment to a reviving hope of eternal life. Forsake without delay those sordid pleasures of sin which the sinner shall soon lose, and by faith receive that holy consolation which every true believer will eternally enjoy.

Ought sincere believers to endeavor, with all diligence, to attain establishment in the assurance of faith as a primary means of attaining established comfort? It follows that every believer should constantly strive to attain a strong faith. Without a strong and a lively faith, the Christian may have comfort, but he cannot have settled comfort; he cannot be habitually cheerful; he cannot "rejoice evermore;" he cannot cleave resolutely to the promise when providence without, or sense within, seems to contradict the promise. It is only by a strong faith that the believer can live as a child in the family without anxious care or fear (Daniel 3:16–17; Psalm 23:4, 6).

As often as Christ removes the burden of contracted guilt from the conscience, the weak believer lays it on again, and then sinks under it; but the strong believer takes the Savior at His word, and relies with firm confidence on Him for pardon and eternal life. Thus, being strong in faith comforts him.

If his heavenly Father at any time frowns upon him and smites him, he believes His love rather than his own feeling. Weak faith says, "The Lord Jesus can save me if He will," but strong faith says, "He both can and will save me." The strong believer lives not so much upon the comforts of God as upon "the God of all comfort." He draws his consolation from the higher springs, even while the waters of the lower springs are running. And were all his earthly comforts to fail him, he knows that he has still one comfort, which is of infinitely more value than them all: "This God is my God forever and ever" (Psalm 48:14). He trusts firmly for all necessary consolation in his God and Savior who changes not; and therefore no outward changes which befall can effect any considerable change in his spirit. He knows that he cannot be poor so long as his Covenant-God is rich; for all the riches of God are his.

O believer, strive diligently to attain a strong, vigorous, and operative faith. Watch and resist the very first appearances of declension in the life of faith. Hold fast the truth in opposition to errors of every kind. Hold it fast in your understanding and judgment, in your will and affections, and in your confession and whole conversation. "Hold fast the faithful word, as thou hast been taught" (Titus 1:9). Keep the truth, and the truth will keep you comfortable and happy. Seek for an established judgment and a firm faith in all the truths of the glorious gospel.

Should the Christian, in order to arrive at stable comfort, endeavor to be rooted and grounded in love? Then he must study, in the faith of God's redeeming love for him, so to love God in Christ as to be at all times pleased with Him. In proportion as he loves his God and Father, he will be pleased with Him, with all His perfections, and with all His will. And if he is always pleased or delighted with God, he will, in the same proportion, be always comfortable, always delighted in his own soul. To be constantly pleased with God in Christ, and with all the will of God, is, indeed, a difficult and high attainment; but the believer cannot otherwise become so rooted and grounded in love for Him as to attain settled consolation. To love God supremely, and to be so pleased with Him as to be constantly disposed in all things to please Him, are in effect the same. If, then, a good man would attain established consolation, he must, by grace, become firmly fixed in a holy and habitual endeavor always to be pleased with God, and always to please Him. One happy consequence would be that, by trusting and praying only for such things as are agreeable to the holy will of God, he could not be disappointed. Another would be that, loving the providential will of the Lord, he would frequently observe providence, and would perceive such traces of love toward him in providential dispensations as would greatly establish him in spiritual consolation.

While unfeigned love for the brethren is, as has been remarked above, an evidence of union and communion with Christ, it appears at the same time to be an instituted means of establishment in spiritual comfort. By the exercise of sincere love for the brethren, a holy man enjoys communion with them, which heightens his enjoyment of communion with Christ. The more he loves them, the more is he disposed to "cover a multitude of sins" in them (1 Peter 4:8), and to "think no evil" of them (1 Corinthians 13:5). It is want of love for the saints that usually disposes a man so to quarrel and contend with them as to mar his own comfort in fellowship with them. Hence the Apostle Paul exhorted the believers at Corinth to "be of one mind," and to "live in peace," in order that they might be of good comfort (2 Corinthians 13:11). He urged brotherly love and unanimity upon those at Philippi by an argument drawn from the comfort of love (Philippians 2:1–3). The more a believer loves the brethren, the more pleasure he takes in them; and the more pleasure he takes in them, and in their company, the more pleasant will he be to them, and the more disposed will he be to be of one accord, of one mind with them, and, in lowliness of mind, to esteem them better than himself. His love of them, and his delight in their company, will render him very unwilling to deprive himself of the comfort of their society by differing, without necessity, in opinion from them. The diversity of opinions in religion among Christians at this day, and the divisions which ensue, are, I believe, as much owing to the want of perfect love for the brethren as of perfect knowledge.

Ought the believer to be always firm in his resolution to avoid such company as appears to have a tendency to draw him into sin? Then he must learn never to feel uncomfortable, far less to murmur, when men of the world appear not to esteem him. The exercised Christian is always a fool in the account of worldly men, and he will not a little mar his own comfort if he looks for respect from them. He ought never to expect that they will esteem him as a holy man so long as they do not regard holiness itself. Indeed, it would display both ignorance and pride in him to murmur when they slight him. He is unknown to worldly and wicked men; and therefore he should not for a moment be uneasy if he finds himself disregarded by them. Nay, if he would attain establishment in heavenly consolation, he must not suffer himself to be in the least disquieted if he should find that even some of the saints themselves appear to disregard him. He should remember that even the holiest of men can in no higher degree be attentive to him than the Lord is pleased at the time to make them.

Is establishment in humility of mind requisite to a saint's establishment in pure and holy comfort? The believer may hence learn that the more deep and abiding his sense of weakness is, the stronger he is. The strongest believer has, in one sense, no more strength inherent in himself than the weakest. He is as incapable of resisting motions of sin, and of performing spiritual obedience, by his own strength as he was when he first began to know the Lord. In another sense, however, he is stronger and more firmly settled in holy tranquility of soul because he has a more deeply felt sense of his own weakness and unworthiness, and a more constant

dependence on Christ for continued supplies of
grace. Thus he is strong not in himself, but in the
Lord, and in the power of His might; and the
stronger he is in the grace that is in Christ Jesus, the
stronger will his consolation be.

It is also evident from what has been said that, as
the peace which believers have in Christ does not
exempt them from outward affliction in the world,
so they ought to take heed that outward affliction at
no time deprives them of, or even lessens, their inward peace and consolation in Him. Outward and
even inward trouble are dispensed to saints in order
not to destroy, but to increase and establish their
holy tranquility and joy in the Lord Jesus (John
16:33). Afflictions are sent that they may be means of
preparing them to derive increasing degrees of spiritual and strong consolation from His fullness.

When the sufferings of Christ, or any calamities
whatsoever, abound in them, it is not in order that
their consolation may diminish, but that it may
abound by Christ (2 Corinthians 1:5). If afflictions
are dispensed, it is to take smaller comforts out of
the way, or to make them cease to be comforts any
longer, in order to make room for greater ones.
Believers, therefore, when they are under affliction
of any kind, should never suffer their grief or their
fear to hinder them for a moment from trusting and
rejoicing in Christ Jesus, who is a Brother born for
adversity. On the contrary, while they are under
trouble, as well as after they are delivered from it,
they ought to fall in so entirely with the gracious design of God in dispensing it as resolutely to endeavor to confide and to rejoice in the great Re-

deemer. Thus, their hearts will be fixed, trusting in the Lord, and they will enjoy a peaceful and a stable tranquility in the midst of a changing and a troublesome world. Thus, desiring above all things and trusting that the infinitely sovereign, wise, and holy will of God may be accomplished in them, they will rejoice in the cheering thought that, in subservience to the glory of Christ in their salvation, all things work together for good to them (Romans 8:28).

Afflicted believer, your grief, arising from what you feel, either of the plague of your heart or of the pressure of your calamity, should never be suffered to rob you of the comfort and joy which the blessed gospel designs for you in what is there recorded of the person, righteousness, and fullness of the glorious Redeemer. Oh, trust Him; delight in Him; wait for Him, and all shall be well. Consider that to you He takes the curse out of every affliction, and turns it into a real blessing. Give up, therefore, all your concerns into the hands of your faithful Redeemer; and trust that, by His infinite love and manifold wisdom, He will conduct them all for your good. Judge not the love of God by providences, but by promises. As no temporal comfort is good enough to be an evidence of His love for you, so no temporal calamity is afflictive enough to be a sign of His hatred of you.

Has a believer attained established consolation, and would he continue to enjoy it? Then let him take heed that he does not look intensely and excessively upon his evidences of grace. No sooner does a good man arrive at some degree of settled comfort than Satan, if permitted, will tempt him to look with great intensity upon his evidences for heaven. That enemy of his holy comfort will often suggest to him that he cannot be sure enough, that he is deceiving himself, in order that, by occupying him continually with laying the foundation and trying it, he may keep him from diligence in the exercise of grace and performance of duty. Were the believer to be as diligent in exercising himself to have always a conscience void of offense toward God and toward men as in trying his evidences, he would advance more speedily than he does in the assurance of sense. It is, indeed, the duty of Christians often to examine their state and their frame, and to see that they are not deceiving themseves; but not to be doing it alone and incessantly; not to be occupying themselves with that when they are called to faith and love, to patience and holy activity for God. Were those of the saints who are favored with comfortable discoveries of their evidences of inherent holiness to take frequent occasion from those evidences to think of Christ, and to set their hearts the more on His consummate righteousness as the only ground of their title to holiness and comfort, they would thereby attain more assurance of their personal interest in Him, and more establishment in pure consolation.

When the Apostle Paul was assured that Christ already lived in him, he took occasion from that to live the more by faith on the righteousness and fullness of Christ. "I live," said he, "yet not I, but Christ liveth in me; and the life which I now live in the flesh, I live by the faith of the Son of God, who loved me, and gave Himself for me" (Galatians 2:20). At the very time in which the same Apostle had his eye fixed upon his having the excellent knowledge of Christ Jesus, he had his heart taken up with the righteousness of Christ (Philippians 3:8–9). If the believer, then, would maintain solid and stable comfort, let him think more of the Lord Jesus, and delight more in Him and His righteousness and fullness than in his own evidences of grace. To pore upon his own inherent holiness more than upon His imputed righteousness would soon interrupt and lessen his tranquility of mind. Evidences are, indeed, delightful to an exercised Christian; but Christ ought to be far more delightful to him.

Such of the saints as are favored with strong and stable consolation may hence learn to express their gratitude for this inestimable blessing by the frequent exercise of holy joy. They should abound much in the lively exercise of joy and praise. When their souls are satisfied as with marrow and fatness, their mouths ought daily to praise the Lord with joyful lips. Their lips should greatly rejoice when they sing unto Him, and their souls which He has redeemed. Every stream of divine consolation which flows in ought to lead them up to the uncreated Fountain of joy, and to excite them to the exercise of rejoicing always in the Lord. They should place their happiness and their delight more in that which is in Christ, and in the promise, than in anything which they find in themselves.

Rejoice, O believer, in the Lord Jesus. Make Him the consolation of your soul. Try how much of Christ may be enjoyed by you upon earth, to prepare you for the full and endless enjoyment of Him in heaven. Let it be your continual study to enjoy as much of heaven upon earth as possible. To be *in* Christ and to rejoice in Him are heaven below; and to be *with* Him, to behold His glory, is heaven above.

Trusting in your gracious Redeemer, who "rejoiceth over thee to do thee good" (Jeremiah 32:41), ask yourself every morning, "What have I to expect from my dear Redeemer this day to afford me joy?" This question will, under the consoling influences of the holy Comforter, tend to make you cheerful and thankful at the commencement of the day. How exhilarating will it be to your soul when you can answer, "My gracious Redeemer will today, according to His promise, be with me to strengthen, to help, and to uphold me; to work in me by His Holy Spirit both to will and to do of His good pleasure; to fulfill in me all the good pleasure of His goodness, and the work of faith with power; to guide me continually with His counsel, and to grant me all the inward and outward comforts which He sees I need. He will this day afford me communion with Himself in His grace, in His word, and in His providence. Perhaps He will cheer my soul even with the sweetness of sensible communion and ineffable joy. He will at least this day bring me nearer than before to the perfection of holiness, to the end of my faith, even the complete salvation of my soul."

Rejoice, then, O believer, every day and all the day. Rejoice in hope. "Hold fast the confidence and the rejoicing of the hope, firm unto the end" (Hebrews 3:6); and let your whole life be a continued expression of grateful praise to the Lord Jesus for all that He has done, is doing, and will do for your soul.

Finally, are some of the heirs of salvation favored

in a good degree with settled comfort? Let them take occasion from it to meditate frequently on that fullness of inexpressible and endless joy into which they are soon to enter. Oh, the ineffable, rapturous joy with which they shall see Jehovah and the Lamb, and become perfect in holiness! Believer, the greatest consolation which you have enjoyed, or which you can enjoy here, is but a small drop in comparison to that boundless ocean of eternal joy which will overflow your soul in the pure regions of eternal day. Oh, what inexpressible, transporting bliss is prepared for you! What a weight, what an eternal weight, what an exceedingly exceeding and eternal weight of glory is, by redeeming grace, secured for you! Does not thy heart long ardently for this? Does it not rejoice, and even exult in the cheering prospect of endless felicity, of inconceivable joy? Does it not look beyond all transitory shadows for "that blessed hope, and the glorious appearing of the great God, even our Savior Jesus Christ" (Titus 2:13)? Oh, set your affection on things above, where Christ sits at the right hand of God, amidst all the splendors of His exalted state, and all those flaming ministers who surround His throne.

By frequent meditation on that glorious rest which "remaineth for the people of God," you now enter into rest (Hebrews 4:3, 9). You enjoy more and more of holy tranquility, of heavenly consolation. To rejoice in hope of the glory of God is to experience the sweetest and purest joy, joy which shall enable you to rise superior to the inordinate love of life and the disquieting fear of death. Consider your death as that by which you will not depart *out* of life, but rather *into* life; and expect from the hands of your faithful Redeemer such living comforts in your dying moments as will raise you above the terror of death, and cause you to triumph over the darkness of the grave.

Though a believer may have fears and conflicts of soul when he is in the near prospect of death, yet, commonly, these are all over before the solemn moment of death comes. His spiritual enemies are usually made to be still as a stone while he is passing through the river of death (Proverbs 14:32). Jesus, our great High Priest, has dipped His feet in those waters. The stream therefore is divided to you who are by faith united to Him. The channel is dry. You may discern the footsteps of your almighty Redeemer in the bottom, and endless felicity on the other side.

Having already tasted the sweetness of pure consolation, you should long, with ardent and increasing desire, for the marriage supper of the Lamb. He has, by ten thousand thousand instances of kindness, so endeared Himself to your heart that you should not be fully satisfied until you have the full enjoyment of His immense and everlasting love—until you see Him as He is.

Enjoy the unclouded light of His countenance, and be crowned with the unfading brightness of eternal glory. Let your present consolation, then, excite you often to meditate on, and ardently to long for, that consummate felicity which awaits you in the pure regions of everlasting light, love, and joy. For yet a little, a very little while, and you, "the ransomed of the Lord shalt return, and come to Zion with songs and everlasting joy upon thy head; thou shalt obtain joy and gladness, and sorrow and sighing shall flee away" (Isaiah 35:10).